EXTRA-DIMENSIONAL UNIVERSE

EXTRA-DIMENSIONAL UNIVERSE

WHERE THE PARANORMAL BECOMES THE NORMAL

JOHN R. VIOLETTE

HAMPTON ROADS
PUBLISHING COMPANY, INC.

HR
for the evolving human spirit

Cover design by Jane Hagaman
Cover digital imagery © 2004 by Getty Images/Comstock Images

Excerpts reprinted with the permission of Scribner, an imprint of
Simon & Schuster Adult Publishing Group, from
Abduction: Human Encounters with Aliens by John E. Mack.
Copyright © 1994 by John E. Mack, M.D. Also reprinted by the
permission of Russell & Volkening as agents for the author.
Copyright © 1994 by John Mack.

Hampton Roads Publishing Company, Inc.
1125 Stoney Ridge Road
Charlottesville, VA 22902

434-296-2772
fax: 434-296-5096
e-mail: hrpc@hrpub.com
www.hrpub.com

If you are unable to order this book from your local
bookseller, you may order directly from the publisher.
Call 1-800-766-8009, toll-free.

Library of Congress Cataloging-in-Publication Data

Violette, John R.
 Extra-dimensional universe : where the paranormal becomes the normal /
John R. Violette.
    p. cm.
  Summary: "Presents an expanded framework of space, time, and consciousness
that for the first time scientifically explains how paranormal phenomena such as
UFOs, near-death experiences, and other mystical phenomena can exist"—Provided
by publisher.
  Includes bibliographical references and index.
  ISBN 1-57174-446-0 (5-1/2 x 8-1/2 tp : alk. paper)
  1. Parapsychology. I. Title.
  BF1031.V56 2005
  130--dc22

                                           2005004237

ISBN 1-57174-446-0
10 9 8 7 6 5 4 3 2 1
Printed on acid-free, recycled paper in Canada

to my parents

Contents

Acknowledgments

Interior illustrations by Al Cabral, graphic arts/photographer, New Bedford, Massachusetts. Permission to reprint selected passages by Raymond E. Fowler and Simon & Schuster. In addition, there are many references and quotations from sources either in the public domain or that fall into the category of "fair use for comment and review." All sources are credited in the text and/or endnotes section, and my appreciation for all.

Also, I wish to thank Booklocker.com, where this work first came out in book form, and Richard Leviton, senior editor at Hampton Roads, for noticing it.

Introduction

UFOs and abductions, psychic phenomena, mystical and near-death experiences—these things just cannot happen, not in the world of three dimensions of space plus time that we know. And yet they do happen. This is why researchers of the paranormal are speculating more and more that these are experiences of something beyond our world, some kind of higher dimensional reality.

Unfortunately, this is where it begins and ends. A few words, a few sentences about higher, inner, other, or extra dimensions, expanded frameworks or parameters of space-time, but never with an explanation as to what this means, or how it could possibly be, not to mention how this would then "explain" the phenomena. In fact, toward this end, there has never been an actual extra-dimensional theory or framework, even tentatively, put forth. Indeed, most references to them are about the need for one.

Extra-Dimensional Universe is the answer to that need, and the framework for such a theory.

PART I

A New Framework of Space, Time, and Consciousness

1

The Theory

A young couple take a moonlight walk along a private beach. They stop, gaze up at the night sky, and see something they will never forget. From out of nowhere, a strange, spherelike object radiating a brilliant white light appears directly overhead. To the couple's astonishment it changes to a triangular shape *in a fraction of a second;* then moments later, like the Cheshire cat, it just vanishes. But how? Where did it come from, and go? And how can a solid object change into a completely different shape instantaneously?

UFO sightings like this, though this one is of the stranger variety, are not rare. They demonstrate the most startling aspect of the entire phenomenon: UFOs violate—transcend—the world of space as we know it, leading some of the world's most renowned researchers to conjecture that UFOs come from beyond our space, from a larger space-time continuum, of which ours is just a part. Moreover, many physicists now also suspect there are more than three dimensions of space. In fact, extra-dimensional theories are the hottest new topic to emerge in theoretical physics in over fifty years.

A high-school girl has a terrifying dream the night before a field trip. In it she sees a bus full of classmates in a bad accident in which one of her friends is injured. Shaken by the realness of the premonition, she refuses to go on the trip and warns her friend. But her warning is not heeded, dismissed as silly, and the accident happens just as she saw it.

Psychic phenomena such as this not only violate our normal idea of space, but our idea of time itself. How can this be? Can our time also be just part of a larger world of time? It seems that to understand the paranormal at its deepest level, we must first acknowledge, as many researchers now do, that we need a new, broader framework of space and time—a new worldview.

Amazingly, only about five hundred years ago the standing worldview was still that of a flat Earth. Only about four hundred years ago, it was that the Earth was the center of the universe, that all the stars and planets revolved around it. By now you can see that our problem has always been underestimating the size of the universe and overly exaggerating our place in it. But a revolution, of sorts, followed. About 350 years ago, Newton had it all figured out. The universe was like a giant machine of three dimensions of space plus time, the workings of which he described in breathtakingly precise terms. But then in the early 1900s, Einstein showed that there was another variable that must be included in any depiction of space and time, *and on equal footing:* consciousness.

Two thousand years ago, a lonely figure in a distant land has a sudden explosion of consciousness, the effects of which will transform the world forever. He realizes, knows directly with a new kind of consciousness, that everyone and everything in the world, indeed the world itself, is just part of a larger reality, a virtual "kingdom" by comparison with ours. He begins to teach, as all religious giants have, that beyond our space and time, beyond the limitations of normal consciousness, exists a vaster reality, which can only be known with *another, expanded consciousness.* Yet the real significance of this has been ignored ever since. For Einstein clearly demonstrated that space, time, and consciousness are interwoven, in effect dependent on one another. But even with the recent interest in expanding our space-time structure, the fact that consciousness itself must be likewise expanded has been completely overlooked, until now.

A New York City police detective lies dying amid the carnage of a drug bust gone haywire. But as his consciousness slowly fades, suddenly it is lifted up out of his body, then through a kind of tunnel to another place, another world. His consciousness now somehow enlarged, he "knows" with a new type of sense. He becomes aware of a larger self and reality, one his normal state had never allowed him to see. Stranger still, here old ideas of space and time are suspended, transformed into a different, larger structure he cannot quite grasp. Where am I? Is this what it's like to die? he wonders. Not bad. But it is not yet his time. Suddenly, the expansion of consciousness halts, begins to contract, and he descends back to his original state. He will recover, but never again think of the world in the same way.

And neither must we. For every time our worldview has changed—been expanded—it has been for the same reason. There are conflicting data that cannot be incorporated into the old model, which must then be broadened to accommodate them. The conflicting data now are reports of the paranormal. We either need a still broader model that can include them, or, as the diehard defenders of every worldview always propose, we can simply ignore them and maintain the status quo. But that is becoming harder to do; reports of paranormal experiences have reached astonishing proportions. There are now over 100,000 UFO reports on file worldwide, and a 1998 Gallup poll showed eight percent of Americans, about 20 million people, claim to actually have seen one.

Furthermore, there are now thousands of people who claim to have been "abducted," even taken beyond our space-time, by aliens. The number of psychic experiences has been estimated at over 50 million worldwide. Another Gallup survey (1999) found 46 percent of subjects reporting "an unusual or inexplicable spiritual experience." Just a few profound mystical experiences have given birth to every religion known to Man. The International Association for Near Death Studies (IANDS) reports that 14 million people in the United States may have had a near-death experience.

Einstein pointed out that it takes only one contradictory fact to demolish a scientific theory. So if just one of these accounts is true and our current space-time framework cannot explain it, we need another, broader framework that can. This I shall bring forward as the extra-dimensional universe theory.

Our world is part of a larger, extra-dimensional one; that is, our world has an extra dimension of space. We do not detect this extra dimension because it is hidden and included in our concept of time. But it can be detected, naturally and effortlessly, by expanded consciousness. Let me explain.

There are three distinct levels of consciousness on Earth: sensation, simple consciousness, and self-consciousness. The first two have, over the course of many millions of years, evolved to the third, higher level. Each has its own framework of space-time. Take a snail as an example of the first. It lives in a world of one dimension of space plus time. The other two dimensions of space all around it are translated, by its faculty of sensation, into one dimension of space or time.

But a higher animal like the dog, with a higher faculty and simple consciousness, mentally extracts from time another dimension of space and lives in a larger world of two dimensions of space plus time. Get the picture? Time is a collection of extra dimensions of space either not apprehended, or imperfectly apprehended; each level of consciousness sees them bit by bit, moving constantly past, fused with time. So it is with the dog and the third dimension. His simple consciousness translates the third dimension of space into either one of the other two, or time.

But we have a higher mental faculty still, self-consciousness. By virtue of it we've extracted yet another dimension of space from time, or put another way, extracted from the transcendental or paranormal aspect of reality yet another normal aspect. We live in a world of three dimensions of space plus time. The question is: is there still a higher faculty, one that can extract another dimension of space from *our* time? And if so, would our paranormal, in this expanded framework, then become the normal?

There is such a fourth level of consciousness, evolving slowly in our race, tortuously so over eons, as all other faculties have before it. It goes hand in hand with the apprehension of a fourth dimension of space extracted from time. A brief taste of this faculty is the mystical experience in which one's consciousness expands into and realizes a broader continuum of space and time. Lesser glimpses of the faculty, just a bit of it at any one time, are psychic intuitions such as telepathy, clairvoyance, and precognition. (How one can then "see" the future will become clear shortly.) This higher faculty conceives in a fashion beyond sensation, simple- and self-consciousness, logic, concepts, and even language. This is why those who have paranormal experiences have such a hard time describing how they "know." All they can say is, "I just know." And still other traces of this higher faculty are responsible for other kinds of psychic phenomena, such as psychokinesis, poltergeists, healings, and apparitions.

Now what if a race of beings on another planet has acquired this faculty completely? They would be like gods to us, as far above us as we are above animals. They would live in a different, larger world of space-time. Using that extra dimension, they could perform feats that seem like magic to us, coming and going into and out of our space at will, and abducting humans into that realm as easily as we, by using the third dimension, could snatch a bug from the surface of a pond. This is the alien consciousness behind the UFO mystery, which we'll meet face-to-face in the abduction phenomenon.

Finally, if our world is just part of a larger world, then each of us in turn must have a larger self that resides in that world. This becomes apparent in the near-death experience, when normal consciousness, all but faded out, awakens to the realization of its larger self in extra-dimensional space. These people know there is an existence beyond our normal space and time. They have been there. This is also why they no longer fear death: they know it is not the end.

The point is this. There are no UFO phenomena per se, no psychic phenomena, no near-death phenomena, and no mystical phenomena. There is just a reality phenomenon. Our world is enveloped in a larger one, the workings of which are beyond our senses and level of consciousness, and so these workings when encountered are treated as paranormal. But in the broader scope of extra-dimensional theory, they are in fact quite normal. To clearly see how this is so, we must first examine all our preconceived notions of space, time, and consciousness and put them to rout. We'll look at the building blocks of our scientific worldview and watch them quiver, shake, and give way under the glare of the new light. Then, these obstructions removed from our view, we can see at last the true vastness of the universe, the supernatural laid bare as the natural, and our old world and selves as just shadows cast by the greater world and life beyond.

The history of Man shows that we have continually overstated our position in the universe, not only by underestimating its size, but also by regarding our location as its absolute focal point. It was at first a tremendous blow to our ego to accept that the Earth was not the center of the entire cosmos. What we must now accept is that Man is no more the center of the conscious or psychical world than he is of the physical world. Our world may *appear* to have three dimensions of space plus time, but watch what happens. . . .

2

Worlds of Space

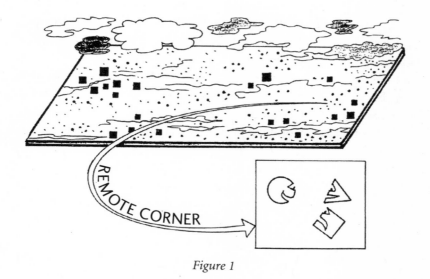

Figure 1

What's this picture about? A world, but one totally unlike ours, a flat world of two dimensions of space plus time, a hypothetical plane world, complete with plane beings who live on it. Now this may at first seem odd, so perhaps it will be easier to picture this world as existing on a vast sheet of paper, on the surface of which the inhabitants—flat squares, circles, triangles, etc.—can move freely about in any two directions, but not up or down, for they know nothing of the space above or below them.

Let us suppose that, save for this one shortcoming, the inhabitants are much like us. They are resourceful and inventive, have formed a civilization, learn and love, raise children, grow old and die, and even have religion, philosophy, music, and science. In fact, their plane world scientists have made remarkable strides and now feel they're on the verge of having a complete understanding of the entire universe—all in two dimensions of space plus time.

But their science cannot explain everything. Strange things are happening in this world: paranormal phenomena, which some plane beings attribute to a higher realm of existence. Others just scoff at the idea, calling the phenomena the stuff of pipe dreams and prophets. But we are in a position to *know,* for we dwell in that higher realm, the third dimension, and can see all that happens on their flat, two-dimensional surface.

Let's think of this world of two dimensions of space plus time as a map, or blueprint, which we can use to understand the paranormal in our higher world. It is like a musical scale, that can be transposed into a higher or lower key, while the relationship of the notes remains the same, or a Rosetta stone for understanding the paranormal. In a remote corner of the plane world, a conversation has just taken place.

"Another dimension of space! Absurd," said the Square.

"Is it?" said the Circle as he continued with his presentation. "You know some of our top scientists now think there may be more than just two."

"Yes, but those are just crazy theories, mathematical . . . [searching for the right word] . . . hocus-pocus, and entirely unproven," said the Square, an avowed skeptic. He then thumped his hand against a nearby object and stammered: "If there's a third dimension of space, why can't we see it, touch it, like the other two?"

"It may just be too small," interjected the Triangle, echoing the trend of modern research to portray possible extra dimensions as too tiny to see.

"Actually," said the Circle, "it's because it is outside of space as we *know* it. Look, we know that there are two dimensions of space, length and width, and they are at right angles to each other, that is perpendicular, right?"

"Right," replied the Triangle, a renowned scientist on the plane world and open-minded about such matters.

"Well," continued the Circle, "I propose a third, likewise at a right angle to the other two, and—"

"But there is no such direction; one cannot even conceive of it," interrupted the skeptical Square.

"I agree; we can't conceive of it," said the Circle. "That is the whole point. It is beyond our senses, beyond our powers of perception. One needs a higher kind of 'sense,' a higher power of mind, a higher faculty, to see it, which brings me to the point of this discussion. I shall demonstrate how such an extra dimension and higher faculty can account for all the strange goings-on we've been hearing so much about of late, the so-called paranormal."

"You mean reports of plane beings who profess supernatural powers, being 'elevated or uplifted,' as they call it, into some other level of reality and seeing the insides of things in our world or knowing about events taking place far away, even seeing the future?" asked the Triangle, his interest piqued.

"That, and more; in fact, much more," said the Circle.

"Oh, but that's all rubbish anyway," growled the Square. "Those people are all deluded, or frauds."

"Not necessarily," said the Triangle. "A colleague of mine at the Plane World Academy of Science has informed me that such abilities are all but proven in the lab under the strictest conditions imaginable. Funny thing though, they still have no idea just *how* they work!"

"This I wish to remedy," confidently stated the Circle. "And, I said there was more. You must have also heard the tales of aliens from some other world coming to ours, and doing so in such a way that seems impossible, just appearing and disappearing from out of nowhere, even taking plane beings away with them and—"

"That does it," said the Square abruptly. "You can't possibly believe that. Besides, there's just no way it can be. It's not possible; it's pure fantasy."

"Not so fast, Square," said the Triangle, suddenly finding himself in the unexpected and undesirable role as mediator. "My first inclination is to agree with you, but let's see what the Circle has to say. You know there are many plane beings of sound repute who have either seen these aliens themselves or personally know others who have, and they are convinced of it, even though they may not publicly say so. Go on, Circle."

"Okay," Circle continued, "but tell the Square to keep an open side to this, will you, and I promise to give him, if nothing else, something to howl about with his cohorts at those skeptics club meetings. Here's the *pièce de résistance*. When I explain how these paranormal phenomena work, you'll understand still others, ones that have always been thought of as religious in nature, and beyond our science, such as the religious experience itself and the age-old question of life after death."

"That's a tall order to fill," cautioned the Triangle, but he was intrigued by the sheer scope of what the Circle was proposing.

"Impossible," said the Square. "Religion and science are in the nature of things directly opposed to each other, contradictory, 180 degrees apart. One is a matter of faith, the other a matter of fact."

"True enough," the Circle conceded, but quickly added: "This is only because there has been no framework, physical or conceptual, that can unify both of them." He then announced he was ready to begin his presentation in earnest, and brought out some drawings he had with him. "Look at this [see figure 2]," he said to his audience (the Triangle watched attentively, the Square eyed the drawing suspiciously) "and think of it as a world, but one totally unlike ours, a world of one dimension of space plus time, a hypothetical line world, complete with line beings who live on it."

Figure 2

"Hmm," thought the Triangle out loud, as he bent nearer for a closer look.

"Harrumph," grumbled the Square. "What of it?"

"Well," said the Circle, "first of all, it is not one-dimensional, is it? For we know that for anything to actually exist, it must have extension in two dimensions. That is, these beings and their world are possessed of an extra dimension, of which they are completely unaware."

"This is childish," said the Square; "they would surely know that there was a second dimension, just by moving off either side of the line and entering it."

"But let us imagine that they have no freedom of movement in the second dimension, nor any kind of consciousness of it, in short, no means of detecting it," proposed the Circle. "Their world is in effect limited by their conception of space. The bottom line is that their world is two-dimensional, but they are aware of only a smaller, one-dimensional part of it."

"Okay," agreed the Triangle. "And now?"

"Now," said the Circle, "just think of the possibilities. I mean, advanced beings like us, by using the second dimension, can perform physical operations in this one-dimensional world that must seem miraculous to the line beings. For example, look at this drawing [see figure 3]. As you can see, it is the same as the first except I have marked the line beings with letters to show their front and back sides. Now you must admit, if to them there is no space outside their world, there would be no way for them to move except forwards and backwards, and no conceivable way for them to change their position or orientation in this world. That is, if the A in creature AB, or the C in CD face forward, there is no way they can realign themselves so that they face backward. Right?"

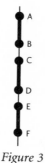

Figure 3

"Yes, that's true," replied the Triangle.

"But," said the Circle, "a two-dimensional being like myself could very easily, by utilizing my freedom of movement in the second dimension, do this [see figure 4]." Here the Circle reached out, detached the CD figure from the line, and spun it completely around. "Now, how do you think the line beings would interpret this?"

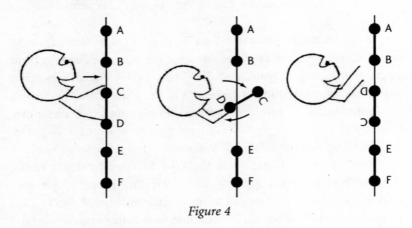

Figure 4

"Well, I . . . I'm not sure," said the Triangle; "I mean if they had no conception of the second dimension, then . . . well . . . I don't know. How?"

"Since they could not interpret it in terms of space that they know of, it would be like being turned inside-out," explained the Circle.

"Are you implying," said the Triangle in an incredulous tone, "that if there is an extra dimension to our world, it lies in an inside-out direction?"

"Yes and no . . . or rather, no and yes," said the Circle, correcting himself. "It might not lie in that direction, just as it doesn't for the line world; but as with the line beings, that's how it would *appear* to us. All extra dimensions appear to those in lower space as in an inside-out direction."

"Very profound," said the Square sarcastically. "But what has this to do with the paranormal?"

"Plenty," answered the Circle. "Can't we easily see through the second dimension the side of a line being which to him is his *inside?* And so couldn't a line being who had the power of seeing in two dimensions, like us, see the insides of things in his world? Likewise, haven't plane beings, when possessed of this higher, supernatural power, claimed to see the insides of things in our world? And haven't there even been reports of plane beings so empowered who have actually turned objects inside-out?"

"Lunatics, all of them, or frauds," muttered the Square contemptuously.

"Well, it is known that such reports do exist," said the Triangle. "And though rather abstract, I guess an inside-out direction is at a right angle to the other two dimensions."

"Good," said the Circle triumphantly, "but I'm just beginning. Now, look at this." He stuck one hand through the line world between two of the line beings. "How do you suppose they would see this?"

"I suppose they would see something just appear in their world," said the Triangle.

"An alien, perhaps?" suggested the Circle. "And, not coincidentally, appearing just as the aliens are said to appear in our world. All of a sudden—they're just there. And, just as we could easily grab a line being and carry him off through the second dimension to examine him at length, an alien race from a third dimension could do the same to us."

"Ridiculous," said the Square. "You are proposing something that can't possibly be to explain things that don't even exist."

"Actually, Square, I think it makes some sense," said the Triangle. "At least it provides a kind of theoretical framework to go on. Please continue, Circle."

"I shall indeed," he stated. "Here is a matter of the greatest importance—the nature of time itself. You must agree that we don't know what time is, but let me give you a hint of its real nature by demonstrating how time is perceived on the line world."

The Circle pointed to another drawing (see figure 5) and produced a ruler with different color segments along it—red, blue, and yellow. He passed the ruler through the line in front of the CD being and said: "Behold! Motion in time on the line world is merely motion in a second, extra dimension."

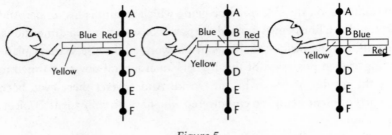

Figure 5

"What's this?" demanded the Square. "Explain yourself more clearly."

"Of course," said the Circle. "As I pass the ruler in front of the line being, this is what he would surely see: At first nothing, then all of a sudden a red point, then a blue one as the blue segment is reached, then a yellow one which disappears from view. The one-dimensional being can see nothing more than a point which changes color in time before vanishing. He can but dimly perceive any two-dimensional object, just a bit at a time, as it encounters his primitive level of consciousness. The point is motion in higher space; by that I mean our second dimension is to the line being motion strictly in time. Our second dimension of space is to him fused with, or included in, his idea of time. Indeed all extra dimensions exist, to those in lower space, in time."

"Very interesting," said the Triangle; "I never would have thought along those lines. So if there's a third dimension to our world, it is in an inside-out direction, or rather appears to be, and hidden or included in our idea of time, which is why we can't detect it. Our 'time' is motion in this third dimension, right?"

"Right," confirmed the Circle.

"Ludicrous . . . preposterous," said the Square. "Why time is . . . just . . . time and nothing else, anywhere."

"No. Actually, it's just the opposite," said the Circle. Time is *every-thing else*. It's not what it is but what it isn't. What cannot be perceived in space lies hidden in one all-inclusive dimension of time."

"But if this is the case, where do we go from here?" asked the Triangle, frustration beginning to show in his voice. "If this extra dimension is there, how do we . . . how can we . . . actually perceive it?"

"The only way to directly perceive an extra dimension," said the Circle, "as I earlier postulated, is to extract it, mentally, from time, with a higher faculty, a new and completely different kind of consciousness. Given this, the space sense would expand to include an extra dimension."

"Oh, who's ever heard of such things—higher faculties, extra dimensions. It's just too weird," moaned the skeptical Square.

"Hold on, Square, we're getting to the good part now," said the Circle. "Imagine, if you will, gentlemen, that a line being, say the same one I just passed the ruler in front of—CD—has a sudden, tremendous leap of consciousness, so that he can see the world in a two-dimensional way like us. Of course he would not have the benefit of two-dimensional perspective, as we do, since this is acquired gradually over many years. But nonetheless, some things would be unmistakable, perhaps those just discussed.

"For instance, (1) he would know that he and his line world had another aspect or dimension that he had been unaware of, and that he had always lived within and been part of this larger world. (2) He'd understand that many things that were impossible under the law and order of the line world, such as miraculous physical maneuvers, were indeed possible in a broader reality. (3) His consciousness so expanded, broadened as it were, he could now see his own inside, that is, his side, and those of other line beings. In fact, he'd probably think that the way to this higher world lies 'within.'

"There's so much more. If we grant the line being two-dimensional 'vision,' he would possess knowledge that must seem supernatural to the other line beings. For example, he could now see objects and events on other, remote parts of his line or world, that which we call ESP; and time—ah, time: just think of how it must seem to him now. He could now perceive motion in the second dimension, motion that to him before was motion in time. Therefore, he could now actually see, at once in space, that which was before relegated to his past and future. Indeed he could predict aspects of the future, such as what color would next appear in the line world as I passed the ruler through—that remarkable phenomenon we in our world call precognition."

"Just hold on now," said the Square; "I thought you said he would have only a limited grasp of this higher knowledge."

"Quite true," countered the Circle. "But a limited grasp is all that's needed for what I have outlined. In fact, because his new sense is so limited, the line being would be prone to some distortion and even error with it. For example, he may think, because he is so overwhelmed by the experience, that he has ultimate knowledge or is in direct communion with God, and because his sense of time is torn asunder, he'd probably think that in this higher realm time does not exist."

"Why, that sounds like what plane beings say when they have these mystical experiences," said the Triangle. "Union with the divine, a realm where there is no time."

"Good," said the Circle. "You're beginning to see the point, the relation between my little analogy and the paranormal in our world."

"I think so," agreed the Triangle. "And I suppose this line being then becomes a religious leader, a god among men, on his line?"

"Not really, although that is one possibility," said the Circle. "It is much more likely that this taste of two-dimensional knowledge will quickly fade and he will return to his original state of consciousness, bewildered by the experience. You see, when he has the higher faculty, he assimilates information and comprehends it in a new manner. But when the faculty fades, he must translate those sweeping insights and revelations into his woefully restricted one-dimensional consciousness, just to try and understand them in his own mind. He may even question if the experience was real, as it must seem so bizarre when assessing it from his normal point of view. But if, upon reflection, he does accept it, his attempts to convey it to his line friends will appear awkward and nonsensical. They will probably just think he has a lively imagination, or is deluded. The higher knowledge is completely different in nature and incapable of being expressed in lower concepts and terminology. It is ineffable."

"Yes, those in our world who claim such mystical knowledge do say it cannot be expressed in words," agreed the Triangle. "But now, tell me," he asked, leaning closer in eager anticipation. "What about life after death?"

"Okay," answered the Circle. "First, I showed that the line beings possess two dimensions, one they are aware of and one they are not; and the greater part of them actually exists in the second dimension.

Now when a line being dies, the part of him that exists on his line is gone, but what of the greater part? Must it not continue to exist in higher space? Suppose that this greater part has a consciousness as well, one the line being is unaware of. In fact, when the line being had a leap of higher consciousness, what if it was only a recognition of that higher self and consciousness, which allowed him to see the world in a two-dimensional way?

"The point is that the greater part and its accompanying conscious-ness still exist after his 'exit' from the line world. Isn't this like the experiences of plane beings who have almost died yet survived? They maintain they no longer fear death because they know it is not the end, but a beginning, the beginning of a different existence beyond our old constraints of space and time."

"New Age drivel," sneered the Square. "I won't hear of it."

"I don't know," said the Triangle. "As with other paranormal phe-nomena, there have been a lot of plane beings now who have had such experiences. I personally know of some in very prestigious positions in our society. Unfortunately, though, they won't speak of it, probably because they fear a response like yours, Square. But what's funny is they seem different after, transformed, in a spiritual kind of way, if you know what I mean. In fact, in this way it's strangely reminiscent of those who've had mystical experiences, or even encounters with these aliens."

"They have tasted the higher consciousness and reality," said the Circle. "All of them, one way or another, and they will never be the same again."

"Well maybe they're just crazy, too," said the Square. "I've had enough of this. But I do have one question for you, Circle. Let's see you answer this. Back to the aliens and these abductions, if there are any. Why? What on Plane Earth for? What could they possibly want?"

"Very well," said the Circle solemnly. "I would rather not have spo-ken of this. But since you ask, the answer is not good, and to make matters worse, it is twofold and the two parts contradict each other. Let me explain. If these beings are three-dimensional, then they naturally possess the higher faculty that goes hand in hand with the perception of this third, extra dimension, and they undoubtedly have complete mastery of it. The problem is that the logic this faculty uses is by its very nature contradictory to us, or ineffable, as our logic would be to line beings. A full treatment of it is better left for another time [see chapter 3].

"But for now by firsthand accounts of these abductions, the numbers of which are growing by the day, here is their plan. One, they say our plane world is in great danger, depleted of its most basic resources and poisoned by the waste products from our great machines. They say we are self-destructive and heading for a day of reckoning, a doomsday we will not survive. They know this because they live in a larger world of space-time and can see our time, our future path, laid out in space along a third dimension. They say we were once line beings, but 'changed' into the way we are now, and that we were supposed to change again into something like them. But we haven't; we've resisted it, and in the process we have defied a basic natural law of the universe, something they call 'evolution.'

"But it is against their policy to intervene in our affairs or help us in any direct way. Therefore, and here's the amazing part, they abduct plane beings, take procreative fluids from us, and combine it with fluids taken from their own race, to somehow produce a half alien, half plane-being race. This race, better suited for survival, perhaps even possessing the higher, extra-dimensional faculty itself, will then replace us here or somewhere else, after our destruction. They say this way our genetic seed will be preserved as will biological diversity.

"Now for the other part. It seems they are trying to cultivate in those abducted plane beings a sense of that higher faculty, or at least point them in the right direction, which is within. They say that if we had sought out this higher power in ourselves, which we should have by now, we would not be in the fix we are. If we do somehow develop it, we may yet avoid our demise. These are two parts of one larger purpose. I know it's contradictory, and may even seem absurd, but this and only this is the sign of a three-dimensional race and intellect."

"Wow," said the Triangle. "That's surely a lot to digest."

"Completely ridiculous," scoffed the Square. "Two purposes, both at odds with each other, that are really one purpose! Who can believe such claptrap?"

"You miss my point," persisted the Circle. "Let me repeat. A three-dimensional alien consciousness must, I say, *must*, appear ridiculous to us. Moreover, do not many of our own scientists now proclaim that our world is in such a crisis stage and our future threatened?"

"Yes, they do," said the Triangle soberly.

At this point, the Circle began to gather up his drawings, signaling that the presentation was over. He apologized for ending on such a somber note, but added, "It's just as well, for this should be taken seriously; in fact, you might say it's a matter of life or death—ours." Then, turning to his audience, he said, "Well, what do you think of my theory?"

"Quite frankly," answered the Triangle, "it strains my belief system. But on the other hand, there is much to like about it. It covers a number of unexplained phenomena—indeed, all the paranormal—with one sweeping hypothesis; I like the economy in that. Also, and more along the lines of my specialty, I know you are preparing to apply the theory to our most baffling scientific riddles, those dealing with elementary particles, that seem to have run into a wall of late. If that shows promise, then, well, let's say I look forward to that presentation."

"How about you, Square?" the Circle asked.

"Pseudoscience," the Square shot back without a moment's hesitation. "Philosophical fiddle-faddle. An extra dimension? One that our level of consciousness can't detect? Why there's nothing more to the universe than, well, the way it appears to be. And the paranormal? I'll explain that for you right now: lies, hallucinations, and wishful thinking. There! That's my theory! And I'll die before I subscribe to any of this kind of nonsense."

The purpose of this story is to show the implications of adding an extra dimension to a world of space and time. Now I'll take over for the Circle and complete the plane world analogy from my supernatural, "god-like" vantage point, the third dimension.

Even though the plane beings consider their world two-dimensional, it is not. Every part of it, no matter how small, thin, or flat, is actually three-dimensional. To exist as anything more than just an abstract image, there must be *some* extension in the third dimension.

For example, this page, and the ink that comprises the words you are now reading, are three-dimensional. So the plane world and all within it, unbeknownst to its inhabitants (just as the Circle implied), is extra (three) dimensional.

The Circle showed how the beings on the line world, unable to conceive of a second dimension of space, would interpret it as in an inside-out direction, and so this is how plane beings would interpret a third dimension. For what happens when we look either up or down into their world, a direction they cannot conceive of? We can easily see the insides of things there. How incredible this must seem to the plane beings; if they wish to see what lies inside objects, structures, or beings in their world, they must cut their way through the perimeter to the inside, much as we must do in our world to see the interiors of three-dimensional objects.

Further, the Circle, by rotating a line being in an extra dimension, turned him inside-out. Can we do likewise to a plane being? Look at figure 6; it's our old friend the skeptical Square—a perfect subject—and he's facing the left. Now, the only way for him to face the right is to spin completely around, but this would leave him upside-down. Yet with the use of a third dimension, we can simply reach down and flip him over, making him face the right while still right-side-up.

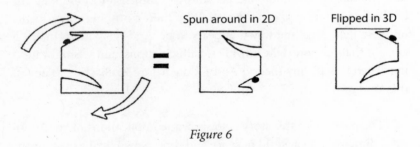

Figure 6

Just think of how the Square with knowledge of and movement in only two dimensions must interpret this: it could only be inside-out. Even so, supernatural physical operations like this can be carried out with ease through an extra dimension in any world of space and time.

Now what if you and I are extra-dimensional aliens who wish to examine a plane being at length? Couldn't we just reach down into their world, suddenly appear there, and cart him off into the third dimension? Here we could take physical samples, even tinker with his psychological make-up. When we return him, how do you think other plane beings would react when he recounts his incredible experience? "Impossible!" they might say. "Aliens! Other dimensions! Experiments! Higher consciousness! It can't be, therefore, it isn't." Besides, they might think it ludicrous we wouldn't first want to present ourselves to their plane world politicians and scientists, as they would do if and when they encountered another plane world with intelligent life.

All extra dimensions exist in time, the Circle said. He showed that the line beings' time was really motion in an extra (second) dimension; he speculated that it would likewise be so for plane beings. Let's see. We'll take the same type of ruler with the red, blue, and yellow sections the Circle used and lower it through (or in front of) the plane world, as in figure 7. Now what do the plane beings see? A red *line* suddenly appear in their world, which changes to a blue one, and then a yellow one before disappearing.

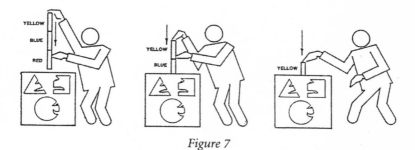

Figure 7

The motion in higher space, that of the ruler, can only be experienced bit by bit, inseparable from time. The plane beings cannot perceive any three-dimensional object as it is, or even imagine its true appearance or function in higher space, for they can only detect the tiniest part of it at any one moment in their space.

This time let's consider a different kind of object: a sphere. I'll take a basketball and lower it through (or in front of) the plane world, as in figure 8. What do the plane beings see? At first just a point, which then expands into a longer and longer line until the midpoint of the ball passes through the plane.

Figure 8

Then the line contracts, appearing shorter and shorter until just a point is visible again, then nothing. It simply disappears. Here's the amazing part: If we reverse the process and raise the sphere through the plane world, it appears in exactly the same sequence: point, growing into a line, contracting into a point which disappears. The implications of this are profound. It means that even though motion in higher space may be in different directions (as it could have been with the ruler as well), the plane beings, or any race of beings in any lower space, translate it into only one direction—linear time from past to future.

Now what would it be like if a plane being, say the open-minded Triangle, had a sudden expansion or elevation of consciousness—a mystical experience—so that he could now see in three dimensions? First, he is sure to understand that the world of space is vaster and stranger than he ever imagined. And his old sense of time? It would not apply, for he could now behold time, the past and future, as motion laid out in higher space. In fact, he could predict the future.

For example, he could see, if the ruler were passing through his plane world, that after the red line would come a blue one, then a yellow. He could infer that this is just motion in a higher space, but this would be an extremely insightful deduction on his part, even for the erudite Triangle. It is much more probable that, since he could see the past, present, and future at once here, he would think that time does not exist in this larger realm.

He is also sure to grasp that he has a larger self that exists in this domain, and that this larger self must still exist, beyond the plane world, when that life ended. Indeed, he would see the higher reality as a virtual "kingdom," a land beyond time and even death.

All this and more the Triangle now conceives by virtue of a new mental faculty, one beyond the old senses and thought processes—a higher sense that brings immediate supernatural powers and vision. For example, he could now see the insides of things on his plane world; in fact, he would probably say that the gateway to this higher level of reality lies within, or in an inside-out direction. From this higher vantage point, be could also see things and events in many and remote parts of the plane world; he would have clairvoyance. Further, he would understand that physical maneuvers impossible in the plane world are possible in such a larger one; he may even perform some.

But this higher, mystical vision is very strange. Everything takes on a new form, a new perspective. He organizes input in a more sweeping fashion, and many things he always thought of as separate and distinct now seem joined and connected. For instance, with only two-dimensional consciousness, every circle, triangle, or square was separate and unique; but now he grasps an idea of plurality and sees the overall connection between them, that all triangles are one, all squares one, all circles one; all is one. So he may think to himself. In other words, reality will appear infinitely broader but infinitely simpler as well; he will have a tendency to condense it into fewer, more general conceptions.

Failing to realize that his new sense is just a higher, normal power of mind, he may think his new vision is ultimate, divine, that he has seen God, that Heaven has opened up before his eyes. After all, compared to his old state he is practically omniscient now, and isn't omniscience the attribute of God? This is what it must be, communion with God!

But all too soon the vision fades, the higher sense swoons, and the Triangle's consciousness plummets back to the plane world. Now what? Did this really happen or am I crazy? he wonders. But in the end he knows—he has seen the real world, the vaster one, the kingdom; it is the old one that is distorted, constricted, and incomplete. This strength of conviction though, will not help him convince his fellow plane beings. For the higher world must be described in lower world terminology and concepts. Imagine him trying to explain to the skeptical Square that all squares or triangles, which are normally thought of as completely different, are really one. His attempts will come across as paradoxical and absurd because the experience is ineffable.

In these analogies with the line world and plane world, their realities are just part of a larger extra-dimensional reality, and a higher faculty is needed to see this. Yet clues to the situation reveal themselves in many ways. If there is an extra dimension to our world and a higher faculty by which we can perceive it, how should this be revealed to us? In the same ways as in these lower worlds. These ways will become apparent later in the chapters on consciousness and time and will be unmistakably demonstrated with the paranormal. Four points will be clearly shown.

1) **Our world is extra-dimensional.** As a line and square must have extension in a third dimension to exist, everything in our world—man, woman, animate and inanimate object—must have extension in an extra dimension to exist. In fact, the greater part of us exists in higher space. We live on two different levels simultaneously, unaware of the larger self and world. The Russian philosopher P. D. Ouspensky, whose early philosophy is a cornerstone of extra-dimensional theory, put it this way in a 1908 essay "The Fourth Dimension":

> We may have very good reason for saying that we are ourselves beings of four dimensions and we are turned towards the third dimension with only one of our sides, i.e., with only a small part of our being. Only this part of us lives in three dimensions, and we are conscious only of this part of ourselves. Or it would still be more true to say that we live in a four-dimensional world, but are conscious of ourselves only in a three-dimensional world. This means that we live in one kind of condition, but imagine ourselves to be in another.[1]

What happens when these conditions change? When we die and our local consciousness exits our world and merges with its larger self and consciousness in extra-dimensional space? Here is a near-death account from Raymond A. Moody, Jr.'s, 1975 groundbreaking work *Life After Life.*

> Now, there is a real problem for me as I'm trying to tell you this, because all the words I know are three-dimensional. As I was going through this, I kept thinking, "Well, when I was taking geometry, they always told me there were only three dimensions, and I always just accepted that. But they were wrong. There are more." And, of course, our world—the one we're living in now—*is* three-dimensional, but the next one definitely isn't. And that's why it's so hard to tell you this. I have to describe it to you in words that are three-dimensional. That's as close as I can get to it, but it's not really adequate. I can't really give you a complete picture.[2]

Dr. George Gallup, Jr., best known for his Gallup Poll, wrote *Adventures in Immortality,* based on a survey of near-death experiencers. One of their most common responses was "the impression of being in an entirely different world."[3] Gallup, comparing his findings with those of other near-death researchers, concluded that, overall, the "results have been highly suggestive of some sort of encounter with an extradimensional realm of reality."[4]

Dr. Kenneth Ring, professor of psychology at the University of Connecticut and a leading researcher in the field, also regards the experience as a transition to another, larger realm of existence. This from his *Life at Death:* "These experiences clearly imply that there is something more, something *beyond* the physical world of the senses, which, in the light of these experiences, now appears to be only the mundane segment of a greater spectrum of reality."[5]

Why can't we detect this extra dimension? Ring hints at the answer here: it's "beyond the physical world of the senses." Like the beings of the plane world, we have no capacity to move in this other direction and no means by which we can sense or otherwise become conscious of it. We are anchored, mentally and physically, to our three-dimensional world. Our normal level of consciousness is simply inadequate, and our science, born from this consciousness, is just as limited. This may at first sound surprising, accustomed as we are to regarding the reach of science as boundless, but Denis Postle, in *Fabric of the Universe,* points out how our science is *only an extension* of our senses and consciousness.

> Science is the discipline in the West which is most concerned with establishing what does exist and what is merely wishfulness on the part of an observer. We forget, or never come to know, that science is no more than a range of devices—some material, some mental—which extend one or more of the senses or functions of mind into areas of space or time to which they would otherwise be unable to penetrate. The images and symbols of language extend memory; computers and computer language extend memory capacity and speed of thinking; space probes extend the distance at which sight and touch can operate; equations extend thinking itself.[6]

Our world is indeed extra-dimensional, over and above the current scientific worldview, which is only the latest in a long line of "approximations" of reality. In fact, when we look closely, we'll see hints of this extra dimension right at the limits of our worldview—in the realm of the very large, cosmology, and the very small, quantum physics, where bizarre and contradictory experimental results cry out for a new interpretation. In chapter 9, I'll show how extra-dimensional theory can resolve paradoxes in this field that have defied solution since the 1930s.

2) **Impossible physical maneuvers become normal.** If there really is an extra dimension, shouldn't we expect to occasionally see miraculous events happen in our world, just like those in the plane world? Objects suddenly appear from out of nowhere, get larger, change color, change shape, get smaller, and disappear? These would be incredible occurrences, so much so that they could scarcely be believed. Yet they do happen.

UFOs are known to do all these things. This is in part why Dr. Jacques Vallee, perhaps the field's most influential theorist, says, "The standard extraterrestrial theory of UFOs is not good enough, because it is not strange enough to explain the facts."[7] Vallee now believes that

UFOs are the product of a nonhuman consciousness, operating "on properties of space-time we have not yet discovered"[8] or "in a multi-dimensional reality of which [our] space-time is a subset."[9] Sound familiar?

What of the aliens behind the UFO phenomenon? They live, mentally and physically, in an extra-dimensional continuum of space-time. In the abduction phenomenon, we'll see that they have complete possession of that higher faculty, even the hints of which are supernatural to us and seem to involve mystical knowledge and psychic powers. They enter closed rooms without the disturbance of walls, doors, or windows, just appear there and carry off and later return their subjects the same way. Carry them off where? Into another world, an extra-dimensional one. John E. Mack, M.D., professor of psychiatry at Harvard Medical School, in his 1994 *Abduction,* relates that many abductees speak of aliens entering our world by "breaking through from another dimension"[10] and abducting people into a larger reality. Mack says:

> . . . there are phenomena and experiences reported by abductees for which we can conceive of no explanation within a Newtonian/Cartesian or even Einsteinian space/time ontology . . . abductees sense that their experiences are not occurring in our space/time universe . . . [plus] . . . a consciousness abductees experience of vast realities beyond the screen of this one. . . ."[11] They experience that they have moved into another reality, but one that is, nevertheless, altogether real.[12]

Raymond E. Fowler, another abduction researcher, believes aliens "exist in a timeless realm, and travel between different planes of existence,"[13] at times "emerging into our space/time frame."[14] Sounds like how the Circle might depict us. The direction abductees report they are taken in to get to this other reality? Mack's interviewees describe it in terms such as "worlds existing within worlds, and in the transition from one reality to another, you feel like you're contracting and expanding at the same time."[15] "Energy . . . folds into itself, and you're just somewhere else . . . everything folds, inverts into, and folds inside itself."[16] The direction is inside out.

We can find examples of impossible physical maneuvers closer to home, right in our normal world, accomplished by some humans with a special knack for wielding just a little bit of extra-dimensional consciousness in psychic phenomena such as teleportation (the movement of objects through solid walls and other barriers or around them through some other space) and psychokinesis (the manipulation of objects by means other than normal or through a medium imperceptible to us). When we see how these work, we'll understand another phenomenon, one for which such maneuvers are the order of the day: the mysterious and spectacular poltergeist.

In a line or plane world, we can turn an object inside-out by using an extra dimension. Can someone in our world turn a physical object inside-out? We'll see how in chapter 6. Meanwhile, here's a description of higher consciousness by Edward Carpenter. Or is it by a line being? Or a plane being? "[A]nother and separate faculty . . . a sense of inward light, unconnected of course with the mortal eye, but bringing to the eye of the mind the impression that it *sees*, and by means of the medium which washes, as it were, the *interior* surfaces of all objects and things and persons—how can I express it?"[17]

3) Our time is motion in extra-dimensional space. This is translated by our consciousness into a sequence of fragmentary perceptions in but one direction, past to future. This allows us to sense order in the world as cause and effect. But the perception of an extra dimension reveals this motion, indeed both cause and effect, as laid out at once in space. In *Tertium Organum* (1912), Ouspensky describes it:

> Our usual psychic life proceeds upon some definite plane (our normal world) and never rises above it. If our receptivity could rise above this plane it would undoubtedly perceive *simultaneously*, below itself, a far greater number of events than it usually sees while on a plane. Just as a man, ascending a mountain, or going up in a balloon, begins to see *simultaneously* and *at once* many things which it is impossible to see simultaneously and at once from below—the movement of two trains toward one another between which a collision will occur;

the approach of an enemy detachment to a sleeping camp; two cities divided by a ridge, etc.—so consciousness rising above the plane in which it usually functions, must see simultaneously the events divided for the ordinary consciousness by *periods of time*. These will be the events which ordinary consciousness *never* sees together, as: *cause* and *effect*; the work and the payment; the crime and the punishment; the movement of two trains toward one another and their collision; the approach of the enemy and the battle; the sunrise and the sunset; the morning and the evening; the day and the night; spring, autumn, summer and winter; the birth and the death of a man. The angle of vision will enlarge during such an ascent, the *moment* will expand.[18]

This is what happens with the onset of higher consciousness—the moment expands to include an extra dimension of space, which has our past and future laid out along it. Mystic Lama Govinda, in *Creative Meditation and Multi Dimensional Consciousness*, describes the mental transition to higher space the same way: "The way in which we experience space, or in which we are aware of space, is characteristic of the dimension of our consciousness. . . . And if we speak of the space-experience in meditation, we are dealing with an entirely different dimension . . . In this space-experience the temporal sequence is converted into a simultaneous coexistence, the side by side existence of things . . ."[19]

That is, the higher faculty mentally extracts from time an extra dimension of space where the past and future now become side by side. This explains much about the paranormal: that a small glimpse of this consciousness can be a glimpse of the future (precognition) or the past (postcognition), and how the more complete samplings of this consciousness (the mystical and near-death experiences) give the impression that this higher reality is timeless. For example:

In this state, there is no time, there is an immediate perception of the past, present, and future as if on the present moment.[20]

> I found myself in a state of widened and deepened con-
> sciousness, a consciousness of a higher dimension . . . While in
> this state, the past, present and future are simultaneously
> knowable.[21]

One describes a mystical experience, one a near-death experience. But which is which? It's hard to tell, for they both describe the same thing arrived at in different ways.

4) A higher faculty is the key that unlocks the door to higher space. Let's now go through it slowly in mathematical fashion, dimension by dimension. First, a line connects all points along that one dimension, right? What could be simpler? Now, to take that line and trace out a plane, we must move the line in a perpendicular direction, making a square, and the second dimension connects and is that which connects all lines in the plane. Right again? But that's not all.

In making the plane, *every point* in the line had to move in that second dimension. So the second dimension is not only that which connects all lines in the plane, but all points as well. Now, if we move the plane in a third perpendicular direction (the same length), we have a cube, and the third dimension connects all planes in the cube. But again, not only every plane but every line and point as well, for to form the cube, every point in the plane had to move in that third dimension. What does this mean?

An extra dimension connects and is that which *connects all three-dimensional objects and every point in them*. This makes conceivable that which would before be inconceivable, that apparently separate physical objects and people are united through this medium, and that things separated by enormous distances of space are here close together. Now, imagine that this extra dimension were to become a factor of consciousness. One would have knowledge that seems supernatural.

An isolated piece of this knowledge one gets at a time may come through as telepathy or clairvoyance. What of the embrace of this all-connecting, interpenetrating oneness suddenly and unexpectedly appearing as in a mystical or near-death experience? It's overwhelming. Nothing could prepare one for it. The mind reels under the impact. Not only this, but to experience a vast kingdom where the past and future exist together, where there's no time! Compared with ordinary reality and consciousness, it must seem miraculous, divine, and ineffable.

"How can I express it?" Edward Carpenter said, after he "saw" this from an inward-out direction. Said Moody's NDEr of her extra-dimensional encounter, "It's so hard to tell you. I have to describe it to you in words that are three-dimensional. That's as close as I can get to it, but it's not really adequate. I can't really give you a complete picture." These are normal, typical reactions. In fact, virtually all accounts of higher consciousness make reference to its ineffable nature. Our normal concepts and language lack the necessary symbolism to portray it. "I can't even explain it. There is no feeling you experience in normal life that is anything like this,"[22] said another NDEr. The *Tao Te Ching* (mystical text of China) simply says: "It cannot be defined."[23]

Ineffable. Not completely. There is a way to capture the essence and even logic of the higher faculty. We'll see it in the next chapter.

According to extra-dimensional theory, our world is part of a larger reality that requires a higher faculty to perceive it. But this in itself is nothing new. Mystics through the ages have known this and wise men have inferred it from their teachings. In fact, this revelation is at the core of every religion (the core only, throw away everything else). It has come to be known as the Perennial Philosophy, a generalized mystical outlook adopted to varying degrees by many of the greatest minds in history, including Plato, Newton, Einstein, Spinoza, Schrödinger, Schopenhauer, Jung, William James, and others.

The basics of the Perennial Philosophy are:

1) Our normal world of matter and consciousness is but a part and manifestation of a vaster Divine Ground, without which our world could not exist.

2) Man has a dual nature—the familiar ego, and a higher self, or spirit, which dwells within this higher ground.

3) Besides knowing about the higher ground by inference, it is possible to know it by a higher form of knowledge such as direct union or mystical experience.

4) Man's main purpose in life is to direct himself toward his higher self, which leads to unification with the Divine Ground.

Here is an early account of an extra dimension and its accompanying higher consciousness. In *The Republic* (circa 370 B.C.), Plato presents the simile of the cave. He prefaces this story by arguing that in our present condition (then), what we take for reality is mere illusion, but there is a higher wisdom that can perceive the world as it truly is. The tale, told through a dialogue between Socrates and Glaucon, is an analogy of how one's point of view changes with an extra-dimensional perspective.

> Socrates: And now, let me show in a figure how far our nature is enlightened or unenlightened. Behold human beings living in an underground den, which has a mouth open toward the light and reaching all along the den; here they have been from childhood, and have their neck and legs chained so that they cannot move, and can only see before them, being prevented by the chain from turning round their heads. Above and behind them is a fire blazing at a distance, and between the fire and the prisoners there is a raised way; and you will see if you look, a low wall built along the way, like the screen which marionette-players have in front of them, over which they show the puppets.
>
> Glaucon: I see.
>
> Socrates: And do you see, men passing along the wall carrying all sorts of vessels, and statues and figures of animals made of wood and stone and various materials, which appear over the wall? Some of them are talking, others silent.
>
> Glaucon: You have shown me a strange image, and they are strange prisoners.
>
> Socrates: Like ourselves, and they see only their own shadows, or the shadows of one another, which the fire throws on the opposite wall of the cave?
>
> Glaucon: True; how could they see anything but the shadows if they were never allowed to move their heads?
>
> Socrates: And of the objects which are being carried in like manner they would only see the shadows?

Glaucon: Yes.

Socrates: And if they were able to converse with one another, would they not suppose that the shadows they saw were real things?

Glaucon: Very true.

Socrates: And suppose further that the prison had an echo which came from the other side, would they not be sure to fancy when one of the passers-by spoke that the voice which they heard came from the passing shadow?

Glaucon: No question.

Socrates: To them, the truth would be literally nothing but the shadows of the images.

Glaucon: That is certain.

Socrates: And now look again, and see what will naturally follow if the prisoners are released and disabused of their error. At first, when any one of them is liberated and compelled suddenly to stand up and turn his head round and walk and look toward the light, he will suffer sharp pains; the glare will distress him, and he will be unable to see the realities of which in his former state he had seen the shadows; and then conceive someone saying to him that what he saw before was an illusion, but that now, when he is approaching nearer to being and his eye is turned toward more real existence, he has a clearer vision—what will be his reply? And you may further imagine that his instructor is pointing to the objects as they pass and requiring him to name them—will he not be perplexed? Will he not fancy that the shadows which he formerly saw are truer than the objects which are now shown to him?

Glaucon: Far truer.

Socrates: And if he is compelled to look straight at the light, will he not have a pain in his eyes which will make him turn away to take refuge in the objects of vision which he can see, and which he will conceive to be in reality clearer than the things which are now being shown to him?

Glaucon: True.

Socrates: And suppose once more, that he is reluctantly

dragged up a steep and rugged ascent, and held fast until he is forced into the presence of the sun itself, is he not likely to be pained and irritated? When he approaches the light his eyes will be dazzled, and he will not be able to see anything at all of what are now called realities.

Glaucon: Not all in a moment.

Socrates: He will require to grow accustomed to the sight of the upper world. And first he will see the shadows best, next the reflections of men and other objects in the water, and then the objects themselves; then he will gaze upon the light of the moon and the stars and the spangled heaven; and he will see the sky and the stars by night better than the sun or the light of the sun by day?

Glaucon: Certainly.

Socrates: Last of all he will be able to see the sun, and not merely reflections of it in the water, but he will see it in its own proper place, and not in another; and he will contemplate it as it is.

Glaucon: Certainly.

Socrates: He will then proceed to argue that it is the sun that gives the seasons and the years, and is the guardian of all that is in the visible world, and in a certain way the cause of all things which he and his fellows have been accustomed to behold?

Glaucon: Clearly, he would first see the sun and then reason about it.

Socrates: And when he remembered his old habitation, and the wisdom of the den and his fellow prisoners, do you not suppose that he would congratulate himself on the change, and pity them?

Glaucon: Certainly.

Socrates: And if the prisoners were in the habit of conferring honors among themselves on those who were the quickest to observe the passing shadows and to remark which of them went before, and which followed after, and which were together; and who therefore best able to draw conclusions as to the future, do you think he would care for such honors and glories, or envy the possessors of them? Would he not say with Homer, "Better to be the poor servant of a poor master,"[24] and to endure anything, rather than think as they do and live after their manner?

Glaucon: Yes, I think he would rather suffer anything than entertain these false notions and live in this miserable condition.

Socrates: Imagine once more, such a one suddenly coming out of the sun to be replaced in his old situation; would he not be certain to have his eyes full of darkness?

Glaucon: To be sure.

Socrates: And if there were a contest, and he had to compete in measuring the shadows with the prisoners who had never moved out of the den, while his sight was still weak, and before his eyes had become steady (and the time which would be needed to acquire this new habit of sight might be very considerable), would he not be ridiculous? Men would say of him that up he went and down he came without his eyes; and that it was better not even to think of ascending; and if anyone tried to loose another and lead him up to the light, let them only catch the offender, and they would put him to death.

Glaucon: No question.[25]

In this account the cave dwellers and their world have an extra dimension of which they are unaware. This is analogous to our world as a three-dimensional cross-section of a larger reality, as their shadow world is a two-dimensional image of a three-dimensional one.

So what is space? Space is simply the form or structure of the outside world as it *appears* to our senses. Or it may be more accurate to say that space is the structure we ascribe to the world to make sense of it on our particular level of consciousness, like the plane beings or the dwellers in Plato's cave. It is our representation, our map, of reality, and as a map is a two-dimensional abstraction of a three-dimensional world, so our three-dimensional space-world is likewise an abstraction of a larger, extra-dimensional one.

Levels of Consciousness

"I think, therefore I am," said the philosopher,[1] and this is now a common expression. But what does this mean? How do we think? We probably don't give it much "thought."

We're all conscious. But what is consciousness? Are there different kinds? How do animals think? Do they? And if they don't, does that mean they don't exist? Why should we care how a dog thinks? Or a snail? What does this have to do with the paranormal or space and time? They obviously live in the same space-time world we do. It seems logical. But they don't! We all live in different ones, and yet the same, larger one. Illogical? Yes, but true. I'll show you. In the largest, extra-dimensional world, our logic becomes absurdity, absurdity becomes higher logic, and the paranormal becomes the normal.

In 1872, Richard Maurice Bucke, a prominent Canadian doctor, was visiting friends in England when he had an experience that would forever change his life and his outlook on consciousness. The event is described here by Bucke, writing of himself in the third person.

He and two friends had spent the evening reading Wordsworth, Shelley, Keats, Browning, and especially Whitman.

They parted at midnight, and he had a long drive in a hansom. His mind, deeply under the influence of the ideas, images, and emotions called up by the reading and talk of the evening, was calm and peaceful. He was in a state of quiet, almost passive, enjoyment. All at once, without warning of any kind, he found himself wrapped around, as it were, by a flame-colored cloud. For an instant he thought of fire, some sudden conflagration in the great city. The next [instant] he knew that the light was within himself. Directly afterwards there came upon him a sense of exultation, of immense joyousness accompanied or immediately followed by an intellectual illumination quite impossible to describe. Into his brain streamed one momentary lightning-flash of the Brahmic Splendor which ever since lightened his life; upon his heart fell one drop of the Brahmic Bliss, leaving thenceforward for always an aftertaste of heaven. Among other things he did not come to believe, he saw and knew that the Cosmos is not dead matter but a living Presence, that the soul of man is immortal, that the universe is so built and ordered that without any peradventure all things work together for the good of each and all . . . He claims that he learned more within the few seconds during which the illumination lasted than in previous months or even years of study, and that he learned much that no study could ever have taught.

The illumination itself continued not more than a few moments, but its effects proved ineffaceable; it was impossible for him ever to forget what he at that time saw and knew; neither did he, or could he, ever doubt the truth of what was then presented to his mind. There was no return, that night or at any other time, of the experience.[2]

This account is fairly typical of the mystical or religious experience. Bucke, a student of the human mind, reasoned it had nothing to do with mysticism or religion as such. He considered it, psychologically, as a new mental state yet unrecognized by science.

He searched through available literature to find signs of the same state in others, and found them in the writings of the Buddha, Jesus, Paul, Plotinus, Mohammed, Dante, Edward Carpenter, William Blake, Walt Whitman, and others. What struck him was that all of these men, living in different times and cultures, had basically the same vision of reality when endowed with this new sense, even though it was given various names such as nirvana, ecstasy, Christ, the Spirit, the Father, and Gabriel. Bucke concluded that these experiences of illumination were initiations to a higher, distinct form of consciousness—a new faculty. He eventually wrote a book, *Cosmic Consciousness,* published in 1901, in which he set down what he believed to be the meaning of it all. Bucke's theory, as outlined in his now classic work, is as follows:

There are four grades or levels of mental function in our world, lower gradually evolving into the higher. The first is sensation, found in lower animals; the second is simple consciousness, found in higher animals; the third is self-consciousness, possessed by humans; and the fourth is a state Bucke called "cosmic consciousness," a level as far above Man's self-consciousness as that is above the animals' simple consciousness.

Bucke argued that consciousness is a sense constantly evolving in all life, and this evolution is marked by spectacular leaps at key points. When a species reaches a certain threshold in its mental development, a distinctly higher form of consciousness will spontaneously manifest itself in a few individuals—the best of the lot—and with the passing of generations it will become more and more frequent until it is finally possessed by the entire species. Thus our descendants as a race will at some point reach cosmic consciousness, just as our ancestors progressed from simple to self-consciousness.

The main feature of cosmic consciousness is its completely different way of knowing, by direct union with the life and order of the cosmos. Bucke said: "Like a flash there is presented to his consciousness a clear conception [a vision] in outline of the meaning and drift of the universe."[3] This knowledge is so profound and so sweeping that just the briefest flash of it gives one a perspective which never can be obtained by ordinary means; those who have seen it feel compelled to share it, pass it down as best they can in the form of teachings and writings, and in this way accelerate the progress of the race toward the same end. Bucke wrote:

The trait that distinguishes these people from other men is this: Their spiritual eyes have been opened and they have seen. The better known members of this group, who, were they collected together, could be accommodated all at one time in a modern drawing-room, have created all the great modern religions, beginning with Taoism and Buddhism, and speaking generally, have created, through religion and literature, modern civilization. Not that they have contributed any large numerical proportion of the books which have been written, but they have produced the few books which have inspired the larger number of all that have been written in modern times. These men dominate the last twenty-five, especially the last five, centuries as stars of the first magnitude dominate the midnight sky.[4]

Though not as famous as the others from this group, Bucke may well have written just such a book. Ouspensky's *Tertium Organum*, in my opinion, is another. Together they helped inspire my own work. Bucke's genius was to put higher consciousness, and the mystical and religious experience, in a simple evolutionary context, that of a fourth stage of *normal* conscious function. Ouspensky's was to begin to add frameworks of space and time to these stages. Now let's put their views and mine together.

Picture this idyllic scene: It's a sunny spring day in New England, and a young boy, Mark, sits in his backyard with his favorite playmate, a little terrier incongruously named Samson. But Samson is preoccupied; he too has a playmate, a snail he has excitedly discovered. Each of these three creatures represents a separate stage of mental evolution, the first three as described by Bucke: sensation, by a lower animal—the snail; simple consciousness, by a higher animal—Samson the dog; and self-consciousness, by Mark, a human. As you picture this scene, it is obviously in three dimensions of space plus time, as it would be for Mark. But how would it be for Samson or the snail? Entirely different.

The snail lives in a world of one dimension of space plus time. Like the very first creatures on Earth capable of receiving information of the outside world, the snail receives all such information as sensations—and these lie along one axis, pleasure-pain. Every input registers somewhere along this scale, with those at one end of it exciting him to one set of instinctive reactions, and those at the opposite end to others. Everything else in the world exists for him in time.

It is obvious to us as we picture the snail crawling along the ground, and to Mark as he watches it, that the snail is a three-dimensional creature in a three-dimensional world. But the snail with his sensation is only aware of one dimension, and even this one he senses as just one point at a time. The space on the ground he has already covered does not exist for him anymore because it as it can no longer impart sensation to him; similarly for the space ahead of him. They belong to his past and future; they exist only in time. The space above, below, and to the sides of the snail will never exist for him, as it can never excite his sensation. That is, though there are three dimensions of space around him, the snail's idea of space, like a being in a line world, is only along the one dimension where sensation occurs for him.

Samson plays with the snail. He touches it with his paw, then his snout, and the snail recoils in pain. Mark reaches out with a stick and touches it; again it recoils the same way. The snail can't tell the difference in the causes. If Mark and Samson touch it at the same time, he will feel only one sensation—the most intense one. How limited its world is. For the snail as subject must find any object (that which imparts sensation) indistinguishable from the sensation itself. At least this lowly creature has no problem with cause and effect as they are one and the same for it.

The snail may not be traveling in a straight line, but *his space* is as straight a dimension as his linear method of apprehending it. The other two dimensions of space are presented to him *in time*, sensed as a fragment when motion through them, such as a paw, snout, or stick, intersects his dimension of sensation. Motion in two- and three-dimensional space are translated by his limited mental faculty into either sensation or time.

Now imagine that the snail were somehow able to formulate a worldview. What could it be? Only this: Space is the one dimension or line where all sensations or objects exist. Sensations vary in intensity along this axis as pleasure or pain; only this distinguishes them from each other. Time is the separation between these sensations and the intervals by which they change.

Such was the world of the first creatures on Earth, which the snail still represents. But, gradually and painstakingly, over eons and many generations, the central nervous systems of these lower animals grew more refined. More cells were added to their sense organs and nerve ganglia, and finally their capacity to register sensations became so broad and so defined that they could perceive several sensations *at once* and combine them into a larger reception.

What this means is that, by the sense of sight, smell, and hearing, several impressions or images could now be combined at one time into one picture, as in a composite photograph. As these animals continued to evolve, more impressions could be included, simple sensation now openly blossoming into consciousness. These animals, instead of experiencing the world as a series of points along a line, could now clearly apprehend lines and surfaces and the difference between them. They have, by virtue of this new and higher faculty, mentally extracted another dimension of space from what was previously time, extracted by perceiving from the transcendental part of reality another perceived part.

Such animals can now sense two dimensions of space instead of one and can see at once that which before took time to see. For example, Samson relents, the snail reaches its hole, and decides to inspect it. But he must do it point by point, and this takes time. Not for Samson though. He sees the hole, its lines, angles, the whole surface of it as it is, at once.

Let's keep the animals on hold and for comparison see how Mark thinks. Then we'll have a better idea of what Samson and other higher animals' worldview might be, and why.

Mark, like all humans, is self-conscious. Yet he wasn't born that way. In his first few years he actually had just simple consciousness, much like Samson. But at about age three, something remarkable happened. Suddenly, he became aware of something different, apart from, his environment. He became aware of himself, an "I" separate from everything else in the world. This is the foundation of self-consciousness, the concept of self, after which all other concepts are gradually added. The animal senses and knows things; in fact, his senses are usually more acute than ours. But he does not know that he knows; he is aware of his surroundings, but not of himself. Call Samson's name and he responds emotionally to the recognizable tone, the inflection of the voice. But he does not know that he is Samson or that he even "is." He is immersed in his simple consciousness like a figure in a portrait, a fish in the sea. But Mark, with the onset of self-consciousness, can mentally step outside his environment, become aware of distinction and self, and utter those words, "I am."

This is how it happened in an evolutionary scheme as well. Over many millions of years animals with simple consciousness evolved and became capable of ever sharper, more distinct impressions. Eventually, a breakthrough was made. The best specimens of the most advanced species—primitive apish creatures—finally acquired the ability to hold an impression of something in mind even when it was no longer there. Now it could be labeled and communicated to another by a sign or gesture. Of course the first one was "I" then "you," and after this probably the elements of most immediate concern, such as food, water, danger. These are all concepts that represent something in the outside world, mental images formed from sensory images. Bucke describes a concept as "a recept (impression) marked with a sign which stands for it—just as a check stands for a piece of baggage or as an entry in a ledger stands for a piece of goods."[5]

Of course with concepts comes language, a natural consequence of self-consciousness. Language is the expression of concepts by means of mutually understood sounds or symbols, while thought is the silent evaluation of them. Over the course of time, these concepts are organized into logic, mathematics, philosophy, religion, science, and worldviews.

Conceptual thought and communication are made possible by the fact that each concept or sign relates to something different, as opposed to other concepts. Of course by being aware of degrees of difference, we are also aware of degrees of likeness. All concepts, in fact, signify what they do by virtue of their difference from and similarity to others, and when two or more objects seem sufficiently similar, we can fashion them into a more generalized concept—plurals.

Now, back to Samson and his world with, first of all, no plurals. He perceives differences between objects, but here with the sense of first impression his classification ends. He cannot mentally group any of them together, i.e., one man and another are completely different and he can never imagine that they have a general similarity as men. Ouspensky spoke of this in *Tertium Organum.*

> The logic of animals will differ from ours, first of all, from the fact that it will not be general. It will exist separately for each case, for each perception. Common properties, class properties, and the generic and different signs of categories will not exist for animals. Each object will exist in and by itself, and all its properties will be the specific properties of it alone.
>
> This house and that house are entirely different objects for an animal, because one is its house and the other is a strange house.[6]

Ouspensky then imagines animals beginning to dimly sense our logic, and how completely absurd and ineffable it would seem to them.

> Let us imagine that to the animal with the rudimentary logic expressing its sensations: This is this.
>
> That is that.
>
> This is not that.
>
> Somebody tries to prove that two different objects, two houses—its own and a strange one—are similar, that they represent one and the same thing, that they are both houses. The animal will never credit this similarity. For it the two houses, its own, where it is fed, and the strange one, where it is beaten if it enters, will remain entirely different. There will be nothing in common in them for it, and the effort to prove to it the similarity of these two houses will lead to nothing until it senses this itself. Then, sensing confusedly the idea of the likeness of two different objects, and being without concepts, the animal will express this as something illogical from its own point of view. The idea, this and that are similar objects, the articulate two-

dimensional being will translate into the language of its logic, in the shape of the formula: this is that; and of course will pronounce it an absurdity, and that the sensation of the new order of things leads to logical absurdities. But it will be unable to express that which it senses in any other way.[7]

A snail, with just sensation, lives in a world of one dimension of space plus time, even though there are three all around him. A dog, with simple consciousness, lives in a world of two dimensions of space plus time, even though there are three all around him. That is, the dog, though constantly in contact with and actually able to sense a third dimension of space, can deal with *only two at once;* the third is sensed by him in time.

For example: Mark walks through his yard to a wooden box, and Samson, the snail now gone, follows. Samson wants to inspect it, yet he must do so in much the same way that the snail inspected his hole, bit by bit. Samson starts with one side, the front, let's say, and sees a two-dimensional surface. But as he moves around it to the side, and sees another one, the idea of the first surface has left his mind; it is now in his past. He hasn't the faculty to keep the first one in mind *in its absence* as a concept and thus be able to combine it mentally with the others into a three-dimensional image of a box. To mentally grasp any one surface, he must mentally let go of the last one. Without conceptual thought, Samson's world is one of constantly changing surfaces.

That is, although his world is three-dimensional, the dog sees only two at any given time—surfaces—and the third is represented to him as motion. How do we know this? *Because this is exactly what we see.* We see only surfaces with the eye, but our minds, by practicing from infancy, can visualize three-dimensional solids *in the brain.* Look around you. If you see a box, table, chair, or house, the reflected light from them forms two-dimensional images in the eyes, that are then combined into a three-dimensional image in the brain. John Ross of the University of Australia said in *Scientific American,* March 1976: "The visual system in effect constructs three-dimensional scenes from the two-dimensional images formed on the retinas by fitting the visual information into a conceptual framework."[8]

The key word is "conceptual," for it is the faculty of self-consciousness that makes this possible. It allows for the refinement of a skill that has developed so gradually and naturally we take it for granted. You probably don't remember that as a baby you constantly reached out to feel any and all objects around you. A picture of a ball and a real ball, a surface and a solid, were the same at first. But you groped for and felt its third dimension and started to acquire an idea of how such objects must be, must look. That's how you began to see them. The animal, however, lacking this ability to mentally compensate for distorted two-dimensional images, sees everything just as it appears to be. Just as to see the third dimension requires a higher function of mind, to see an extra one requires a still higher function.

The animal learns much of what it does know by attaching emotional colors or tones to situations and objects. It is gradually able to function in the world by building up a large inventory of such associations, one for every object, person, or event. Many animals display remarkable prowess in certain physical acts, which makes it appear that they possess depth perception, but this is due to their primal instinctual programming and is not a *mental* assessment of the situation.

So, just what kind of mental assessment of the world would an animal like Samson have? He would think that the world consists of surfaces encountered in space plus time. And what surfaces! For only when he is at rest and there is no motion around him do these surfaces stay put. But if he or anything around him moves, the surfaces begin to display all kinds of bizarre and complicated motions: twisting, turning, expanding, contracting, narrowing, appearing, and disappearing. Take Samson for a ride in the car and he is mesmerized. He sees the surfaces of houses twisting about, trees turning around, and the panorama in a whirl of motion we know to be illusory.

Back on solid ground, a cube, plane, sphere, or circle look the same to him; only upon approaching them do they seem different, as their surfaces spin differently. To Samson, the motion of lines and surfaces is hopelessly complicated and incomprehensible. He must take each situation as it comes and rely on his instincts and store of emotional responses for guidance. The third dimension of solids is sensed by him as motion, completely embedded in his idea of time.

His idea of cause and effect is just as strange, based on conditioning. If Mark always rings a bell before he serves Samson his food, Samson will associate the bell as the cause, like Pavlov's dogs. If the bell accidentally falls to the floor and rings (with no dinner to follow), Samson will be perplexed but ignore this violation of causality. If the sequence of events is abandoned, Samson's previous idea of cause and effect will dissolve and eventually reform with new information.

The limited space-time worlds of the snail and the dog are direct consequences of their limited levels of mental function. It may not be easy to accept that our space-time world is likewise limited by our level of consciousness, or that our laws (based on observed consistencies) likewise represent a sort of conditioning, but to understand the paranormal we must, or else we will be just like Pavlov's dogs: when violations of our laws happen, we will ignore them; they can't be, so they aren't.

We have *mentally* extracted a third dimension of space from time with self-consciousness, and since the third dimension is that which connects two-dimensional surfaces, we can connect these surfaces *mentally* with depth perception. With self-consciousness we also have concepts. We start with only one—self—but accumulate them throughout our life; in fact, our mind becomes a kaleidoscope of concepts. When we store them, it's memory; compare them, it's reason; communicate them, language; make a science of them, logic; and quantify them, mathematics. Of course, everyone's conceptual mind works a little differently. Bucke says: "The large intellect is that in which the number of concepts is above the average; the fine intellect is that in which these are clear cut and well defined; the ready intellect is that in which they are easily and quickly accessible when wanted, and so on."[9]

Yet overall, as humankind has progressed from generation to generation, our minds encompass an ever growing number of concepts, more complex ones, and sometimes entirely new ones. In fact, in an evolutionary scheme, it seems the mind has built up concepts in much the same way as lower forms of life built up brain cells and impressions. These concepts are continually broadened and unified in the subconscious, which is not particularly concerned with space and time, cause and effect, or logic. It is here that the mind's evolution toward a higher state takes place.

If the waking consciousness, self-consciousness, with all its habits, desires, attachments, and predisposed views of the world, is caught temporarily quiescent and off guard, the subconscious may superimpose a new vision of reality over and above it by extracting an extra dimension from time. Of course this would happen at first only sporadically, in the best specimens of the race, and when they are at their best, in the prime of life. Bucke proposed that the humans with the best prospects to achieve cosmic consciousness are those with exceptional mental, physical, and moral development. In fact, he rates the moral aspect as most important, and a balance of the three next.

Now it comes, a flash of cosmic consciousness and those feelings of peace and joy, the light, that staggering sense of oneness, that higher way of knowing that supersedes our normal conceptual thought, logic, and mathematics, rendering them obsolete. What is this higher way of thought? Can we imagine it? Can we conceive of a logic where $2 + 2$ does not equal 4? Ouspensky could—he called it "transfinite" logic and mathematics.

Imagine it's the first day of school and there are two different classrooms on two different planets. Here on Earth, Mark is ready for his first lesson on basic arithmetic, while on another planet, one where everyone has the higher, extra-dimensional faculty, an alien youth (whose name we can't pronounce) is likewise ready for his first lesson on the same subject. Mark's teacher says: "Now, pay close attention, class. This may seem very simple but it's very important. Here are some fundamentals of mathematics:

"Each and every number, or quantity, is equal to itself.

"Two different numbers cannot be equal.

"Two numbers, equal separately to a third, must be equal to each other.

"A part is always less than the whole."

Mark is already bored. He's a bright kid; he knows this. And who wouldn't? It's so easy.

In the other classroom, the teacher begins: "Now, pay close attention, class. This may seem very simple but it's very important. It is well known that everything in our world, in fact everything in the whole universe, is dynamic and infinite, so this is our foundation and point of departure for all mathematics—infinity itself, which we shall express as i~. Every number begins with this. Thus, if we take any two numbers, such as i~ + 1 and i~ + 10, we see that although different, they are also equal. They both equal infinity. And if we add, subtract, multiply, divide, square, etc., any numbers, the values will change accordingly, but still remain equal at the same time. They will all equal infinity. Consequently, any and all parts of the whole are equal to the whole and, though different, are still and always the same. So, here are some fundamentals of our mathematics:

"A number can be not equal to itself.

"Two numbers, equal to a third, can be different from each other.

"A part may be less than, equal to, or more than the whole.

"All different numbers, in spite of apparent differences, are equal.

"And most important of all:

"Each and every part contains and is the whole."

But this kid is smart, too, and he knows this. In fact, nothing could be more obvious to him, it all comes with his natural mental faculty, acquired at about age three, when his simple "I am," changed into "I am this, and that, and *everything*." This conception, that of the dynamic, inseparable and infinite whole, is the root of cosmic consciousness, just as the conception of self is of self-consciousness.

It is just this conception and logic that Ouspensky illustrates in his transfinite mathematics. It may seem absurd, but doesn't our logic—"this is also that," i.e., plurals—seem absurd to the animals' simple consciousness? Transfinite logic is the foundation of higher consciousness and the unifying principle of higher space. It's the whole contained in each and every part; and it's unmistakable to anyone who's tasted cosmic consciousness (for now, through the mystical experience).

The Buddha said: "This unity alone in the world is boundless in its reality, and being boundless is yet one. Though in small things, yet it is great; though in great things, yet is small. Pervading all things, present in every minutest hair, and yet including the infinite worlds in its embrace; enthroned in the minutest particle of dust . . . it is one with Divine knowledge."[10]

Eastern mystic Sri Aurobindo said: "Nothing to the supramental (higher) sense is really finite; it is founded on a feeling of all in each and of each in all."[11]

Plotinus: "Each part always proceeds from the whole, and is at the same time each part and the whole."[12]

Chinese philosopher Fa-Tsang: "Each one again contains the others, includes the others—each contains infinitely multiplied and remultiplied delineations of objects."[13]

And of course, just as in transfinite mathematics, no matter how any part is multiplied or divided, it is still one, infinite Whole. The Upanishads: "Indivisible, infinite, the Adorable One."[14] The Bhagavad-Gita: "Entire amidst all division."[15] Indian Yogi Shankara: "The Atman is one, absolute, indivisible."[16] Plotinus again: "The One, possessing no (geometrical) magnitude, is indivisible in its power."[17]

It is the apprehension of an extra dimension of space, extracted from time, that makes this possible, for this new medium connects and is that which connects *everything* in our three-dimensional world, that which we normally see as separated by space and by time. Lama Govinda makes both these points: "This space, however, is not the external 'visible' space, in which things exist side by side, but a space of higher dimensions, which includes and goes beyond the three-dimensional one. In such a space, things do not exist as separate units but rather like the interrelated parts and functions of one organism, influencing and penetrating each other."[18] And regarding time: ". . . the 'one-after-another' is transformed into 'the-one-within-the-other' . . . Thus the universe and the experiencer of the universe are mirrored in every phenomenon . . ."[19]

Ouspensky offers a simple way to picture how things that are different and separate in lower space can be connected and be parts of one body in extra-dimensional space; he uses a plane world analogy:

If we imagine our plane being to be inhabiting a horizontal plane, intersecting the top of a tree, and parallel to the surface of the Earth, then for such a being each of the various sections of the branches will appear as a *quite separate* phenomenon or object. The idea of the tree and its branches will

> never occur to him . . . Yet in our space, from our standpoint, these are sections of branches of *one* tree, comprising together one top, nourished from one root, casting one shadow.[20]

The corollary to this is that it applies to mental things (concepts), as well as physical things (objects). That is, concepts that are different and even opposed to each other in lower space may be parts of one larger concept in higher space, as in transfinite logic. Therefore, the logic and purpose of beings on a higher level than us, as in UFO phenomena, will seem inexplicable, absurd, and illogical, just as our logic seems that way to the animals' simple consciousness.

But there is another aspect, at first just as illogical, to the apprehension of the infinite whole that we can all understand; it is not merely dynamic—it is alive. On this point, Bucke wrote:

> He does not come to believe merely; but he sees and knows that the cosmos, which to the self-conscious mind seems made up of dead matter, is in fact far otherwise—is in truth a living presence. He sees that instead of men being, as it were, patches of life scattered through an infinite sea of non-living substance, they are in reality specks of relative death in an infinite ocean of life. . . .[21]
>
> This consciousness shows the cosmos to consist not of dead matter governed by unconscious, rigid, and unintending law; it shows it on the contrary as entirely immaterial, entirely spiritual and entirely alive; it shows that death is an absurdity, that everyone and everything has eternal life; it shows that the universe is God and that God is the universe, and that no evil ever did or ever will enter into it; a great deal of this is, of course, from the point of view of self-consciousness, absurd; it is nevertheless undoubtedly true.[22]

Note also here the hints of transfinite logic (where what we normally think of as separate becomes one): "the universe is God and God is the universe" and though all this is "undoubtedly true," it is from our standpoint "absurd." Absurd to us because ours is the consciousness of self *only;* but the higher consciousness is the *consciousness of consciousness,* within a broader tapestry of life; this life in turn is within an infinitely expanded scope of time—eternity. Isn't this the focal point of all the world's religions which are based on experiences of cosmic consciousness? For example, in the East, Mohammed says: "Allah! There is no God save Him, the Alive, the Eternal."[23] And Christianity—the first Epistle of John: "I write . . . of the Word of Life. And the Life was made known and we have seen, and now testify and announce to you, the Life Eternal which was with the Father, and has appeared to us."[24]

Life after death? For eternity? Not in our world of three dimensions of space plus time. In the larger, extra-dimensional one, maybe. Yet if so, what kind of life? One with our memories and identities? For if not, is it really life or just mindless existence? We'll see which in chapter 8.

The snail lives in a world of one dimension of space plus time. Samson, by virtue of his higher mental faculty, lives in a larger one that includes the snail's. Mark, with self-consciousness, lives in a world of three dimensions of space plus time. There's a larger one still—an extra-dimensional one that includes ours, just as ours includes the others. It's accessible by a higher faculty of mind, the faculty that all mystical and near-death experiences spring from, that all psychic phenomena derive from, and on at least one other planet (as we'll see in chapter 7), that a whole race possesses as naturally as we possess self-consciousness.

4

What Time Appears to Be, and What It Really Is

Saint Augustine once said: "What, then is time? I know well enough what it is, provided that nobody asks me; but if I am asked what it is and try to explain, I am baffled."[1] How many of us might answer the same way? To think about time can be a strange experience. It is something we are intimately and constantly connected with, and yet we just normally take it as it is, a self-evident, unavoidable fact of life. If we were to describe time as "what is measured by a clock," it is because it appears that obvious. But this will no longer do, so let's establish what the concept of time implies, then strip away its mystery and see what lies behind it.

Time is simply motion or change in space. Our earliest ancestors knew this and did the only thing they could do—measure it. Each time the sun rose it was their reference point; they divided this cycle into one half day, one half night. Each time the change of seasons had run its course, and the sun and other celestial bodies returned to their former positions was another good reference point, the year, which they divided into four seasons. This was just the beginning.

Starting with the day and the year, Man gradually organized and systematized his concept of time, breaking it down into ever more defined segments. Sundials, water clocks, and hourglasses came into use, and by the thirteenth century A.D. mechanical clocks arrived, even if at first wildly erratic by today's standards. But steady progress eventually made it possible to accurately divide the hour into minutes and seconds. Still, this was not good enough.

Each region had its own time system, determined by the rising and setting of the sun. These had to be combined, coordinated, and indexed into a worldwide system of timekeeping. Now the whole planet is synchronized to the nearest one thousandth of a second with the use of atomic clocks, and the watch is the most mass-produced object in the world with more than five hundred million of them sold a year.

Time is motion in space, and our index for measuring this motion is the solar system. The interval it takes for the Earth to completely orbit the sun we count as a year; divide this into twelve smaller units and we have months. The time it takes the Earth to revolve around once on its axis we count as a day; divide this 360 degree rotation into 24 segments and we have hours. Divide the hour into 60 smaller units and we have minutes, divide these again by 60 and we have seconds, and so on if we wish. A second, minute, hour, day, and year are just measurements of how much the Earth has moved since the last measurement.

Our normal idea of time is minutes, hours, and months, and not degrees of rotation or positions in orbit. This way of thinking is so ingrained in our culture and personal lives that we feel compelled to preserve the system. In reality, the Earth sometimes spins a little bit faster or slower, and it takes about 365 1/4 days to orbit the sun, but we compensate for this by adding an extra day to the calendar every four years, making a leap year. Thus we interpret motion in space as time and translate its measurement into a timekeeping system, which has almost come to be seen as the real thing, instead of the representation it actually is.

Time is motion and is indissolubly connected with change or events in space. But this motion actually occurs *outside our space*, somewhere else; we see only the results by the *effects* on our space. So in our idea of time exists everything else that does not exist for us now in space. Everything that ever was or ever will be in space: what a vast realm! It may seem strange to describe time as what isn't (everything not now in space) rather than what is, but this lets us begin to envision the possibilities of what may be behind our idea of time.

We study only the appearance of time by noting its direction and meticulously measuring its rate of flow. But we are at a loss to understand anything of its intrinsic nature because we don't see what lies behind its surface. This mystery goes unnoticed by most because time *seems* so obvious and self-evident. But it is just this obviousness that keeps us from looking at it more deeply. Overcoming this predisposition is the first step in coming to a truer understanding of time, just as overcoming the obviousness that the Earth was flat was the first step in coming to a truer understanding of the world of space. Richard Morris, in *The Nature of Reality,* admits: "Time, after all, is one of those elusive things that we all think we understand, but which may contain mysteries that we have not yet fathomed."[2] French psychologist Pierre Janet hit the nail on the head, as he wondered (in *From Anguish to Ecstasy,* vol. 1): "Will not man someday make progress in time similar to that he has made in space?"[3]

There are three very different schools of thought on the nature of time and space. First, at one end of the spectrum is the mystical stance, probably best typified by Eastern religions but actually including all mysticism, East and West. This maintains that all we take for real, including time and space, is illusory when seen from the broader perspective of the larger, true reality. Our world is at best a fragment of this vaster realm, and to some extreme factions it is a complete illusion. In the true reality, often described as multidimensional in nature, and known *only* by expanded consciousness, our space fades away, and there is no linear flow of time. All is one, now!

For example, in the East, the Upanishads say: "He is One, without beginning, middle, or end; he is all-pervading."[4] And in the West, Thomas Aquinas wrote: "Now although contingent events come into actual existence successively, God does not, as we do, know them in their actual existence successively, but all at once . . . Hence all that takes place in time is eternally present to God."[5]

The mystical experience, as reflected in these quotes, is generally taken to be one of divine union with God. But why such an interpretation, just because it so different from and so far above normal consciousness? There's no question it's an awesome event, seeing for the first time a much larger and timeless world, unified with each and every part of it through a new sense, with feelings of rapture and joy. Yet the unveiling of a higher though quite normal mental faculty suddenly apprehending an extra-dimensional reality could account for all of this. Think how stupendous and divine the first flashes of self-consciousness must have seemed to our apelike ancestors and what little understanding they must have had of them.

Edward Carpenter makes just this point:

> In the far past of man and the animals, consciousness of sensation and consciousness of self have been successively evolved—each of these mighty growths with innumerable branches and branchlets continually spreading. At any point in this vast experience a new growth, a new form of consciousness might well have seemed miraculous. What could be more marvelous than the first revealment of the sense of sight, what more inconceivable to those who had not experienced it, and what more certain than that the first use of this faculty must have been fraught with delusion and error?[6]

Nevertheless, it is understandable that the general mystical outlook is that the higher world cannot and need not be described, only experienced, and that the experience is of ultimate reality—communion with God.

Second, the other extreme is positivism, or the scientific stance. It holds that our world is indeed real, in fact *the* ultimate reality, as outlined by our perfectly "correct" idea of space. As for time, science does not inquire into its hidden nature, but simply describes it as is, i.e., when it seemed to begin, how it seems to relate to space, and the fact that it seems to point in only one direction, past to future, as described by the scientific arrows of time. But let's now look at these scientific descriptions in a new way, in an expanded framework of space, time and consciousness, and see that they are not at all what they seem. They indeed point in one direction, but a different one from what we thought. They point to an extra dimension, and the third different school of thought—extra-dimensional theory.

The first of the three arrows of time is the psychological arrow, which is simple enough: We remember the past and await the future. Unless you're like Merlin from T. H. White's *The Once and Future King,* who remembers the future but not the past, or the White Queen in Lewis Carroll's *Through the Looking Glass,* whose memory "works both ways," it must seem an obvious fact of life. But is it?

How then, can one explain the phenomenon of precognition, of which there are tens of thousands of impressive accounts and, even more impressive, almost irrefutable, laboratory evidence as well? This must mean that information of the future exists *somewhere* now and is accessible by some other kind of consciousness. Which way does the arrow now begin to point?

The explanation is that motion in our time is really motion in a higher space. In this larger, extra-dimensional world, everything we normally see in time exists at once, laid out in space; we just can't see it in our normal state of consciousness. We merely sense the passage of this extra dimension through our space an instant at a time, as a momentary and fleeting sensation we call the present. What we have just sensed has disappeared into the past. What we wait to sense has not yet appeared.

The psychological arrow of time is just our own limited way of apprehending a much broader reality, to make comprehensible what would otherwise be incomprehensible. For without this, life would present itself to our normal minds as unfathomable chaos, like music with all the notes sounding at once. The past, present, and future are *qualities* we impart to the world to separate it, break it down into a sequence of bits and pieces, and bring it into focus for our particular level of consciousness. A continuous flow from past to future enables us to perceive a structure in life, an unfolding of events, cause and effect, and this is necessary to have any meaning or perspective on our conceptual level, three dimensions of space plus time.

The beginning of time, according to widely accepted scientific theory, was the Big Bang, which may have occurred some ten to fifteen billion years ago. At that time, the universe was much more compact than it is today, so much so that it was contained in a very dense, very tiny region, virtually the size of a point. But there was then a tremendous explosion, and this primeval fireball rushed outwards in all directions at great speed. Over eons this primordial matter eventually coalesced into galaxies, stars, planets, life, and us.

An interesting point is that the Big Bang was not only the beginning of time, but of space as well. That is, the universe did not expand into existing space but rather space itself expanded, hand-in-hand with time. However, some questions immediately arise: What existed before the Bang—and when—if there was no such thing as time? Must there not have been some kind of available space for the universe to have expanded into? These questions cannot be addressed by science, but they can by extra-dimensional theory.

Reality is extra-dimensional and our perceived universe is only a cross section of it, just as a square is only a cross section of a cube. The larger, extra-dimensional reality had to have been in existence before our universe unfolded along its space. Time, though motion in higher space, generally speaking, is more specifically the interaction between an extra-dimensional space and ours, so our time was created moment by moment as our space rolled along and contacted that higher space. As long as there was motion within higher space, there was something comparable to time before the Bang.

Eminent physicist David Bohm (1917–1992), a modern-day leader in his own way of the extra-dimensional theory, postulated that our familiar universe is just a "relatively independent sub-totality" of a larger multi-dimensional one, which exists in the most real sense, of an "undivided wholeness" of both matter and consciousness. In his acclaimed 1980 *Wholeness and the Implicate Order,* Bohm speculated how our world of space-time could have begun by unfolding from that vaster realm.

In our approach this "big bang" is to be regarded as actually just a "little ripple." An interesting image is obtained by considering that in the middle of the actual ocean (i.e., on the surface of the Earth) myriads of small waves occasionally come together fortuitously with such phase relationships that they end up in a certain small region of space, suddenly to produce a very high wave which just appears as if from nowhere and out of nothing. Perhaps something like this could happen in the immense ocean of cosmic energy, creating a sudden wave pulse, from which our "universe" would be born. This pulse would explode outward and break up into smaller ripples that spread yet further outward to constitute our expanding universe.[7]

In Bohm's example of the wave rolling over the sea, essentially a new two-dimensional cross section is added to an extra (three) dimensional body. Of course in reality our entire three-dimensional universe was added to a larger, extra-dimensional one. Yet another profound aspect of Bohm's theory is that it predicts that each and every part of our normal world contains within it complete information of the multidimensional whole or "implicate order." Sound familiar? Mystics have always maintained that in the higher world, and seen from that perspective, everything is one, and that the whole is contained in every part of our world.

For example, Plotinus said, "Every thing contains all things in itself, and again sees all things in another, so that all things are everywhere, and all is all. Each thing likewise is every thing."[8] And the *Tao Te Ching* said: "Every being in the universe / is an expression of the Tao [whole]."[9] This transfinite conception is part of the near-death experience as well. One NDEr says he "simultaneously comprehend[ed] the whole and every part."[10] Another recounts the experience this way: "God was me and I was God. I was part of the light and I was one with it. I was not separate. I am not saying that I am a supreme being. I was God, as you are, as everyone is."[11]

The second major arrow of time is called the cosmological arrow. This is the expansion of our universe proceeding along a line from past to future, which goes hand-in-hand with the psychological arrow of time, in which we remember the past and await the future. The third major one is the entropic arrow of time, also known as the second law of thermodynamics. The first law of thermodynamics states that the total energy of the universe is constant, and thus energy can never be created or destroyed, only changed from one state to another; in other words, you can't get something from nothing. The second law says that when energy is changed from one state to another, whether by nuclear fusion or by burning a piece of paper, a small amount of that energy is rendered unusable, and is in a sense lost. The measure of this lost energy is called entropy.

What this means is that all systems, all processes, everything, suffer organizational decline and thus get worse. Machines rust and wear out, plants, animals, and people grow old and die, even stars eventually burn out. On a cosmic scale, our universe began with a single point of order and is growing more disorganized every second, like a giant clock winding down. Sometimes, it seems this disorder can be overcome; an old car can be restored, for example. But this can only be done when more energy—parts and labor—is brought in from the outside. If the situation includes these outside inputs, there is still an overall decrease in useable energy, or entropy.

The entropic arrow of time is that we see the world moving from past to future as systems move from order to disorder. But this direction becomes cloudy in the realm of the very small. For example, entropy is not something that applies to one or two individual particles but rather to the pattern established by large systems of them. It is a statistical effect, and no single molecule can experience entropy, any more than a single fish can school or a bee swarm. Physicist John Wheeler says: "Ask any molecule what it thinks of the second law of thermodynamics and it will laugh at the question."[12]

Moreover, the laws of physics do not forbid individual particles from traveling backward in time, and it is speculated that antiparticles and tachyons do this. But aren't all these inconsistencies exactly what we should expect? For if our description of time, like our worldview, is just another approximation, there should be inconsistencies at its limits, as we begin to see here.

Mainstream science contends that the three major arrows of time—psychological, cosmological, and entropic—complement one another, and it makes the case for time being a one-way street, an iron-clad property of reality. But mainstream science is still undecided as to *how* they relate to one another. Attempts to correlate the entropic arrow with the cosmological lead to enigmas such as: How is it that if entropy increases with time and the universe's expansion, then at the time of the Big Bang the universe was in a state of thermal equilibrium, which is maximum entropy? This plus the fact that the formation of the universe seems to violate the first law of thermodynamics, i.e., you can't get something from nothing. How does gravity in an expanding universe relate to entropy, seeing that one can't determine the entropy of a gravitational field or demonstrate that entropy even applies to gravity?

What we are left with is the fact that motion in our world *seems* to be in the same, single direction. But isn't this just the way it *seemed* in the plane world? Even if we passed a ruler or sphere through it *from different directions,* the inhabitants translated that motion in extra-dimensional space into motion *in one direction* in their space. That was the only way they could perceive motion in extra-dimensional space, and this is the only way we are capable of perceiving it, as motion in time from past to future. This is simply the way it must be if we are to have any sense of order, such as cause and effect, in our relatively independent subtotality of three dimensions of space plus time.

Our time is motion in extra-dimensional space, apprehended by us bit by bit as it passes through and contacts our space. We know this as the present, the ever-changing sensation of now. But it is a strange thing, fluid and elusive like quicksilver; we feel it, but can't quite grasp it. Can science?

Science describes the present in terms of a relationship to space by Einstein's theory of relativity. Special relativity (1905) says there is no one "now" common to everyone. This seems to contradict common sense, because when an event occurs in our world, we usually agree on the time. But each observer sees the event only when the light reflected from it reaches him, and someone farther away actually sees the event a little later than someone closer; this also applies if observers are moving at different speeds relative to the event. But all these distinctions are so slight that for practical purposes they don't exist because we live under circumstances where any speed involved is very slow compared to the speed of light (186,282 miles per second). With motion close to this speed however, the differences become pronounced.

Before relativity theory was developed, time was considered to be absolute, flowing through space like a river, at a constant speed and the same everywhere. But in relativity, there is no such thing as absolute simultaneity of time or space. They are both deceptively subjective, and everyone's now is a different space-time coordinate from everyone else's. One person's present is another's past, and still another's future.

Special relativity says our world has four dimensions, three of space and one of time. So time is a dimension, *like those of space*. This seems to suggest that on both sides of our now, the past and future exist in some *real* sense along that time dimension, just as a town we pass along the road exists *in space* before and after we pass it. The present is just the one point we see before us at the moment. And if our time, under relativity, is like this, an axis constituting the fourth dimension, then our present must be, what? A moving point along this axis? It was described this way by mathematical physicist Herman Weyl, in his *Philosophy of Mathematics and National Science.* "The objective world simply is; it does not happen. Only to the gaze of my consciousness, crawling upward along the life line of my body, does a section of this world come to life as a fleeting image which continuously changes in time."[13] It starts to sound mystical, as did Einstein when, in a personal letter written shortly before his death, he said: "For us believing physicists the distinction between past, present, and future is only an illusion, even if a stubborn one."[14]

More important, where does the motion, the change, for this moving point, the now, come from in the four-dimensional blocklike world depicted by special relativity? Einstein worried about this. He once told a colleague that "the problem of the Now worries me seriously . . . that the experience of the Now means something special for man, something essentially different from the past and future, but this important difference does not and can not occur within physics."[15] He was right. Our now is the fleeting awareness of motion from outside our continuum, that of an extra dimension apprehended relatively, bit by bit as it passes through our world in time.

The other prominent part of special relativity is the way in which space, time, and mass are affected as speed increases. As seen from a fixed point of reference: (1) space shrinks (in the direction of motion);

(2) time slows down (time dilation); and (3) mass increases. Einstein deduced that since the mass of a body increases as its motion increases, and motion is a form of energy (kinetic energy), then the increase in mass comes from its increased energy; hence the famous equation $E = mc^2$, with c being the speed of light.

Thus mass and energy are equivalent with mass being simply concentrated energy. The most well-known consequence of this is that as an object is accelerated towards the speed of light, its increase in mass presents more and more resistance, until at the speed of light it would have infinite mass and be immovable. Einstein saw the speed of light as a universal natural law, and according to relativity nothing can ever be accelerated to or beyond this speed.

But the ultimate nature of light itself is unclear, and in fact today it is best understood as vibrations in a fifth dimension. To us, it is basically the limit (supposedly) at which information can be transmitted or received. So is light speed the limit of time itself, or just the limit of our perception of it *as is?*

If our time is motion in extra-dimensional space, then it is perceived as such, i.e., motion, right up to our *limit of sensing it* as the speed of light. That is, below this speed we still process information in linear fashion, with the self-conscious mind and its extension, science. But if we could transcend our limitation of perception, we would see this extra dimension in its entirety and our time laid out along it at once in higher space. This is just what one sees in the mystical or near-death experience, by virtue of expanded consciousness. A mystic says: "[There is] a simultaneous eternity of Time in which past, present, and future exist together."[16] An NDEr comments: "It was just all there at once, I mean, not one thing at a time . . . but it was everything, everything at one time."[17]

In an extra-dimensional reality, information is received at greater than light speed: "everything at one time." But the curious thing is that this larger world is by no means devoid of light, but just the opposite. It's described as a world of unearthly brilliance, of radiant and divine light. In fact, this is one of the most consistent features of all mystical and near-death experiences. It is reported in UFO abductions as well, although to a lesser degree as abductees are usually inside a UFO while in higher space. Theoretical physics provides a clue as to how this can be. Physicists have speculated there is a particle called the tachyon that always travels faster than light speed and which would abound in an extra-dimensional continuum. In the 1930s, an interesting discovery was made, which Nick Herbert reports on in *Faster than Light:*

> Russian physicist Pavel Cerenkov discovered (in 1934) that whenever an electrically charged particle travels faster than light's phase velocity, the particle gives off light—now called Cerenkov radiation. A fast particle's Cerenkov radiation is analogous to a jet plane's sonic boom when it exceeds the speed of sound. Cerenkov radiation is a kind of "optic boom." . . . Since tachyons always travel faster than the speed of light in a vacuum, a charged tachyon is expected to emit Cerenkov radiation continuously. Charged tachyons could be recognized by that special glow.[18]

So the higher, extra-dimensional faculty may apprehend information carried throughout higher space by tachyons, which have that "special glow." The Bhagavad-Gita said: "Suppose a thousand suns should rise together into the sky; such is the glory of the Shape of Infinite God."[19] And the Upanishads: "Thou art the fire, / Thou art the sun."[20] An NDEr: ". . . it was a brilliant, glowing, breathtaking white light. It was brighter and whiter than looking at the sun . . ."[21]

Kenneth Ring comments on this NDE light phenomenon as follows: "At this level of consciousness—where we are no longer constrained by the sensory systems of the physical body—we are presumably sensitive to a higher range of frequencies, which may appear to us as light of extraordinary brilliance and unearthly beauty . . . it is perhaps at least noteworthy that virtually every description that purports to convey a sense of 'the next world' depicts 'a world of light.'"[22]

We are below this threshold of perception, where information in higher space is glowing and immediate, and time stops. Nevertheless, it is inevitable that as we get very close to it (the speed of light), *time slows down,* or dilates, and other properties of our world, such as space and mass, become correspondingly distorted.

Still there is another reason why science is dead set against anything surpassing the speed of light. Because it is the highest velocity at which information can be transmitted, any information traveling beyond it would be effectively able to reach into the past and affect an event prior to its original cause. Thus science has imposed on reality the causal ordering postulate, or COP, which forbids this. It is not however, part of Einstein's relativity and was only introduced later, to explain *definite* faster-than-light quantum connections (another extra-dimensional phenomenon) while preserving the sanctity of relativity and the current worldview.

The COP permits these connections but not any kind of intelligible signal, thus maintaining the normal order of cause and effect. But if relativity's description of time is not a universal law but *another* approximation, a statistical effect valid below the speed of light in our relatively independent subtotality, we might expect to see occasional violations of causality in our world, in fact, right in everyday life. This we find in precognition, which also violates the psychological arrow of time.

In 1915, Einstein presented his theory of general relativity which further describes time and space. It says that not only are time and space relative, but the framework of space-time itself is relative to the distribution of matter in the universe. Matter curves space and causes time to flow at different rates. Consequently, gravity is no longer thought of as a force acting upon objects, but a measure of the local space-time curvature, and objects in gravitational fields simply follow the path of least resistance. Time starts to slow down as gravitational fields grow stronger, and the effect becomes significant when gravitational forces are extremely strong. Gravity taken to its known limits, a black hole (a massive collapsed star that even light cannot escape from), becomes a singularity where time and space become fused. Here, just as at the speed of light, we reach a barrier where conventional laws of physics no longer apply.

General relativity essentially says that space and time are curved by gravity, which would seem to indicate that our universe is a three-dimensional surface curved in four- (extra-) dimensional space, just as the outside of the Earth is a two-dimensional surface curved in three-dimensional space. However, physicists maintain that this is not so with relativity, that *only* the geometry of our normal space, i.e., its mathematical representation, is curved. This, like the COP, would safeguard relativity and the current worldview. But John D. Ralphs, in *Exploring the Fourth Dimension* (1992), refutes this:

> If it is possible for a three-dimensional space to be curved without involving a fourth dimension, then it must be equally possible to construct (either physically or mathematically), a curved two-dimensional surface which does not require the existence of a third dimension. To the best of my knowledge, this has never been attempted, nor is it imaginable . . . Unless such a surface can be demonstrated, the idea is unacceptable.[23]

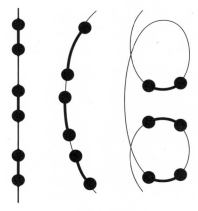

Figure 9

Indeed, look at figure 9: here line worlds are just as easily curved or even spiral instead of straight. Yet the line beings would experience them as all the same. Imagine the line world scientists, who suspect their space may be curved, but maintain it is not through a second (extra) dimension—"It's just the mathematical representation of our space that's curved," they say. But this clearly can't be. Their one dimension of space is not an absolute property of reality, but rather just the way their consciousness is capable of representing an extra-dimensional reality to them.

 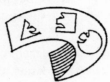 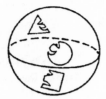

Figure 10

Now look at figure 10. Here plane worlds can be flat, curved, or even spherical; and the plane beings would experience them as all the same. After all, even we humans with three-dimensional consciousness thought for centuries that the Earth was flat. The plane beings' idea of space and any kind of plane world geometry is not representative of *true* reality; it is the only way they can grasp an extra-dimensional reality, albeit in limited scope. In both examples, a higher faculty is needed to perceive that extra dimension their space is curved in. The same applies to us.

Mainstream science, however, is convinced that relativity is the final worldview, or at least an almost final one. There is still one last piece remaining to be fit into the puzzle: the Grand Unification Theory (G.U.T.) or Theory of Everything (T.O.E.), a problem Einstein labored on until his death in 1955. This is a theory that, if realized in the form of an equation, will incorporate everything in the universe from its beginning to its end, and will thus be a description of God. Here God shall be composed of the four fundamental forces (we know of) in the universe, the strong nuclear force, weak nuclear force, electromagnetism, and gravity. But though some of the pieces fit nicely together, others don't, and the Holy Grail of physics remains elusive, at least in the standard four-dimensional space-time continuum.

Many physicists now contend that the pieces can be made to fit in a larger space-time framework, an extra-dimensional one with ten or eleven dimensions. Here light is explained as vibrations in the fifth dimension, and is there and beyond unified with gravity and the other forces. But these extra dimensions are theoretical and not at all like the other three. They are very tiny, curled up, almost to nothing. Why? Two reasons.

First, because we seem not to experience signs of them in our world, that is, as in objects appearing from nowhere, changing shape and color, getting larger or smaller, or disappearing. Needless to say, theoretical physicists hot on the trail of the Theory of Everything are not likely to consider the possibility of UFOs, teleportation, and poltergeists, and how they may or may not fit into their theories.

Second, because according to our mathematics, there can't be an extra dimension of space as we *know* it. For instance, if the Earth's orbit were calculated with a normal fourth dimension of space (like our other three), it would spiral into the sun. Physicists know that *mathematically* there can't be an extra dimension like the other three. So, extra dimensions must either be *outside the range of science* or extremely small. Thus they are proposed as just large enough to incorporate the necessary field activity but tightly rolled up and tucked away safely out of sight.

But remember, our mathematics is merely an extension of our level of consciousness, self-consciousness, and therefore hopelessly inadequate to portray an extra dimension. We need a higher faculty even to apprehend it, and then, we would no longer describe reality with the by-products of self-conscious thought, logic, and mathematics; it would be described by a new and higher language, with logic and mathematics in turn by-products of that higher faculty.

Bohm stops just short of this, saying: "It is important to emphasize that 'the law of the whole' (multi-dimensional reality) will not just be a description of current quantum theory to a new language. Rather, the entire context of physics (classical and quantum) will have to be assimilated into a different structure, in which space, time, matter, and movement are described in different ways."[24]

Visionary that Bohm was, he leaves out the most important factor, the one needed to perceive an expanded structure of space-time in the first place, namely, expanded consciousness. This brings us to extra-dimensional theory.

This view of time, space, and reality actually started with German philosopher Immanuel Kant (1724–1804). Kant proposed that there is a real physical world, but we don't know it nearly as well as we think; in fact, we scarcely know it at all. It is largely beyond our powers of perception, and the best we can do is impart a simple form to it—space. Beyond this facade lies the real world, but it can only be known as it truly is with a higher and direct form of perception, a "living union" between subject and object.

Kant's view of time is the same. There is something real behind it, but our level of consciousness prevents us from seeing it as it really is. Instead, we see reality as through a narrow slit: that infinitesimal part we are now seeing is the present; that which we have already seen is the past; and that which we have not yet seen is the future. Our time sense presents the underlying reality to us in linear fashion, in effect reducing it to an endless series of separate moments, the relations of which we regard in terms of cause and effect. Thus causality is not a universal principle but rather a condition *we impose* on the world to reduce it to a structure we *can* grasp. And this of course, allows for our sense of time to be only an imperfect sense of higher space.

Kant's theory has provoked debate between mystics (especially extreme and fringe factions, who use it as testimony to the fact that all reality is illusory) and positivists, who cannot stand Kant and dismiss him as a mystic. But they both miss the point. Kant is only saying that our physical world is *not all there is* and that to see the rest we need a *higher faculty* than we now possess. Kant's philosophy was later applied to different levels of space, time, and consciousness by P. D. Ouspensky in *Tertium Organum* (1912); the basics of both views are part of extra-dimensional theory.

The number of spatial dimensions that any being or race of beings perceives at once depends on its level of consciousness. Dimensions not directly perceived are sensed in imperfect and fleeting fashion, in time. In other words, what cannot be apprehended in space is done so in time. To mentally extract an extra dimension of space from time and add it to one's normal field of space, a new and higher faculty of mind is needed.

Our unique sense of time is a function of our level of consciousness, and we use it to measure that which we cannot measure in terms of height, length, and breadth. This is clearly shown by special relativity, which firmly established time as just such a function of consciousness, self-consciousness. This is the point. For it is only our self-conscious mind that lives in the present and experiences that sensation of now. It alone senses motion in time; time does not exist for the subconscious or any other kind of latent consciousness we may have. We live within the confines of reality as sensed by our self-conscious mind.

But our now is actually an awareness of the future becoming the past, a split-second before we can even register the change. The present is behind us before we know it; we only recognize it momentarily in the *process of being recorded as the past.* This means that the past and future are just as real as the present and exist somewhere beyond the scope of our now. Ouspensky in *Tertium Organum,* says: "The past and the future cannot not exist, because if they do not exist then neither does the present exist. Unquestionably they exist somewhere together, but we do not see them."[25]

So in the broadest sense, everything that ever was, still is, and always will be, and everything that will be or can be already exists somewhere. What a vast realm! Of all this we see but the tiniest fragment at a time, and even this after the fact. The self-conscious mind is stuck in this position. A higher consciousness escapes. Eastern mystic J. Krishnamurti explains how overcoming the constraint of the self-conscious mind leads to an expanded view of time. "The center (self-consciousness), the observer, is memory. The center is always in the past. . . . It is a memory of what has been. When there is complete attention (higher consciousness), there is no observer. . . . Life is broken up and this breaking up of life, caused by the center 'me,' is time. If we look at the whole of existence without the center 'me' there is no time."[26]

The Patanjali Sutras, as described by I. K. Taimni, relate essentially the same view. "The present . . . has no reality. It is a mere concept for the ever-moving dividing line between the past and the future. . . . Actually, the present has become the past before we realize its presence and, therefore, ever eludes us. But, though it has no reality of its own it is a thing of tremendous significance because beneath this dividing line between the past and future is hidden the Eternal Now, the Reality which is beyond Time."[27]

To us, space appears everywhere at once, and if time is motion in extra-dimensional space, then our time should appear likewise with a glimpse of *that* space, i.e., time would appear to stand still, to not exist. This is exactly the way mystics who have seen it, and NDErs who have been there, describe it. The ancient Greek philosopher Parmenides said: "Nor was it ever, nor will it be; for now it *is*, all at once, a continuous one."[28] An NDEr says: "I had a very acute awareness of everything that had ever happened, everything that was happening, or everything that would happen."[29]

There are some loose ends to tie up—big ones! Under extra-dimensional theory, our time—past, present, and future—is laid out along an extra dimension; that's why, with the perception of this, time appears to no longer exist. But if this is the case, if the future exists somewhere now (as the NDEr said, as "an awareness of everything that would happen"), is our fate, indeed every moment of our lives, already fixed and predetermined? Are our personal stories already written as we just move through a script we are powerless to change?

Under extra-dimensional theory this is not the case. The future is not set in stone but rather represents an expanded view of what will occur if events in progress remain *unaltered* on the path we are heading along. This is what the person having a mystical or near-death experience sees. However, the experience is normally so brief and the expanded view of time so overwhelming that this distinction isn't made. But Lama Govinda perceived it. He maintains that higher consciousness sees all time along an extra dimension, but the future only in a state of as yet unrealized probabilities. He describes the past: ". . . it loses its time-quality and is converted into something which we can only call a higher dimension of space, for the simple reason that all that apparently has happened in time is seen or sensed simultaneously, and therefore experienced as timeless presence . . ."[30]

As for the future, Govinda writes: ". . . a higher space-dimension, in which things and events exist simultaneously, though imperceptible to the senses. They are in a state of potentiality, as invisible germs or elements of future events and phenomena that have not yet stepped into actual reality."[31]

Govinda essentially says that although the past and future are laid out along an extra dimension, the future represents *probabilities* inherent in the direction we are moving but that are not yet finalized. This is not predetermination. As a perfect example of this let's look at precognition from Louisa Rhine's *Precognition and Intervention:*

> A mother dreamed that two hours later a violent storm would loosen a heavy chandelier to fall directly on her baby's head lying in a crib below it; in the dream she saw her baby killed dead. She awoke her husband who said it was a silly dream and that she should go back to sleep as he then did. The weather was so calm the dream did appear ridiculous and she could have gone back to sleep. But she did not. She went and brought the baby back to her own bed. Two hours later just at the time she specified, a storm caused the heavy light fixture to fall right on where the baby's head had been—but the baby was not there to be killed by it.[32]

This demonstrates that even though the course of events may bespeak a certain conclusion, changes still can be effected. Of course it helps to have a flash of higher consciousness to see what lies ahead.

Actually, the idea of predetermination is the main reason why precognition is unacceptable to many, over and above any scientific considerations. It's philosophically objectionable, for a predetermined future, its critics say, would negate the meaning of our existence. Indeed, where would be the purpose, the freedom of choice, the sport in it all? But there are far too many cases like the above in which individuals make use of premonitions to prevent disaster. These point to an extra-dimensional interpretation, not predestination.

Here is another loose end. Is this extra dimension that our time lies along the last, the ultimate? After all, the perception of it is of time standing still, as not existing. But let's look closer. In *On Indian Mahayana Buddhism*, D. T. Suzuki describes the general mystical outlook on time in the higher reality:

> In the spiritual world there are no time divisions such as the past, present, and future; for they have contracted themselves into a single moment of the present where life quivers in

its true sense. . . . The past and the future are both rolled up in this present moment of illumination, and this present moment is not something standing still with all its contents, for it ceaselessly moves on.[33]

The mystical outlook on time actually implies an extra dimension. For if motion in time is motion in higher space, then this explains all our time—past, present, and future—as laid out at once or contained in one moment, and then *more motion*, i.e., this moment still "quivering" or "moving on." In fact, virtually all mystical accounts describe something like this—one dynamic and ever-changing "now," or one present constantly "recreating itself anew." (This is exactly how we could describe our time!) This suggests further change, motion, although of a different sort and in a still higher dimension.

Near-death experiencers report something comparable. Ring, in *Heading Toward Omega,* notes that "even though there is no *time* in these [NDE] experiences, there is a certain feeling of progression."[34] One NDEr, for example, says: "[It] seemed to be in a sequential nature, more or less. I say more or less because time itself seems to have disappeared during this period."[35] This "sequence" or "progression" is likewise motion or change, not like ours, but it is some kind of change nonetheless. Since all change is motion in higher space, this residual motion must represent movement within another extra dimension, still not apprehended in either the mystical or near-death experience.

What would time be like to a race endowed with complete possession of the higher faculty? Far different from ours but still some kind of time. Later, in the UFO abduction phenomenon, we'll find that the aliens who have this faculty and live in a larger, extra-dimensional reality say that the human concept of time is localized, that time with them is not like time with us. Our past and future are the same as today to them. They know about our time, but their time is different!

PART II

The Paranormal as the Normal

The Mystical Experience: Dawn of a New Species

I know you. You're in the prime of life, intelligent, and a seeker. Something strange is tugging at you, pulling you, calling you like a siren. Something vast and mysterious; much larger than this life and world. It's spiritual, yet in no way religious. It touches—no, almost touches—you. You reach out, but can't quite grasp it, even describe it. Yet it's somehow very important.

What you feel is the mystical impulse, the stirring within you of a potential higher form of consciousness, a consciousness by which you can know *directly* that larger life and world. You feel it because you're one of the best of the race, at your best, in your prime. In the scheme of evolution, you are now on center stage, a candidate to cross a remarkable threshold and become a new species of human.

That's the good news. The bad news is that only one in many millions ever makes it (many are called but few chosen), and even then just temporarily and imperfectly. These are the forerunners of the next step in Man's evolution. Many of them you've heard of, some are household names, and a few have changed the course of history. They have inspired every religion known to Man, and yet these religions have been from the start completely and utterly wrong. For not only have they distorted, both intentionally and unintentionally, their founders' teachings, they have attributed their supernatural experiences to visions granted by God, when they were not. They were brief and unexpected glimpses into a larger, extra-dimensional world by the awakening of a higher mental faculty that in its first act of knowing suddenly extracts an extra dimension of space from time.

Jesus one day "saw the heavens rent asunder,"[1] and from then on spoke of a vast "kingdom not of [beyond] this world,"[2] a kingdom that could not be "beheld" anywhere except "within you."[3] Mohammed likewise described "the heavens with the clouds . . . rent asunder,"[4] and from then on spoke of a much larger world, known by a higher power that was "All-Embracing, All-Knowing."[5] It could see at once "[all] that is before them and [all] that is after them,"[6] by comparison with which "the life of this world is but comfort of illusion."[7]

In fact all those who have been so introduced to this new faculty describe having seen something like a higher plane of existence, another level of reality, or a vast, timeless realm lying beyond our space-time world, and seen in a new way, a way whereby all is infinite, alive, and One. Isn't this exactly what we should expect, by now, when an extra dimension is apprehended with its accompanying sense? For one thing, and perhaps the most telling, that which was before separated in time, the past and future, is now seen at once along that extra dimension; therefore, time, as previously known, does not exist.

Here are selected quotes from mystics and mystic texts that affirm this:

- The Upanishads: "Thou art beyond (our) time."[8]

- Chinese philosopher Fa-Tsang: "When myriad phenomena (in our world) arise, they must be at the same time, in one space—noumena (the larger world) has no before and after."[9]

- Chinese Zen Master Hui-Hai: "(with expanded consciousness) you stop thinking that things have a past or a future, and that they come and go."[10]

- Lama Govinda: "Vision . . . is bound up with the space of a higher dimension, and therefore timeless."[11]

- Zen Master Dogen: "It is believed by most that time passes; in actual fact, it stays where it is. This idea of passing may be called time, but it is an incorrect idea, for since one sees it only as passing, one cannot understand that it stays where it is."[12]

- Sri Aurobindo: "The mind of ignorance (self-consciousness) lives . . . successively in each moment."[13] But the higher consciousness "maintains in itself at once . . . whole sight what appears to us as the past of things, their present and their future."[14]

- The New Testament, Paul: "For the things that are seen (in normal fashion) are temporal, but the things that are not seen are eternal."[15]

- Revelation: "I am the Alpha and the Omega, the beginning and the end, says the Lord God, who is and who was and who is coming."[16]

- The Apostle Peter: "But, beloved, do not be ignorant of this one thing, that one day with the Lord is as a thousand years, and a thousand years as one day."[17] (Note also the transfinite logic here.)

- Thomas Aquinas: "We may fancy that God knows the flight of time in His eternity, in the way that a person standing on top of a watchtower embraces in a single glance a whole caravan of passing travelers."[18] (In other words, from an expanded view.)

- Jewish philosopher Philo Judeaus: "Periods of months and years and of time in general are ideas of men, who calculate by number; but the true name of eternity is today."[19]

- Christian mystic John of Ruysbroeck perhaps sums it up best with this typical expression: "He contemplates Himself and all things in an eternal Now."[20]

Of course the higher faculty that apprehends this extra dimension has its own form of conception, wherein both the "one after another" in our time and the "one beside another" in our space become the "one within another" in higher space (as an extra dimension connects all points of three-dimensional space). This transfinite conception, that of the whole contained in each part, is the very mental process by which an extra dimension is perceived, and it is also unmistakably present in the mystical experience.

Here are more quotes in support of this:

• The Bhagavad-Gita: "Part of myself is the God within every creature . . . yet seems to be separate."[21]

• The *Tao Te Ching*: "The Tao can't be perceived [normally]. / Smaller than an electron, / It contains uncountable galaxies."[22]

• Fa-Tsang: "Great knowledge, round and clear, looks at a fine hair and comprehends the ocean of nature; the source of reality is clearly manifest in one atom, yet illumines the whole of being."[23]

• Chinese sage Lop'u: "When you hold a grain of dust, you are holding the universe in your hand. A golden lion, in all its splendor, is you."[24]

• Chinese Zen Master Huang-Po: "On seeing one thing, you see all things . . . When you see a grain of sand, you see all possible worlds, with all their vast rivers and mountains. When you see a drop of water, you see the nature of all the waters of the universe."[25]

• Sri Aurobindo: "The infinite and eternal Self of things is an omnipresent Reality, one existence everywhere . . . it can be met, seen or felt in its completeness in each soul or in each form in the universe . . . the Infinite can be felt in an infinitesimal atom or in a second in Time . . . for the Divine is in all, and all is the Divine."[26]

• The New Testament, Paul: "One God and Father of all, who is above all, and throughout all, and in all."[27] Compare with Heraclitus (fifth century B.C.): "From all, one; and from one, all."

• Paul again: "For just as in one body we have many members, yet all the members have not the same function, so we, the many, are one body in Christ, but severally members of one another."[28]

The mystical experience is the momentary breakthrough of a higher evolutionary faculty that apprehends an extra dimension of space. But if so, how did it all get so distorted, so wrong? Why has its real nature been overlooked and instead held to be a vision of God, a gift bestowed upon a chosen few? Why do we now have so many religions with so many symbols, doctrines, rules, and regulations all claiming to be the only, true one? Three reasons.

First is that the mystical experience by its very nature lends itself to gross distortion. The person finds it impossible to grasp it intellectually even in one's thoughts. That is, there is distortion right off in transposing the higher conceptions into the lower. This is compounded when the person tries to convey the transfinite nature of the experience in normal, conceptual terms. *Our* concepts are only possible attempts at expressing an *impossible* conception. The result is absurdity and failure. The experience is ineffable. This is why the *Tao Te Ching* says: "The way that can be told / Is not the constant way; / The name that can be named / Is not the constant name."[29]

Nevertheless, such powerful experiences cannot but be conveyed. Inevitably differences in interpretation arise over their true meaning, and further differences of opinion over these, hence further interpretations, and ever more distortion. The only way to make sense out of this worldwide mess is to look for the main elements to see if there is a pattern. There is.

The Perennial Philosophy says our world is part of a larger one, which requires a new sense to see, and our purpose is to get in touch with our larger selves within that world. Simple enough, and perfectly in tune with extra-dimensional theory. Here, our space-time world is part of a larger, extra-dimensional one, which requires a higher faculty to see; we are naturally programmed, or naturally selected, by evolution to progress towards it and our higher selves.

The second reason why the extra-dimensional nature of the phenomenon has been overlooked is that the mystical experiences that shaped world religion occurred about two thousand years ago when most people had little use for notions of space and time and no theory of evolution. Their concerns were with social behavior and religion. Remember that this new vision is as incomplete and unrefined as the first few flashes of self-consciousness are to any child. If you remember your first thoughts of your new world, I'm sure they weren't "Hey, there are three dimensions of space plus time." (In fact, many still don't know this! If you stopped a hundred people on the street and asked them how many dimensions of space there are, I'd bet you'd get some astounding responses.)

The most striking thing about your first perception was probably the sheer novelty of the perception itself. This is how it is with the higher faculty as well. But since almost all the workings of the world we now know as basic laws of nature were at that time attributed to acts of God or gods, it is understandable that the first interpretation, and the inevitable distortion, would be along those lines. Any later mystical experiences would likely be put into the same familiar context.

The third reason is where the intentional part comes in. It is the implication for an expanded, eternal life in the larger world. Virtually all mystical experiences (the consciousness of consciousness) include this apprehension. (Mohammed: "That is life, if they but knew."[30] Paul: "Your life is hidden with Christ in God. When Christ [comes] your life will appear."[31] Jesus: "I am the way, and the truth, and the life."[32]) It is easy to see how the promise of life after death can be exploited to convert and hold people to one's cause. It is the main draw and justifies all the rules and regulations (a fair trade), and in the process it establishes a complicated hierarchy, as it were, of middlemen—brokers—between man and God.

The situation becomes: "If you want eternal life, go through me." Yet this is exactly what the founders of these religions tried to do away with! Jesus not only rejected all external rites, he openly denounced the priests of organized religion, seeing them as obstacles to any real sampling of the Kingdom. "But woe to you, Scribes and Pharisees, hypocrites! Because you shut the kingdom of heaven against men. For you yourselves do not go in, nor do you allow those going in to enter."[33] Compare this with what the Buddha said: "Leave then dogmatic views and their attendant strife."[34]

No one who has had a mystical experience has ever taught that life after death (beyond our space-time) had to be acquired or granted; it's just the opposite, that everyone possesses it naturally. Bucke calls it "a sense of immortality, a consciousness of eternal life, not a conviction that he shall have this, but the consciousness that he has it already."[35] This is what the great religious leaders wanted, for everyone to see this for themselves. But the fact is, they didn't quite know how to bring it about as their own experiences came so naturally and effortlessly. The Buddha said: "Please don't think that when I attained enlightenment, there was anything I attained."[36] Compare this with Plotinus: "We must close our eyes and invoke a new manner of seeing . . . a wakefulness that is the birthright of us all, though few put it to use."[37]

These evolutionary prodigies assumed naively that if people did the same thing they did, lead a good, healthy, moral life, they would acquire the higher sense the same way they did, spontaneously. Jesus said: "The Kingdom of God comes unawares"[38] and "watch therefore, for you know neither the day nor the hour."[39] Mohammed said: "It cometh not to you save unawares . . . Knowledge thereof is with Allah only."[40] The *Tao Te Ching*: "[The Tao] arrives without being summoned."[41]

Toward this end, Mohammed preached only "righteous conduct," the Buddha the Middle Way, and Jesus said to "love one's neighbor as oneself." Simple as that, but look at what we ended up with, especially in the West. Jesus preached the Kingdom of Heaven, and we got the Church. Leo Tolstoy, in *The Kingdom of God Is within You,* said: "But Christ could certainly not have established the church, that is, what we now understand by the word, because neither in Christ's words, nor in the conception of the men of that time, was there anything resembling the concept of a church, as we know it now, with its sacraments, its hierarchy, and above all, its assertion of infallibility."[42]

Nevertheless, Bucke, seeing the situation for what it was, felt that the natural order of things would ultimately prevail and foresaw an idealistic future when the entire race had the higher faculty (the Coming of the Kingdom) and all formal religions had vanished.

> In contact with the flux of cosmic consciousness all religions known and named today will be melted down. The

human soul will be revolutionized. Religion will absolutely dominate the race. It will not depend on tradition. It will not be believed and disbelieved. It will not be a part of life, belonging to certain hours, times, occasions. It will not be in sacred books nor in the mouths of priests. It will not dwell in churches and meetings and forms and days. Its life will not be in prayers, hymns, nor discourses. It will not depend on special revelations, on the words of gods who come down to teach, nor on any bible or bibles. It will have no mission to save men from their sins or to secure them entrance to heaven. It will not teach a future immortality nor future glories, for immortality and all glory will exist in the here and now. The evidence of immortality will live in every heart as sight in every eye. Doubt of God and of eternal life will be as impossible as is now doubt of existence; the evidence of each will be the same. Religion will govern every minute of every day of all life. Churches, priests, forms, creeds, prayers, all agents, all intermediaries between the individual man and God will be permanently replaced by direct unmistakable intercourse.[43]

Bucke wrote this in 1901. But times have changed, and something's gone wrong. In the 1970s, Gopi Krishna, a mystic-philosopher from Kashmir, India, offered the same line of thought. He said that the mystical experience was a prelude to a higher evolutionary faculty (as in *The Biological Basis of Religion and Genius* and *The Secret of Yoga*) but with a drastically different outlook for the future.

He proposed that evolution is driven by one higher law of nature, which is both spiritual and biological (that which is different in our space is one in higher space, or transfinite). The spiritual part is the development of the lower into the higher; the biological part is a force called kundalini, an energy which, when activated in an individual, flows from the base of the spine to the top of the head, causing a psycho-physiological effect—the mystical experience. The significance of this is that it is a physical phenomenon, operative in a larger world, but with real physical effects in ours.

Gopi Krishna maintained that when the mind and body are in an exalted, "ready" state, they become a sort of open channel, and the higher energy, kundalini, rises up—a natural consequence of a natural, though higher law. Centuries earlier, Meister Eckhart, describing here the onset of the mystical experience, suggested the same:

> God *must* act and pour himself into you the moment he finds you ready. Don't imagine that God can be compared to an earthly carpenter, who acts or doesn't act, as he wishes. . . . It is *not* that way with God; where and when God finds you ready, he *must* act and overflow into you, just as when the air is clear and pure, the sun must overflow into it and cannot refrain from doing that.[44]

So much for divine intervention. This in-pouring of energy helps explain a key feature of the mystical experience—the sensation of inner fire and light that usually kicks off the whole episode. Gopi Krishna wrote of this: "I felt a stream of liquid light entering my brain through the spinal cord . . . The illumination grew brighter and brighter."[45] (Remember Bucke's "flame-colored cloud"—the fire and light within.) As a physical phenomenon, the effect sometimes can actually be seen by those nearby. Jesus, for example, was often described as physically aglow when he united with the Kingdom. "And he was transfigured before them: and his face did shine as the sun, and his garments became white as light."[46] "As he was praying the fashion of his countenance was altered and his raiment became white and dazzling."[47]

Gopi Krishna's kundalini is another name for the physical mechanism I offered earlier for the radiant light seen in mystical and near-death experiences: tachyons, charged particles in extra-dimensional space that naturally have a "special glow" and carry information at faster-than-light speed. They are one and the same phenomenon, and it works here like this: When tachyons/kundalini enter our space via a portal of primed consciousness, the result is a blinding light within and glowing aura about the person (the oft depicted halo of saints and mystics?). As one's consciousness expands into extra-dimensional space, it sees this energy, radiating naturally in higher space, everywhere. Gopi Krishna describes his expanded consciousness at this point as "immersed in a sea of light,"[48] a description in keeping with all mystical accounts.

Here are some mystical sources that support this view:

- Peter in the New Testament: "The coming of the day of God, by which the heavens, being on fire, will be dissolved, and the elements will melt away by reason of the heat of the fire!"[49]

- The First Epistle of John: "God is light."[50]

- The Bhagavad-Gita: "brilliant like the sun; like fire, blazing, boundless."[51]

- The Upanishads: "That being I worship as effulgent. He who meditates upon Brahman as such becomes effulgent."[52] "The wise know him who assumes all forms, who is radiant, who is all-knowing, who is the one light that gives light to all. He rises as the sun of a thousand rays, and abides in infinite places."[53]

- The *Tao Te Ching:* "Can you cleanse your inner vision / until you see nothing but the light."[54]

- Mohammed: "Allah is the Light of the heavens and the earth . . . Light upon light, Allah guideth unto his light whom he will."[55]

In an interesting aside to this and a hint of things to come, Mohammed says that while the righteous will be rewarded by the light and fire, those who are undeserving (disbelievers) will be overwhelmed and consumed by it. "And as for those who do evil, their retreat is the Fire . . . Unto them it is said: 'Taste the torment of the Fire which ye used to deny.'"[56] Compare this with Christianity's concept of the fires of Hell and the radiant bliss of Heaven. (I'll explain how this works, and why, in chapter 8.)

Gopi Krishna maintains—as Bucke did—that all the spiritual training in the world cannot bring about the higher faculty in someone;

it can induce only the dimmest glimpses of it. The real thing is reserved for the best evolutionary specimens, who have from birth a rare ingredient, an innate capacity for it. Even in those cases where the faculty did arise during training, the individual probably had this capacity from the beginning, needing only a stimulus to bring it out. Gopi Krishna acknowledges this may not seem fair to those who devote their lives to such practices, and who in their despair blame the teacher, system, or even the justice of the divine being they strived toward, but calls it a "hard historical reality."

> Why there should be such a (despairing) reaction is based on the mistaken idea that all our spiritual endeavor is a means to please or propitiate the Lord and to seek His grace in order to cross over to the other shore. It is not an anomaly that while, in the intellectual sphere, out of millions who devote their lives to the various sciences and arts and make colossal sacrifices to win distinction in them, only an extremely few rise to the stature of a Shakespeare, a Kalidasa, an Omar Khayyam or a Confucius. The rest reasonably attribute the rise to exceptional natural talent, based on some still unknown biological law. In the spiritual realm the seekers after God do not often take the same reasonable view and, instead of attributing their failure to a law of nature, assign other causes for it.[57]

Both Krishna and Bucke recognized that, perhaps paradoxically, there is one way to accelerate and even trigger the coming of the higher faculty—by listening to or reading the words of others who have acquired it. (Bucke wrote his book, full of quotes about cosmic consciousness, with this end in mind.) Jesus' words certainly seemed to have acted as a catalyst on some of his disciples, and even on a Christian persecutor, Paul, who soon after Jesus' death, had an unmistakable taste of it.

Startled by a blinding light, "he was caught up into paradise and heard words that man may not repeat."[58] He was "united" with a "new world" and a "new order"[59] that "made foolish the wisdom of this world."[60] In a rare act of perspicuity, he described it as being "able to comprehend with all the saints what is the breadth, the length, the depth, and the height."[61] In other words, a fourth, extra dimension! Paul then realized that Jesus' teachings about a vast kingdom known by a new way were the real thing and he became the great Apostle Paul.

That the words of those who have been there can actually rub off, and bring out the higher faculty in someone, has been acknowledged by others as well. The Upanishads state: "The awakening which thou hast known does not come through the intellect, but rather, in fullest measure, from the lips of the wise."[62] And the Buddha: "If an intelligent man be associated for one minute with a wise man, he will soon perceive the truth, as the tongue perceives the taste of soup."[63]

Such power to elevate with the spoken word can help explain the enormous appeal that all the great religious leaders had. For if all humans have within a tendency to progress toward the higher state, they cannot help but be naturally and powerfully drawn to those who have been there. Gopi Krishna describes it as: ". . . the outcome of a deeply rooted urge in human beings to show respect to one naturally endowed with a lofty attribute of the human mind necessary for the evolution of the race."[64]

But here Gopi Krishna's mood turns dark. While Bucke felt that flashes of the higher faculty would become more and more common, Gopi Krishna says just the opposite has happened—they have dwindled from ancient and even medieval times. How can this be?

His explanation is that Man is increasingly living under conditions that oppose and obstruct the natural blossoming of higher consciousness, in effect violating the law of evolution; he predicts this will lead to disaster. Krishna says that though all the great religious leaders and mystics have told us what to do to allow the higher faculty to come naturally (lead a balanced life and not be unduly attached to sensory and material pursuits), we have gone in the opposite direction. We're consumed by these pursuits. Hopelessly greedy and materialistic, we lust after the very things they have always told us to avoid.

For example, Paul: "Mind the things that are above, not the things that are on earth."[65] And, "be not conformed to this world, but be transformed in the newness of your mind."[66] Again: "But the sensual man does not perceive the things that are of the Spirit of God, for it is foolishness to him and he cannot understand."[67] Jesus: "Amen I say to you, with difficulty will a rich man enter the Kingdom of heaven. And further I say to you, it is easier for a camel to pass through the eye of a needle, than for a rich man to enter the kingdom of heaven."[68] Mohammed: "Rivalry in worldly goods distracteth you."[69] The Buddha: "One is the road that leads to wealth, another the road that leads to Nirvana."[70]

Gopi Krishna sees other global problems, such as moral and intellectual decay, constant political upheaval, and the specter of technological mass destruction, as further signs of a degenerating world society and as side effects of resisting the law. He feels that only the recognition and eventual transition to higher consciousness can change the course of events, but he does not see this happening. He maintains that even though the mystical impulse is still there in millions of people (you've felt it), it is frustrated and thwarted, denied its natural outlet; many end up seeking it in dead-ends such as occult practices, corrupted religions, and drugs.

In reference to the drug aspect of this, Andrew Weil, in his controversial 1972 book *The Natural Mind,* proposed that all human beings have an inherent drive to experience altered states of consciousness, a drive first expressed in children by such things as whirling about to dizziness and squeezing each other to faintness. Eventually, these activities are curtailed by adults, and the child is conditioned by society to be "normal." But the repressed drive is still there and may later surface in alcohol and drug use, which in turn may lead to addiction.

Weil's theory, in the expanded perspective of extra-dimensional theory, makes more sense. Here, every human has an innate tendency to progress toward a higher kind of consciousness. Children instinctively sense this, and even after rigorous cultural programming the subconscious urge remains; frustrated, they seek any route, even destructive ones.

What it boils down to is this: We are all extra-dimensional, but aware of only a three-dimensional part of ourselves. Our evolutionary purpose—to unite with our larger selves by developing the higher faculty—is something we as a race have not been able or willing to do. Thus, cut off from our greater selves, we are increasingly unfulfilled, frustrated, and self-destructive. Roger Walsh, in *The Spirit of Shamanism,* looks at it from the viewpoint of the Perennial Philosophy:

Within our collective trance we act blindly and destructively, as might be expected of anyone whose awareness is distorted and constricted. Our behavior is said to be driven by greed and fear in ways destructive to ourselves, our fellow human beings, and our planet. For the perennial philosophy then, our global crises can be traced to our shared insanity . . . We do not recognize this as a trance because we all share in it and because we live, says the perennial philosophy, in the biggest cult of all: *culture.*[71]

The mystical experience, as the emergence of a new and higher mental faculty, is the highest possible aspiration of Man, the most valuable natural asset any individual, or any race, can have. On this point Jesus said: "The kingdom of heaven is like a treasure hidden in a field; he who finds it hides it, and in his joy goes and sells all that he has and buys that field."[72]

It is the most important natural phenomenon in the history of mankind and essential to our very survival. Yet what have we done with it? Either ignored its profound implications or distorted its nature beyond recognition. Each and every religion it has given rise to is further removed from its root, and more the dogmatic institution it was meant to replace. Followers obediently repeat credos, receive their faith, and kill and crusade to defend its "sanctity." We have forgotten the *cause,* and worship the grossly distorted *effect.* It is insane. Do we even have the capacity to recognize the real thing today?

Eighteenth-century English artist and mystic William Blake tried to "open the immortal eyes of man inwards"[73] to "cleanse the doors of perception of the race," so Man could see reality as it really is—"infinite."[74] Many thought him a madman, and yet no one captured the true transfinite sense as eloquently as he did:

> To see the world in a grain of sand
> And heaven in a wild flower
> Hold infinity in the palm of your hand
> And eternity in an hour.[75]

These lines are recognized now as pretty phrases. But they are a perfect description of the mental process required to perceive what Bucke calls "by far the larger world . . . equally real [as ours]"[76] or what Gopi Krishna calls "the dimension just one step higher" than ours, which "is real only in the human state of consciousness."[77]

Imagine a race of beings on another planet who have acquired this faculty. What would they think of us? In the discussion of the UFO abduction phenomenon later, we'll see. These aliens say that we are more than just physical beings. We have a higher side to us, one essential for our survival, but we have not realized it because of lack of interest and research. As they can see our future path laid out in extra-dimensional space, they can see our impending fate, and it's one far worse than Gopi Krishna imagined. Life on Earth as we know it will cease to exist. John Mack says:

> What the abduction phenomenon has led me (I would now say inevitably) to see is that we participate in a universe or universes that are filled with intelligences from which we have cut ourselves off, having lost the senses by which we might know them. It has become clear to me also that our restricted worldview or paradigm lies behind most of the major destructive patterns that threaten the human future—mindless corporate acquisitiveness that perpetuates vast differences between rich and poor and contributes to hunger and disease; ethnonational violence resulting in mass killing which could grow into a nuclear holocaust; and ecological destruction on a scale that threatens the survival of the Earth's living systems.[78]

What do the abductees think about this? Mack again: "Abduction experiencers come to feel deeply that the death of human beings and countless other species will occur on a vast scale if we continue on our present course and that some sort of new life-form must evolve if the human biological and spiritual essence is to be preserved."[79]

The mystical experience gives us inklings of the next—intended—step in Man's evolution. But we either don't see it or don't care.

6

Psychic Phenomena

When we have a new understanding of time, we will understand ESP.
All the pieces will fall into place.
— Dr. Gardner Murphy, former president of the
American Society for Psychical Research[1]

These kinds of things cannot happen: telepathy, clairvoyance, pre-cognition—yet millions of people have experienced them. Psycho-kinesis, poltergeists, apparitions, and healings should be just as impossible. Yet millions have witnessed them. Any one such phenome-non pokes a hole in our standard worldview of space, time, and con-sciousness. Together, they make a shambles of it. These things cannot happen in the world *as we know it*, but in an extra-dimensional world, *they must happen*.

All psychic phenomena derive from the same source—the higher faculty that apprehends an extra dimension. Bucke sensed this but said he lacked the "time and necessary ability"[2] to include it in his book. Gopi Krishna was explicit about it. He repeatedly emphasized that the same consciousness that could "look beyond [our] space and time"[3] was responsible for *all* psychic phenomena; and that various kinds of it were often included in the mystical experience. "The moment transcendence occurs . . . other windows in the mind open . . . [which] can bring to him knowledge of events occurring at a distance, as also visions of the past and future. His utterances may become prophetic and he may acquire the healing touch."[4]

In other words, the different kinds of psychic phenomena are just different facets of higher (extra-dimensional) consciousness, just as language, mathematics, depth perception, and the use of tools are different applications of our three-dimensional self-consciousness. What this means is that if you had full possession of the higher faculty, you would have the *full* complement of psychic powers, which of course no *human* being has ever had. Even the best of us get only partial possession of them, which is likely to yield a part of the spectrum at a time. The Apostle Paul said:

> Now there are varieties of gifts, but the same Spirit . . . To one through the spirit is given the utterance of wisdom; and to another the utterance of knowledge . . . to another faith . . . to another the gift of healing . . . to another the working of miracles . . . to another prophecy . . . to another the distinguishing of spirits . . . But all these things are the work of one and the same Spirit.[5]

Still, virtually all psychic phenomena happen without any possession of the higher faculty, per se. Here's how. We know that as consciousness has evolved in the human race, a few individuals have leaped over the threshold to a higher type of consciousness, i.e., extra-dimensional. But not just individuals evolve, whole species do; many more of us must be close to that threshold, and in fact have been for thousands of years. Millions of people, though still under-qualified for a full-fledged taste of the higher faculty and a mystical experience, are capable of having smaller pieces of it, fragments of extra-dimensional consciousness that filter down into our normal state, fragments we know as telepathy, clairvoyance, precognition, psychokinesis, and the experience of poltergeists.

Telepathy

Telepathy is the process by which someone gets information directly from the mind of another. It's a bit of the higher, more sweeping faculty that Mohammed says "embraceth all things in his knowledge,"[6] a piece of that facet of higher consciousness that is naturally telepathic. For example, Jesus "needed no evidence from others about a man, for he himself could tell what was in a man."[7] It is an isolated fragment of the extra-dimensional "consciousness of consciousness." Such a fragment, in the form of a spontaneous telepathic intuition, often involves a person feeling or just knowing what is at that time happening to someone else, usually someone they are close to. For instance:

> We had just moved to Kansas, and my mother was visiting in Colorado. At 3:15 A.M., October 11th, I wakened suddenly with a terrible choking sensation, as though I could be dying. My breath was coming in dry sobs; I looked out the window, and noted the town clock was chiming 3:15.
>
> I rushed into my daughter's room, wringing my hands crying, "Your Grandma is dead." My daughter ridiculed my crazy dream as she called it. It was no dream. I had not been dreaming at all.
>
> In a few minutes I fell asleep, exhausted. In the morning my daughter asked, "What was wrong with you last night?" I declared I knew something was wrong with Mother and I was going to be prepared for a call. I unpacked a trunk to get out my winter clothing; then I called Western Union to let them know where to find me when the message came. The family meanwhile teased me about my nightmare. The telegram came at 4:15 P.M. from Colorado: "Bury Mother 3 P.M. Friday 13th, Auburn."[8]

Louisa E. Rhine offered this and other accounts of telepathy in her *ESP in Life and Lab*. Another example is that of a farmer who went into a deserted barn near his property and stumbled upon a large rattlesnake, coiled and ready to spring. At first stunned by the suddenness of the encounter, he recovered in time to kill the snake with a stone and iron bar. At the very time this was going on, his daughter back at the house was seized by a great fear that something was happening to him. Searching desperately but unable to find him, she prayed and waited, until all at once she felt at ease as the fear lifted. When he later returned, they would compare notes on the timing.[9]

Clairvoyance

Clairvoyance is the direct perception of objects or events with no other sending person needed. It is just a different part of the same extra-dimensional consciousness, as described here by Christian mystic St. John of the Cross: "The Holy Spirit illumines in . . . other present or future matters and about many events, even distant ones."[10] It's a trace of the higher sense the Bhagavad-Gita calls "Open vision, Direct and instant,"[11] a fragment of the extra-dimensional consciousness that can perceive *every* object in our world, as that extra dimension connects every point of our three-dimensional space.

Here is such a perception of an object: A young woman was thought to have taken a watch from a bathroom in the boarding house where she was staying. Though innocent, she was upset because the other boarders blamed her. After a week of praying for a way out of this dilemma, she had a dream that the watch was still in the bathroom wedged between the tub's leg and the wall. When she awoke, she went to the bathroom and it was indeed just where she had "seen" it.[12]

Here is another example, this time of an event: "I lived 14 miles from Memphis, Tennessee. One day I went to town to see a movie. I had an uneasy feeling as I entered the movie that something was on fire at home. This feeling grew until I could endure it no longer. I left the movie with an overpowering pull that drew me homeward. Within a mile of home I saw the fields all black and smoking. A boy hunting rabbits had thrown a lighted match in a field and started a fire. It took the fire department and fifty volunteers to save my home."[13]

Precognition

Precognition is seeing a glimpse of the future. Of all psychic phenomena, it is the most flagrant violation of our laws of nature. It shatters the old notions of cause and effect, of linear time flowing from past to future. It's the most impossible phenomenon of all, yet its explanation is the simplest.

Precognition, like telepathy and clairvoyance, comes from the expanded consciousness that apprehends an extra dimension, *with our past and future laid out along it.* But here the glimpse is of what lies ahead for us in that extra dimension. It's a peek into "the hidden knowledge of past, present, and future that is always carried within itself by the eternal spirit,"[14] a glimpse of one small point in "the beginning and the end and the midpoint of times."[15] (This also accounts for another phenomenon, psychic glimpses of the past, or postcognition.)

Many precognitive visions occur in dreams. Here's a famous one: Shortly before his assassination, President Abraham Lincoln had a precognitive dream—of his own death. This account of it was recorded by Ward Hill Lamon, U.S. Marshal for the District of Columbia, who was at the White House when Lincoln related the dream at the prompting of Mrs. Lincoln.

About ten days ago, I retired very late. I could not have been long in bed when I fell into a slumber, for I was weary. I soon began to dream. There seemed to be a deathlike stillness about me. Then I suddenly heard subdued sobs, as if a number of people were weeping. I thought I left my bed and wandered downstairs.

There the silence was broken by the same pitiful sobbing, but the mourners were invisible. I went from room to room; no living person was in sight, but the same mournful sounds of distress met me as I passed along; every object was familiar to me, but where were all the people who were grieving as if their hearts would break?

I was puzzled and alarmed. What could the meaning of all this be? Determined to find the cause of a state of affairs so mysterious and so shocking, I kept on until I arrived in the East Room, which I entered. There I met with a sickening surprise. Before me was a catafalque, on which rested a corpse wrapped in funeral vestments. Around it were stationed soldiers who were acting as guards; and there was a throng of people, some gazing mournfully upon the corpse, whose face was covered, others weeping pitifully.

"Who is dead in the White House?" I demanded of one of the soldiers.

"The president," was his answer. "He was killed by an assassin." There came a loud burst of grief from the crowd, which woke me from my dream. I slept no more that night, and although it was only a dream, I have been strangely annoyed by it ever since.[16] (Lincoln was assassinated a few days later.)

Louisa Rhine also gives several accounts of precognitive dreams in her book. In one, a woman dreamed that her brother-in-law had died and his wife called her long-distance to tell her. When the woman told her husband upon waking, he just laughed. But later that same day, her sister-in-law called to say her husband had been killed that morning while topping a tree, and she was "screaming and crying" exactly as the woman remembered in the dream.[17]

Spontaneous intuitions like these have been reported by people of all ages, cultures, and religions. The majority occur in sane, healthy individuals, and then only once or twice in a lifetime. They are not the stuff of delusions or mental disorders. Nor are they paranormal, at least not in an extra-dimensional world. They must happen. They are exactly what we should expect, inklings of the higher consciousness we as a race are subconsciously struggling to acquire.

The connection between telepathy, clairvoyance, and precognition, now known collectively as ESP, and the mystical experience, its parent consciousness, is unmistakable. How could it be otherwise, for ESP is a natural part of that extra-dimensional consciousness. In fact, reports of ESP can be found in all mystical literature and religious scriptures based on the mystical experience. The difference is that the mystical experience is broader, deeper, more complete with ESP accompanying it, while intuition by itself is but an isolated fragment of the whole.

As with the mystical experience, those who have such intuitions are stunned by them. They are likewise completely unexpected; they "come unawares," or as Paul says, "like a thief in the night."[18] Also, those who have had these apprehensions immediately realize how far removed they are from any normal conception, and it is just this strangeness that makes the strongest impression. This must be so.

Higher transfinite knowledge cannot be grasped or understood by the self-conscious mind. For with ESP, fragments gleaned from the vaster extra-dimensional ground make their way to the threshold of self-consciousness and are there recognized as a sensation, impression, feeling, or intuition. As such, the intellectual conception of it is ineffable; one can only say, "I just know." It is beyond the scope of the self-conscious mind to realize what is being directly apprehended. As the *Tao Te Ching* says: "[an] image without an image, / subtle, beyond all conception."[19]

What these intuitions most resemble is an emotional feeling. They are almost always about people and events important to the experiencer, where there is already an emotional attachment. This suggests that it is the emotional closeness, or "oneness," not the actual distance of space or time that allows for the apprehension. Not that this is the only type of information available with the consciousness of an extra dimension; it's just that with a race capable of only the feeblest traces of higher consciousness, these simply come first.

With these spontaneous intuitions, the perception comes through because it is important to the individual. But how about in the laboratory? Can subjects intuit extra-dimensional information about emotionally meaningless targets on demand in cold, clinical settings? Apparently, to some degree, they can.

In the 1930s, J. B. (Joseph Banks) Rhine and his wife, Louisa, applied scientific methodology to psi research in their landmark Duke University study. From early on, they got significant results with card-guessing tests for telepathy and clairvoyance, even when carried out over great distances. It seemed this mysterious sense was not bound by (our) space. The Rhines wondered if psi could transcend (our) time as well. It did. Tests for precognition were likewise significant, but the Rhines were so concerned with the implications of this (e.g., that ESP could violate the law of cause and effect) that they delayed publication of their results for years.

The Rhines knew that ESP was real. They also knew it was "impossible" under the laws of the standing worldview. J. B. Rhine, in *Extra-Sensory Perception*, wrote:

. . . it may be that quite new principles of reality will have to be found before these new phenomena can be explained. In any case one must be guided by the new facts, of course, and not by the present limits of knowledge . . . It is difficult to think of physics as probably very far from complete in its grasp of world processes. Yet that is the very point that is indicated or strongly suggested by the facts.[20]

Louisa Rhine went further:

Now it is clear that it is not the phenomena that are questionable, rather the theory that the universe is such that phenomena like these cannot occur is incorrect . . . Its answer as far as one can see now must lie in a fundamental rethinking about the structure of the universe; a rethinking that will take account of all the questions raised by the phenomena that show the direct contact of mind and matter.[21]

The Rhines' most profound realization was that it seemed that another part, an *extension,* of our normal self-consciousness could operate outside of our normal space and time. Louisa Rhine wrote in *Mind over Matter:* "Accordingly, since space and time are the main criteria of physicality, it was a breakthrough to find a mental ability that was not bound by them. It meant that the operations of mental life are at least in some degree free from the restrictions of the physical world. This was to demonstrate that mind has a nonphysical element; that it includes an aspect that seems profoundly different from that of the physical world, even while it is all part of a single universe."[22]

J. B. Rhine, in a lecture at London's Guildhall in 1965 sponsored by the British Association for the Advancement of Science, summed it up: "We know now, at least in parapsychology (the field of psi research), that space-time as generally known does not comprehend the whole of the universe . . . man therefore belongs to a bigger universe than he has known hitherto."[23]

In other words, a bigger universe of which our space, time, and consciousness are just a part. Sound familiar? The famous psychologist Carl Jung, who was strongly impressed by the Rhines' experiments, picked up on this connotation, saying that it showed "space and time . . . were dependent on psychic conditions and did not exist in themselves but were only 'postulated' by the conscious mind."[24] (Shades of Kant and extra-dimensional theory.) Jung then tried to tie this in with his own quest for a theory of synchronicity, a force of nature he felt transcended the law of cause and effect. In *The Interpretation of Nature and the Psyche,* he said: "It seems more likely that scientific explanation will have to begin with a criticism of space and time on the one hand, and with the unconsciousness on the other."[25]

Jung was definitely on the right track, but unfortunately, he never got past these basic assumptions. Now for the other side of it. Skeptics who reasoned that since "ESP can't be, it isn't" attacked the Rhines' results for everything from statistical and procedural errors to outright fraud. Most of the claims were either unfounded or exaggerated, but this attitude would nevertheless set the tone for a half-century of more of the same. Researchers tighten up their experiments to eliminate any possible alternative explanation, as pointed out by skeptics; they get more significant results then skeptics attack them again, with a seemingly endless array of "normal" explanations for the results, many more bizarre than the existence of ESP itself. Yet, this is predictable.

In every case where the prevailing worldview is threatened, it is fiercely protected right to the very end. Thomas S. Kühn, in *The Structure of Scientific Revolutions,* says:

> Normal science, the activity in which most scientists inevitably spend almost all their time, is predicated on the assumption that the scientific community knows what the world is like. Much of the success of the enterprise derives from the community's willingness to defend that assumption, if necessary at considerable cost. Normal science, for example, often suppresses fundamental novelties because they are necessarily subversive of its basic commitments.[26]

For example, only parapsychology requires an extra experimenter present to avoid charges of cheating by a sole experimenter, and results are not considered to be statistically significant unless the odds against them being due to chance are at least fifty or one hundred to one; in other, less controversial, sciences, a result is considered significant if it is twenty to one against chance.

Despite all restrictions, researchers were still getting significant results, and in the process wearing down resistance in the mainstream scientific community. In 1969, the Parapsychological Association, an international organization of professional psi researchers, was granted affiliation with the American Association for the Advancement of Science—a major step in the emergence of parapsychology as a legitimate scientific endeavor.

Still, one obstacle remains. Through the years there have been many successful ESP tests, enough to convince most reasonable people that ESP does exist, but these tests are notoriously difficult to duplicate. Established standards of scientific proof demand that at some point an experiment must be duplicated with predictable results. Such an experiment is the Holy Grail of parapsychology and would establish psi as scientific fact. The problem is that even with repeating the same test there are differences in methodology, scoring technique, size of the test, and types of subjects, and all these factors have been known to influence results.

But slowly, these factors are being sorted out, and the influence of each determined; slowly, because the manpower and resources involved in psi research are incredibly small compared to other scientific disciplines. Dr. Richard Broughton, Director of Research at the Institute for Parapsychology (North Carolina) and former president of the Parapsychological Association, estimated in his 1991 book, *Parapsychology: The Controversial Science*, that:

> There are probably fewer than fifty scientists in the English-speaking world and in Europe who conduct parapsychological research on a more or less full time basis. When you realize that there are probably more people involved in this research than ever before, you can see why progress in this field is slow.[27]

Yet it is inevitable. There will be a repeatable psi test, perhaps soon. Dr. Broughton says: "We are now—finally—on the verge of a break-through."[26] *The* breakthrough, because when this happens, there will be nothing left for critics to criticize. It will be irrefutable proof. Mainstream science must accept ESP. But then another problem arises: How to explain it? It is, after all, impossible in the world as we know it. ESP cannot be carried by any physical energy. It is unhindered by great distances of space and all known forms of energy get weaker over distance, and no known energy can transcend time.

We need a larger framework of space-time, right? No; we need a larger framework of space, time, and *consciousness,* a consciousness beyond our normal way of knowing. This is what ESP hints at, for even in the lab, flashes of higher consciousness that result in "hits" elude the detection of the senses and self-conscious mind. When subjects try to say when their ESP is operating during testing, as checked by their correct guesses at precisely those times, they have generally scored no better than when they felt it was not.

The subject is oblivious to the real "sense" at work. The real sense is the higher consciousness that can perceive an extra dimension, and those who have temporarily acquired this—mystics—have always maintained it is beyond the senses and intellect. The Upanishads: "There the eye goes not, / Speech goes not, nor the mind."[29] The *Tao Te Ching:* "Look, and it can't be seen / Listen, and it can't be heard / Reach, and it can't be grasped."[30] Jesus: "Seeing they do not see, and hearing they do not hear, neither do they understand."[31]

J. B. Rhine speculated that ESP was "a later evolutionary acquisition"[32] in the human race, that it was connected with the "analogies of ESP found in religions and mystic lore."[33] Rhine flirted with the truth but missed the larger picture. It is the higher faculty unveiled in mystical experiences that is the later evolutionary acquisition, of which ESP is a lesser manifestation. The experimental evidence for ESP reflects this. These lesser manifestations of extra-dimensional consciousness are as feeble and incomplete in the lab as they are in real life. Good results are just a little bit better than chance and even the best do not yield perfect scores. Also, the evidence for telepathy, clairvoyance, and precognition is about the same, just as it should be if they are all by-products of the one real sense at work, the higher, extra-dimensional faculty.

Everything in our world has extension in an extra dimension. I earlier postulated that indications of this would show up in the investigation of the "very small": we see it here, in the consistent but weak positive results from psi tests. Psi is the extension of consciousness.

Psychokinesis

In the 1970s and '80s, some television documentaries on psychic phenomena featured this strange sight: a stout, middle-aged Russian woman standing in front of a wooden table, concentrating intensely, then gesturing and grimacing: her objective, to try to get some ordinary matches sealed inside a glass case (on the table) to move, using only the power of her mind. If you've seen it, you know what happened next— they indeed moved about.

The woman in the film was Nina Kulagina, a Russian housewife, and the best known PK subject of modern times. Kulagina could move small objects such as matches, cards, and cigarettes, even when they were sealed inside lead-impregnated glass enclosures; she could also deflect compass needles and affect living material, for example slowing down and stopping a frog's heart.

This is psychokinesis, or PK, the ability to move matter and influence objects without touching or affecting them in any normal way. PK first gained wide attention in the nineteenth century with tales of mediums who could levitate tables and move objects about rooms, tales that are difficult to evaluate because of mediumship's long association with fraud. However early researchers compiled lengthy documentation, and the performances of some mediums were impressive.

But there's little doubt about Kulagina. She has been studied extensively in Russia by researchers, committees, and impartial scientific institutes, and there has never been any basis to suspect fraud. In addition, she led a modest life and at no time attempted to profit from her PK abilities.

One might think that such well-documented and oft-repeated performances would prove the existence of PK, but not so. Skeptics, who deny its existence because "it's just not possible," still claim fraud, even when exhaustive measures are taken to eliminate any possibility of it. They maintain that the subject *must* be cheating but in a way that has not yet been detected. Kulagina has been accused of this by some in the West. But when a Soviet journal *(Man and Law)* alleged trickery, she brought legal action against it. Two members of the Soviet Academy of Science testified on her behalf, and in 1988 the court ordered the journal to publish a retraction.

Kulagina's PK was real. But despite all the testing, researchers were never able to explain how it works, or even offer a "conventional" hypothesis for it. They only know that her performances were very taxing physically, as if she had expended a tremendous amount of energy; she lost weight, her blood sugar increased, and her heartbeat rose dramatically. (As she grew older, the experiments became too much of a strain on her; she retired from laboratory testing and died in 1990.)

Here's how PK such as Kulagina's can be understood. Remember these two things: Physical maneuvers that are impossible in any world of space-time are easily accomplished by the use of an extra dimension; and, everybody and everything in our world has extension in an extra dimension. Now, here's how it actually works. The subject moves an object by applying force with her extra-dimensional extension, or "body," to the extra-dimensional body of the target, all of which takes place outside of our normal space and goes unseen (made easier by the fact that all three-dimensional objects are connected in extra-dimensional space).

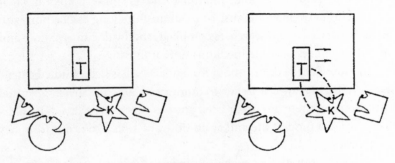

Figure 11

This is just how it is about to happen in figure 11. Here, the Star, Ms. K, is a PK subject, and she will attempt to perform a feat that is impossible on her plane world: move an object that is completely sealed inside a glass case. To observe the experiment, and make sure she doesn't cheat, are our old friends the Square, Triangle, and Circle. The Star is a typical PK subject; she herself doesn't know how her PK works. All she knows is that she can somehow "do it."

K concentrates, stares intently at the target, then begins to gesticulate wildly, whatever feels right at the moment to try to coax her strange motive force into action. Sometimes these efforts seem to help. But other times, and this is one of them, the effect just happens when she has stopped trying. The target moves. It moves because, as shown in the illustration, the Star's extra-dimensional extension (here somewhat arbitrarily portrayed as limbs) touches and moves the target's extra-dimensional extension, moving the target itself. But what the observers and even K herself fail to realize is that it isn't just a case of mind over matter. There's more to it.

PK works the same way in our world. The impetus comes from the self-conscious mind, but the real work is done in extra-dimensional space. This is why it is extremely difficult, almost impossible, for PK subjects to initiate or control it. The person is in fact completely unaware of the higher ground; the smaller, three-dimensional cross-section, the physical body and self-conscious mind, must summon up the strength to move the larger extra-dimensional essence. This is why it takes such a tremendous physical effort to initiate PK, and also why it is so rare an ability.

Physically moving an object on cue, as Kulagina could, is quite a feat. Yet it pales in comparison to the PK more recently produced in China by the mysterious Zhang Baosheng. Zhang, now in his fifties, established himself as the country's top psi subject in the early 1980s. Since then he and his family have enjoyed a luxurious life, with a twelve-room suite complete with chef, nurse, and servants, all courtesy of the State, on condition that he never leave the country.

Accounts of Zhang's abilities are largely based on papers published before 1984. Since then, most research has been kept quiet by the authorities and only sporadic reports have reached the West. But what is known is that Zhang has a special talent for moving small objects and even live insects in and out of sealed containers, i.e., *right through them*—the phenomenon of teleportation. Reports like these have been heard before in psi circles but never with the documentation accompanying those of Zhang. Films and freeze photos show objects such as a pill in the process of exiting a sealed bottle.

This is of course completely "impossible" in our normal world of space, time, and consciousness, but not in an extra-dimensional one. I'll demonstrate, by another plane world analogy.

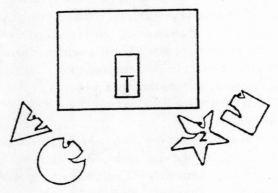

Figure 12

In figure 12, a teleportation experiment is ready to begin. The target object, a small rectangle, is sealed inside a transparent container. The subject, a different Star, Mr. Z, will attempt to move the target out of the container, presumably through solid, two-dimensional space. Again to observe are the Square, Triangle, and Circle.

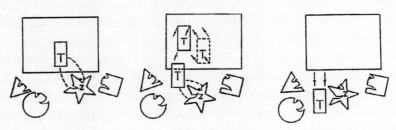

Figure 13

As shown in figure 13, the Star, by utilizing his extension in extra-dimensional space (height), *could* move the target outside of the container just by lifting it up and over and depositing it outside. This is how we might expect it to be done. However, this wouldn't allow the observers to film the target as it exits *through* the container. But there is another simpler way of doing it that would.

Z could pull or drag the target into extra- (three-) dimensional space and over the boundary of the container, which would take significantly less force than to lift and carry it. After all, if we must move a heavy object, it is easier to do so by pulling it along the floor than by lifting it up in the third dimension (height) and carrying it. It is a more economical use of energy, and PK subjects expend prodigious amounts of energy. Moreover, PK may have its own natural tendency to take the path of least resistance.

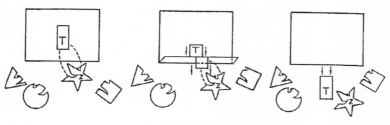

Figure 14

Now in the plane world, this pulling maneuver in three-dimensional space would appear, to the observers, just as in figure 14. Here, as that part of the target closest to the boundary of the container is lifted into an extra dimension, it seems to disappear from the plane world only to appear again on the outside as it is lowered down and continues forward. (Remember that even though the plane beings may build structures such as the container, and it must have extension in a third dimension to exist, they are completely unaware of that part of *any* structure, or even that part of *themselves.*) Now as the target is pulled over the edge of the container, more and more of it appears on the outside, and less and less remains on the inside, until it is completely outside.

Zhang's PK with the bottle is identical to this analogy, except it's done at high speed. The target (pill) appears to be in the bottle one moment, then suddenly outside. But at a film speed of 400 frames per second, it can be seen exiting the bottle, like the target in the analogy exiting the container. The accelerated speed is due to the fact that motion in higher space is seen by us as *motion in time*. This extraordinary feat of PK by Zhang is an extra-dimensional one.

Here is another—the clincher. The target was chemically treated pieces of paper, placed in the bottom part of a test tube, which was then constricted in half. In the top compartment of the tube were cotton wads treated with a different chemical that would react on contact with the one in the target. The top of the tube was then irreversibly sealed. Zhang was able to move the target papers outside of the tube, and the cotton revealed traces of a chemical reaction, suggesting that the papers had passed through the cotton.

In teleportation cases such as this, or with the pill, the only explanation ever offered is that the target is "somehow" broken down at the molecular level, into particles that can pass through those of the barrier, then instantaneously reassembled again into the original object as it exits. But this cannot be the case here. For if the target were broken down molecularly and passed through the cotton, the chemical on the target would exist *at that point* in a broken down, constituent state where it could not possibly react with the other chemical in the cotton. It can't be done this way; but it can be in another, an extra-dimensional way.

Let's assume that Zhang's PK operates as in the last example with the bottle, lifting the target papers into extra-dimensional space and pulling them past the cotton in the top compartment, and finally outside of the container. As before, the movement is through extra-dimensional space and at accelerated speed.

Now for the important part. As the papers are pulled along the edge of extra-dimensional space, they come into contact with the cotton. The two chemicals will leave traces of their reaction, traces that with a porous substance like cotton will be visible in three-dimensional space. But this contact is not on the surface of the cotton; it goes much deeper than that. It occurs on the threshold of our space and extra-dimensional space, and that threshold, which shows evidence of the contact, is *every point in three-dimensional space,* as the papers pass through in an *inside-out* direction.

That is how Zhang's, or anyone else's, teleportation works. All extra dimensions lie in an inside-out direction. That is, all movement or physical manipulations in extra-dimensional space must be evidenced by those in lower space as in an inside-out direction. Remember how in chapter 2 we turned the skeptical Square inside-out by rotating him in an extra, third dimension? In *Lifetide,* distinguished biologist Lyall Watson gives a firsthand account of such a manipulation. When in Venice, Italy, he was introduced to Claudia, a five-year-old with a unique skill (she would later lose it as she matured): turning a tennis ball inside-out. In Watson's words:

> She held it to her cheek, affectionately, and then balanced the ball on her left hand while she stroked it gently with her right as though it were a small furry animal, a dormouse to be aroused from untimely hibernation.
>
> One moment there was a tennis ball—the familiar off-white carpeted sphere marred only by its usual meandering seam. Then it was no longer so. There was a short implosive sound, very soft, like a cork being drawn in the dark, and Claudia held in her hand something completely different: a smooth, dark, rubbery globe with only a suggestion of the same pattern on its surface—a sort of negative, through-the-looking-glass impression of a tennis ball.
>
> It was something I had never seen before, but recognized instantly despite the unfamiliar point of view. It wasn't a bald tennis ball, deprived somehow of its hair, but an everted tennis ball, one turned inside out yet still containing a volume of air under pressure. I squeezed it and it held. I dropped it and it bounced. I picked up a knife from the dinner table and, with some difficulty, pierced the rubber and let the air hiss out. Then I cut right around the circumference and there it was, lining the interior where it had no business being, the usual furry pile apparently none the worse for the wear.
>
> It still disturbs me. I know enough of physics to appreciate

that you cannot turn an unbroken sphere inside out like a glove. Not in this reality.[34]

Not in this reality is right. But in an extra-dimensional one, inside-out is how it must be. It is not supernatural, but perfectly natural. We see it in PK and teleportation; we'll see it in UFO and near-death phenomena. It's the way it works there. Mystics have acknowledged this as well. The Patanjali Sutras, for example, describe the path as an "involution of a part of Itself";[35] and German mystic Hugh of St. Victor is unequivocal on this: ". . . to ascend to God is to enter into oneself, and not only to enter into oneself, but, in some unsayable manner, in the inmost parts to pass beyond oneself . . . going deeper and deeper . . . we must pass through ourselves."[36]

In other words, inside-out!

PK in the Lab

Experimental PK research in this country had, until the 1970s, mainly consisted of dice-tossing experiments, where the object was to will a certain number to come up more often than chance. This is obviously a different kind of PK from what we have been looking at, in that the effect is invisible; it is a statistical one, by which the presence of PK is inferred. The overall results, however, were positive and tended to parallel the success rate of tests for telepathy, clairvoyance, and precognition. This is of course as it should be, for PK, like telepathy, clairvoyance, and precognition, is just another natural facet of the one higher faculty, and so they should be roughly equal in strength.

In the 1970s, PK research was transformed by the advent of random number generators (RNGs) and other similar subatomic devices. This type of testing, known as micro-PK, now dominates PK research because it is completely automatic and can be easily administered, monitored, and evaluated; this device can also be used to test for precognition. Results with both micro-PK and micro-precognition have also been positive, and to the same degree as other kinds of psi tests. Not surprising. Consciousness can affect matter at the subatomic level, and here some parapsychologists actually offer an explanation of how this, but only this, *may* be done in our normal world of three dimensions of space plus time. But as to how it's *really* done, and where, and what kind of consciousness actually does it, I'll show you in chapter 9, Extra-Dimensional Theory and the New Physics.

Poltergeists

It seems a tranquil family setting. A quiet evening at home, parents watching television, teenage daughter on the phone, younger brother doing homework in the next room. All's pleasant, peaceful, but not for long. Suddenly a loud bang comes from somewhere in the house, and the mood changes, darkens. The parents look at each other but say nothing; the girl quickly ends her conversation, and the boy enters the family room, no longer wishing to be alone. Some minutes go by, but nothing further happens. Maybe tonight will be a normal one after all, one of too few in the month since it all started. But no such luck.

The lights dim and flicker, then a barrage of explosive sounds comes from the kitchen. Before the father can get up to investigate, a picture flies off the wall and across the room, landing at his feet. The young boy and girl cling to their parents in fear, praying the commotion will end. Thankfully, it does; and soon, in a few more days, it will be over for good, stopping just as suddenly and mysteriously as it started. The family is relieved. Yet a question will haunt them: What was it?

This family was plagued by a poltergeist, an old German name for noisy ghost. But a poltergeist is not really a ghost, or even a thing; it's more of a phenomenon, a range of disturbances that erupt in a home, usually in a family setting. The disturbances vary from case to case and include loud noises such as raps and blows, objects hurled or moved about, stones falling from within or pelting the outside of the house, objects disappearing and reappearing elsewhere or teleported through walls, electrical disturbances, and to a lesser extent, spontaneous fires, physical attacks (such as biting or pinching), and communication.

Accounts of poltergeists go back thousands of years. In 530 A.D. it was reported that Deacon Helpidium, physician to Theodoric, king of what is now Germany, suffered from a diabolic infestation that caused showers of stones to fall in his house. Jacob Grimm, in his

Teutonic Mythologie, recorded a case in 856 A.D. in Kembden where the house of a priest was plagued by rapping noises and bombarded by stones.

Such occurrences seem to be orchestrated by an intelligence who is rather mischievous, and they were at first blamed on a malicious spirit. Often the local clergyman was called in to banish the demon, and since poltergeist activity normally fades anyway within a period of weeks to a few months, the exorcism might appear to work.

But it's now clear that poltergeist activity centers on a living person, called the agent, rather than a place. When the agent is removed from the setting, the activity ceases (this is how to find out who the agent is); but the phenomena may follow that person to a new location. Researchers believe that the agent subconsciously and *unknowingly* produces the effects by PK, which researchers refer to as "recurrent spontaneous psychokinesis," or RSPK.

Modern investigations have revealed that the apparent agent is usually an adolescent (sometimes a child) who is going through a period of psychological stress. It is assumed that this stress, combined with the inherent strain of adolescence and puberty, causes feelings of frustration and hostility. If these feelings are repressed, they can become mentally damaging. Thus the youth needs a release or way to let off steam—the poltergeist. In fact, in several instances when some of the more obvious stress-inducing conditions were removed, the poltergeist phenomena quickly subsided. According to this view, the poltergeist is a psychological safety valve, and its destructive acts are actually the cure rather than the problem.

It is difficult to accept however, that repressed anxiety alone causes poltergeist outbreaks. If this were all there were to it, we might expect to find one in every home, instead of it being a rare phenomenon. Another problem is how does RSPK work, seeing as no one has offered a "normal" hypothesis for how PK works? Also, how can these agents wield such formidable PK, the likes of which put virtuosos like Kulagina and Zhang to shame, without any signs of the traditional energy depletion?

We need another approach, an extra-dimensional one. Here, the agent gains use of a facet of the higher faculty and conducts the PK in extra-dimensional space. A clue to this is contained in a 1978 survey of 92 cases conducted by William Roll, who has been one of parapsychology's most experienced poltergeist researchers. He found that almost 25 percent of the apparent agents had exhibited some form of dissociative state ranging from trance and mild seizure to diagnosed epilepsy. The significance of this is that these states can make perhaps an isolated facet of the higher faculty more accessible, simply by removing the distractions of normal consciousness, much as meditation may do. But even so, this still leaves the other 75 percent of cases without a dissociative state for access to higher consciousness.

We need another mode of access. We'll find it in the "moral sense," or the way the moral sense is added to one's self-consciousness.

The faculty of self-consciousness is acquired at about age three. But the moral nature, with all its facets comprising one sense, may be thought of as a faculty in its own right, in fact, a higher one. It is acquired later in life, and though the time can vary considerably, it probably averages to be in the early teens, *the age of most poltergeist agents.*

The root of self-consciousness is the realization of distinction, of a separate I, and the awareness of otherness, or "not I." The moral sense has many parts, such as conscience, right and wrong, compassion, and responsibility, but its root, from which all these branches spring, is the ability to see the other side of it, to have empathy for others. After all, what is morality but the capacity to empathize with the consciousness of others, and accordingly treat them as you would have them treat you, a la the golden rule. The moral sense brings a person closer to higher, extra-dimensional consciousness; it is an abstraction and reflection of that living union of subject and object, of oneness.

The development and onset of the moral sense take place in the subconscious, as do all emergent faculties, and it's probably met with anxiety because at first it must seem contradictory. That is, the root of self-consciousness is the realization of distinction, while the root of the moral sense is oneness, to sense others' feelings. So one is separate and one at once; it is paradoxical, and the subconscious mind trying to reconcile these opposites may experience a moral upheaval, or stress at the deepest layer of the psyche. The youth will have trouble adjusting; in fact, this stage of life is traditionally described as being about learning to cope with new feelings.

Let's now also assume that in a few cases, the acquisition of the moral sense is unusually stressful. As the moral sense is an abstracted "feel" of the higher faculty, in rare cases it may open a doorway by which *one* ability of the higher faculty, PK, can be used. Dissociative states provide the same access to higher consciousness, and either of these combined with severe psychological stress in the normal state unleashes the agent's subconscious—extra-dimensional PK lashing out like an angry child. As an angry child, when frustrated, bangs on walls, throws things, slams doors, steals, even bites and scratches, so the agent does the same, under safe cover of the poltergeist.

But how does the agent produce such extraordinary PK, especially when we've already seen how even weak PK causes a physical drain on a subject? The impetus does not come from the self-conscious mind, fettered, as it were, to a world of three dimensions of space plus time. It comes from the subconscious, closer to the threshold of extra-dimensional space where PK is a natural force.

I'm sure you've heard stories of clocks stopping, objects falling, or inexplicable noises just at the moment of someone's death, cases where it's presumed that a person near the clock senses the death and reacts with subconscious PK. No physical drain there, and pretty fair PK to boot. This is why poltergeist agents show no signs of depletion, and also why they can effect such spectacular PK that cannot be explained in a framework of three dimensions of space plus time, but can be with an extra-dimensional one.

Raps, Blows, and Detonations

In a poltergeist outbreak, loud sounds are often heard from the walls or floor, and on occasion from furniture such as tables or chests. The sounds have a percussive aspect, more like detonations than raps or knocks. Often they are signs of more dynamic activity to come, and this is the key to understanding them. An angry child first stomps on the floor and pounds walls *before* throwing things or stealing. The PK agent does likewise, using his extra-dimensional extension.

A four-dimensional object pounding on our three-dimensional space is like a three-dimensional object (a stone) pounding or traveling through a two-dimensional surface such as water. As the stone creates certain physical effects upon contacting the surface, so a four-dimensional body does when contacting our world. These effects are described by John D. Ralphs in *Exploring the Fourth Dimension.*

It (a four-dimensional body entering our world) will displace a volume of air, and may also cause local heating of the displaced air by friction. In either case the effect will be to create a pressure wave radiating outwards, rather in the manner of a small explosion or a balloon bursting. (Such a "step wave" or "impulse" is one of the simplest and most fundamental of sounds.) Any large resonant surface, such as a wooden floor or a large piece of furniture, will "drum" to the impact of the air wave, and the sound will be further modified by the acoustics of the room so that what is heard in an adjoining room will be a hollow bang or thump.[37]

These are sounds typical of the poltergeist, and it is not surprising that they accompany other extra-dimensional activities. (Remember how when Claudia turned a tennis ball inside-out, there was an "implosive sound"?) Here is an account by William Roll, from his *The Poltergeist:*

Suddenly a small glass vase from the kitchen table flew through the open door and fell to the rug at my feet. The vase did not break; nevertheless there was a loud explosive sound. I was facing Mrs. Beck but not looking directly at her. It was possible, therefore, that she might have thrown the vase. However, this would not explain the sound, which was as loud as a pistol shot. I at once examined the vase. There was no sign of foreign substances on it or on the floor. . . . Unusually loud sounds are often reported in connection with poltergeist incidents.[38]

Movement of Objects

Movement is the most common feature in poltergeist cases. Sometimes objects will fall off shelves or slide over counter surfaces, but more often they are seen flying across the room. Some objects behave normally while in flight but others execute seemingly impossible maneuvers, such as floating in mid-air, changing speed or trajectory, making turns at sharp angles, and striking surfaces with an unusually weak impact.

This kind of manipulative prowess suggests constant control of the objects, and since this is clearly impossible in three-dimensional space, it must be maintained elsewhere—in extra-dimensional space. The agent moves the extensions of these objects in higher space and the three-dimensional cross sections show the effects. More complex movements, which require more control, become more common as the poltergeist phenomenon continues and the agent becomes more adept with his "skill."

Many of these movements are accompanied by disproportionately loud sounds, as should be expected with extra-dimensional activity. This explains, for example, how an object can strike a wall with an explosive sound, yet fall to the ground unbroken, leaving the impression of a weaker impact than expected. At other times, bottles explode by themselves. This implies a force from within and an extra dimension in an inside-out direction.

Objects thrown about are usually found to be warm to the touch when handled immediately after. This should also be expected when force from an extra dimension is brought to bear on it. There is local heating produced by friction, as already explained. In spite of all the flying objects and broken glass in poltergeist outbursts, though, there has never been a case of a serious injury. In fact, objects hurtling towards the agent or family members often stop or change direction at the last moment. It is hard to attribute this restraint to the agents themselves, embroiled as they are in psychological trauma, and diverse in temperament and character.

It's more probable that the PK which operates in extra-dimensional space is subject to the laws that govern it. In a framework where all is alive and subject and object are one, some of these may be moral laws, ruling there to the same extent that physical laws do in our world. Thus objects in motion may have a natural tendency to avoid or minimize a forced collision.

Teleportation

In some poltergeist outbreaks, household objects will mysteriously disappear and then reappear elsewhere, sometimes suddenly dropping from the ceiling. They have been known to penetrate walls or other physical objects without causing any damage, even to vanish from locked containers, as in this incident, investigated by Hans Bender, Germany's leading poltergeist researcher, and reported by D. Scott Rogo in *The Poltergeist Experience.*

The oddest phenomenon reported during the case was the inexplicable teleportation of objects. At one time the mistress collected all the poltergeist-teleported items, which had been scattered helter-skelter during a previous bombardment, and placed them in a toolbox. Then she sat on the box in defiance of the poltergeist. Yet, even as she did so, the same items that she had carefully locked away started dropping down from the ceiling, in front of her. They were soon scattered all over the floor. The witness thereupon opened the toolbox, only to find it empty.[39]

I've already shown how PK can teleport objects by using an extra dimension, like Zhang with the pill and bottle. But here the maneuvers are more accomplished and increasingly so as the agent's subconscious gains control of its newfound ability.

Teleportation is an unmistakable sign of an extra dimension. In fact, physicist Ernst Mach, who strongly influenced Einstein, wrote that the sudden appearances of objects in our space would be the best possible evidence for the reality of higher spatial dimensions, unperceived by us. This best possible evidence is the poltergeist phenomenon (and the UFO and abduction phenomena, as we'll see in the following chapter).

As with objects moved by the poltergeist through three-dimensional space, teleported objects are found to be warm to the touch, due to the local heating effect when objects enter our space from an extra dimension. Rogo gives this account from another case: "At the moment that a priest blessed the house, Bender reported, a stone fell from the ceiling and came to rest on a board without any bouncing almost as if it were fastened to a magnet. The priest picked it up and it gave the sensation of being warm."[40]

Stone Throwing

Another tactic of the poltergeist is to bombard the outside walls or roof of a home with stones or pebbles, although sometimes, as in the case above, they may mysteriously fall or be thrown about inside the house. They appear from out of nowhere before falling, and at times pass through solid matter—they are teleported. Stone-throwing is one of the poltergeist's most common tricks, and often it is the only one manifested. The poltergeist agent probably chooses rocks because they appeal to the angry child within. Also, deep psychological stress may provoke a primal expression of hostility, and rocks are Man's most primitive weapon.

Like other objects manipulated by the agent through extra-dimensional space, the stones exhibit weird patterns of flight, are usually warm when handled afterwards, arrive accompanied by pops or other percussive sounds, hit with much less force than expected, and in instances where someone is actually struck, produce no injury. Here is an account of a stone-throwing poltergeist in the jungles of Sumatra, reported by W. G. Grottendieck, a Dutch traveler.[41] The outburst lasted only one night:

After retiring for the night in the house where he was staying, he half awoke to the sound of something falling near him. More noise completely roused him, and he found a cascade of smallish black stones falling to the floor by his bed. When he turned up the lamp, he could see the stones coming right through the roof. He awoke a laborer in the next room and had him go outside to examine the nearby jungle, while he lit up the area with an electric lantern. Nothing was found yet the stones continued to fall. While the laborer searched the other section of the house, Grottendieck went back inside his room to observe the falling stones and try to catch them. But he could not.

It seemed to him they actually "changed their direction in the air as he tried to get hold of them." He managed to climb up a partition-wall of the room to examine the area of roof where the stones were entering. There were no holes in it, but the stones kept coming through; and he was unable to catch them there either. Grottendieck noted the stones fell abnormally slowly, hit the ground with a loud bang, and were warm to the touch—classic poltergeist *and* extra-dimensional characteristics.

Electromagnetic Disturbances

Electrical disturbances are common in poltergeist outbreaks. Lights inexplicably go on and off, appliances start by themselves. This suggests the presence of electromagnetic energy. But from where?

Electromagnetism is one of four elementary forces in our normal world (the others are the strong and weak nuclear force and gravity). To us they appear as separate forces, but physicists now suspect they are unified in an extra-dimensional framework. Likewise, in extra-dimensional theory that which is separate to us is unified and part of one phenomenon in higher space. Thus, from that broader vantage point, these four basic forces are one "normal" force of nature.

Granting this, it is likely that any time this one extra-dimensional force is applied through our space, there are residual by-products, or waste products, from this force (similar to the energy loss with our entropy). Since the everyday workings of our world are predominately electromagnetic, this is where we'd most likely see any such waste products as electromagnetic disturbances. We'll see this same effect, and more, with UFOs.

Fire-Lighting

In a poltergeist outbreak mysterious fires may spontaneously ignite about the home and premises. It is an extremely rare phenomenon, and in such a case, no normal cause is ever found for the blazes. Fire is also electromagnetic energy, and it is probable that as the PK agent learns to control his extra-dimensional force, he can learn to focus its electromagnetic discharge, or waste product, to produce an electrical spark, which then ignites objects into flames. The manipulation of electromagnetic energy seems reasonable inasmuch as we have already seen that Nina Kulagina could deflect compass needles, and in chapter 9, we'll see how extra-dimensional PK can manipulate the weak nuclear force in the lab.

Communication and Intelligence

At times the poltergeist may communicate with people, usually by responding to questions with raps, and display what appears to be a personality. It is these incidents that most often convince witnesses that a spirit entity or demon is responsible.

The apparent independence of the poltergeist comes from the normal subconscious mind's capacity to create another distinct personality to relieve the stress and guilt common to all poltergeist agents. *The Three Faces of Eve* and *Sybil* are books that present well-documented cases in which multiple personalities were consciously displayed; multiple personality disorder (MPD) has become a recognized phenomenon. There is no reason to assume that potentially independent personalities cannot exist in the subconscious of all of us. Therefore, within the poltergeist agent, an aspect of his personality can function independently at the subconscious level where PK is more easily generated.

What tends to support this, as opposed to possession theory, is that this aspect, or alter ego, incomplete in itself, is very sensitive to and actually conforms to the expectations and beliefs of its observers. Treat it as an intelligent entity, and it raps out answers to questions. Confront it as a demon and it starts to behave as one, realizing how it is supposed to act. In fact, in reports of confrontations between demons and exorcists in Western and Eastern cases, the entities always conformed to local customs and expectations. In short, no otherworldly or even extra-dimensional interpretation is necessary to explain this part of the phenomenon.

Physical Attacks

This is another rare phenomenon that may consist of bites, scratches, or pinches which can leave marks on the body, usually that of the PK agent. Most of these agents, however, have a tendency to self-abuse. Thus the marks could be attributed to autosuggestion, inasmuch as similar effects can be produced on volunteer subjects by the use of hypnotic suggestion; both are subtle applications of PK. Attacks on family members, and the agent in some cases, can be carried out by the agent's alternate personality, with the wounds similarly inflicted by PK. Remember that Kulagina could affect living tissue in animals.

In conclusion, the poltergeist is another by-product, though an unwelcome one, of extra-dimensional consciousness. It's a natural consequence of tapping into a force we have in our present state little or no control over. Many mystics have been known to be plagued by poltergeist disturbances, and later we'll see the same ramification in other contacts with that consciousness, such as in UFO abductions and near-death experiences.

Healings

I have a tough time with this subject. There is too much fraud in it, and most of it is virtually impossible to establish as paranormal healing, as opposed to normal healing. Still, I must touch upon it because under extra-dimensional theory, it is possible in three ways and, therefore, must on occasion happen.

First, when one has a mystical experience, that person is galvanized by the higher, extra-dimensional faculty in every conceivable way: morally, spiritually, intellectually, *and physically.* St. Teresa says, "Even the sick come forth from ecstasy healthy and with new strength; for something great is then given to the soul."[42] An energizing of the body's physical processes is a natural consequence of illumination; in fact, the mystical experience itself is in part a biochemical reaction. Now, given this, we've seen that those who have had the mystical experience gain, more or less, the capacity to affect those around them in the same ways that they were originally affected, one of which is physically. So, second-hand exposure to the higher faculty may vitalize or heal people in this way.

Second, one who has had a mystical experience, and thus has the potential capacity to energize and heal, may try to heal someone. The problem is it's virtually impossible. This healing capacity, yet another by-product or facet of the extra-dimensional faculty, must be just as unpredictable, that is as rare, as telepathy, clairvoyance, precognition, and PK are on command—with one possible exception.

That is Jesus, the human who almost assuredly had the greatest acquaintance with the higher faculty. Jesus not only had an unusually deep experience, but returned to it often (also highly unusual), and may even have, for a time, acquired constant use of the faculty, which would make him the only human being ever to do so. Thus he would naturally have had more success in using any facet of it, such as healing, to the point of maybe being able to do it. At any rate, Jesus certainly thought himself capable of such healings; in fact, he could sound cocky about it, boasting of being able to make "the blind recover their sight, the lepers made clean, the lame walk, the deaf hear."[43] Of course with Jesus' unique grasp of the higher faculty, the unintentional rubbing-off effect would be stronger as well, and could have been the thing that did the trick.

Third, a paranormal or extra-dimensional healing could occur as a spontaneous self-healing. In rare cases, a terminally-ill patient's disease will inexplicably go into remission, never to return. Could the person have gleaned a fragment of the higher faculty, in the same fashion as one gleans a fragment of ESP, but just the one needed at the time? Unfortunately, the chances of summoning this extra-dimensional fragment, when needed, are as slim as summoning up any other on demand—a one-in-a-million shot. (Still, could there be any more practical benefit to the cultivation of the higher faculty?)

Apparitions

Imagine you're a real estate agent, and one morning you're sent by a client to appraise an old Victorian house for sale. After examining the grounds and interior, you're impressed: A very distinctive property, you think; it will sell quickly at the right price. But then as you approach the staircase to the second floor, you're startled to see an elderly gentleman in a robe coming down that staircase. Strange, you think. I thought this place was vacant; after all this is an estate sale. And just as you are about to speak to this man, he disappears.

It's spooky; you don't know what to make of it, until you later speak to the owner, informing him you saw someone there, and you ask if anyone else had been at the house that day. You describe the man. The owner has a knowing look. "You're not the first," he says. "The man you've just seen is my father. Four months ago, despairing over the death of his wife, my mother, he took his own life. God, how he loved that house."

This is a typical ghost story. Was it the sprit of the bereaved man you saw, a hallucination, or something else? Actually, it's a combination of two things, both of which are acknowledged by modern researchers, but neither of which can be explained in our normal framework of space, time, and consciousness.

Most apparitions are linked with a death and a place the deceased had a strong emotional attachment to. Researchers have speculated that the emotions and events surrounding the death are somehow encoded in the materials of the building, just as the information of sight and sound can be encoded on a videotape. Then, when atmospheric conditions are right, or the observer's mind is tuned to the correct wavelength, he picks up images of these past events. The more powerful the emotions involved, the stronger the resonance, and the more likely they will be picked up by an observer.

This hypothesis is basically correct; the problem is it doesn't work in our world, but it does in an extra-dimensional one. Here the information of the emotions and events is naturally encoded in each part of the house, as in an extra-dimensional reality, and from that higher point of view, each part of our world contains information of the whole. But how does an observer access that view?

One may glean a fragment of this extra-dimensional information with ESP, made easier by the strong emotional content encoded in the house; remember, it is emotional strength that facilitates an ESP intuition. Also remember the Apostle Paul's description of one part of the higher faculty as "the distinguishing of Spirits." The fact that an apparition is essentially a psi apprehension, that is, dependent on someone being able to intuit it, explains another nuance of the phenomenon—when several people are present, not everyone sees it.

Psychic phenomena are hints and clues that we live in a larger reality, of which our world of three dimensions of space plus time is but a part. On rare occasions we see small parts of that larger world. Now let's meet a race that actually lives in it.

UFOs and Abductions

Or do humanoids and UFOs alike bespeak a parallel "reality" that for some reason manifests itself to some of us for very limited periods? But what would this reality be?

—Dr. J. Allen Hynek[1]

It's amazing what somebody can do with just a little bit of extra-dimensional consciousness—have "impossible" psychic phenomena. With a little more still, as in the mystical experience, one is like a god amongst men. Imagine what a person could do if he were born into this consciousness and had it his whole life and were surrounded by others who had it. Each could learn from the other, cultivate and refine it, and together develop a language, mathematics, logic, and technology based on it. Suppose an entire race on another planet has been doing this for hundreds of thousands of years, for such a race exists!

Our sun is one of about one trillion stars in the Milky Way galaxy, which in turn is one of about one hundred billion galaxies in the visible universe, each with billions of stars. And since many of these stars presumably have planets, there could be trillions of opportunities (just within our relatively independent subtotality) for life to develop and consciousness to evolve.

The argument against another intelligent race visiting us is the enormous distances between stars and the speed limit of light imposed by special relativity. It would take several human lifetimes for us to visit even nearby stars, though those on board would experience a time-dilated trip of only a few months. We have no designs for starships that can even approach this speed. But these are only *our* restrictions, built into our conceptual worldview, a natural consequence of our level of consciousness.

A race endowed with the higher faculty, and as far above us as we are above animals or plane beings in knowledge, would know no such restrictions. Think of how just a new, higher concept can result in a tremendous advance in travel; for example, we cross the ocean in a fraction of the time our ancestors did, not because of faster ships, but because of flight. A higher conception would utilize higher principles, too, ones we cannot even imagine.

Such beings at this level would have means of transport that to us *must* be miraculous. Moreover, in an extra-dimensional reality, they may actually be much closer to we have in stellar distance to begin with. But let's keep it simple. Let's picture a race that has evolved from the same three-dimensional ground as we have but is conscious of an extra dimension and can use it, just as we on the Earth's surface are conscious of and can use a third dimension (height) to erect buildings in it and fly machines through it. Imagine this race is interested in us.

Reports of unusual flying machines have been made for centuries. Witnesses at first described them by comparing them with familiar objects: heavenly chariots, celestial wheels, fiery shields, scrolls, and later as airships or vessels in the sky. During World War II, Allied airmen called them "foo fighters" and thought they were enemy weapons. (It was later learned that German and Japanese pilots also saw them and thought they were Allied weapons.) In recent times, we call them UFOs and envision them as extensions of our technology, as spacecraft.

There are now at least 100,000 unexplained UFO sightings on record worldwide. Skeptics attribute all of them to misidentification of atmospheric phenomena or man-made objects, psychological illusions, and hoaxes. But the sheer number of reports and credibility of the witnesses say otherwise. UFOs have been described in consistent fashion by thousands of reliable and competent observers, including commercial and military pilots (from more than 40 countries), air traffic controllers, and even astronomers—people obviously well-acquainted with normal aerial phenomena and craft.

In addition, there's often corroborating physical evidence: radar trackings, photographs and motion pictures, unusual animal reactions, and electromagnetic effects such as interference with compasses, radio and television transmissions, automobile engines, and electrical equipment aboard aircraft. Physical evidence found at UFO landing sites include imprints/ground markings, residues, damaged trees, cooked soil and grass, and traces of radioactivity. These physical trace cases also number in the thousands, and reports have been catalogued from more than 40 countries.

There is indeed a real phenomenon. Recognizing this, many have adopted what at first seems a plausible explanation: UFOs are spacecraft from another, more advanced planet, visiting the Earth to study it, much as we might expect to do to other planets in our future. In 1954 professor Hermann Oberth, the German rocket pioneer, in an article for *American Weekly* entitled "Flying Saucers Come from a Distant World," stated:

> I have examined all the arguments supporting and denying the existence of flying saucers and it is my conclusion that UFOs do exist, are very real, and are spaceships from another or more than one other solar system. They are possibly manned by intelligent observers who are members of a race carrying out long-range scientific investigations of our Earth for centuries.[2]

This standard extraterrestrial hypothesis was a logical extrapolation of the facts. But over the years, it has become increasingly apparent that there must be more to it. For one thing there is simply too much activity, far more than required for any physical survey of the planet. Also, even allowing for fantastic technological advances, UFOs do not behave as one might reasonably expect. Sometimes they instantaneously appear, as if from out of nowhere, and then just as suddenly disappear. Other times, they grow larger, expanding, then contract into nothing or change from one shape into another in a fraction of a second. They have been known to split in two, then merge again, fly into bodies of water, and even into solid ground. It is just these features that convince some the phenomenon is fantasy. Solid objects in four-dimensional space-time physics simply cannot do these things, *but extra-dimensional ones can.*

In chapter 2 we saw that when a three-dimensional object (like a sphere) passed through a plane world, it was observed by the plane beings as something (a point) suddenly entering their world; and then the object appeared to expand as more and more of it entered their space. On the other hand, if the object, once there, began to move out of their space, it would seem to contract and then disappear.

These are classic UFO and extra-dimensional characteristics. The explanations normally offered for them are that UFOs can somehow materialize or dematerialize at will, or somehow make themselves larger and smaller, or even invisible. But these are simplistic interpretations of what is observed. In reality, the maneuvers seem the way they do—bizarre—because we see only part of the object at a time, and thus have a distorted view of the real activity.

Remember the opening of this book—a UFO magically changing from one shape into another. Here's how it works. In the upper-middle of figure 15 is a three-dimensional wedge-shaped object, a UFO to the plane beings, and capable of the same kind of magic.

Figure 15

Just above it are four of its different cross-sections that would be seen in the plane world as a circle, elongated rectangle or cigar, square, and triangle. Plane beings who encountered the forms at different times, as in the illustration, would never realize that they were just different cross-sections of one extra-dimensional object. And if it happened that during the course of a sighting, one of these shapes suddenly changed into another, they would not know that it was only due to one extra-dimensional object changing position, or rotating, in higher space.

Likewise in our world, a UFO is an extra-dimensional craft which, when shifting position in higher space, appears to change into a different form as a new cross-section of it is presented to us. In fact, the forms in the illustration are meant to suggest the types of UFOs most commonly reported and which have been known to change from one into another: disc and/or sphere, cigar shaped, cube, and pyramid shaped.

Using the same kind of analogy of an extra-dimensional craft rotating in extra-dimensional space but this time with a craft of different shape, say with structural protrusions, it could easily appear to split apart as it rotated through our space, then merge again into one whole as it continued. For example, picture a three-dimensional craft like an airplane rotating through a plane world: one solid object, the body, splits into two or more, wing, nose, struts, only to become one object again. Or, as we've seen before, objects that appear to be different in lower space may be connected or part of one object in higher space.

The electromagnetic disturbances that accompany UFO activity are similar to those that accompany another extra-dimensional phenomenon, the poltergeist. In both cases, electrical circuitry is affected, only to return to normal once either the UFO departs or the poltergeist outburst subsides. I've already shown how this is possible: electromagnetic discharge as a waste product or energy loss when a (more inclusive) extra-dimensional force is applied within our space.

With UFOs however, the effects are not only stronger and farther reaching, as befitting a more powerful employment of energy, there is sometimes an additional waste product—radioactivity. Witnesses have suffered burned skin and eyes, which is consistent with exposure to radioactivity, and radioactivity has also been found at landing sites. But if the power systems of UFOs operate on a higher, extra-dimensional energy force that includes our four forces of nature, we could easily see both electromagnetic and radioactive discharges (strong/weak nuclear *and* electromagnetic implications) as normal, residual by-products.

UFOs also demonstrate flight characteristics unlike anything previously seen on Earth. They can hover motionless, display phenomenal acceleration and deceleration, travel up to 18,000 mph, and make 90-degree turns while traveling at such speeds, an act that would rip a normal physical object apart. A technology that can accomplish these things, i.e., defy inertia and gravity, is not *just* more advanced than ours, it is totally beyond our understanding of physical laws.

A higher form of consciousness and its ensuing level of science would give rise to such a technology, which confounds reality as we know it. The performance capabilities of UFOs reflect this. They are founded on higher principles, operate in accordance with the physical laws of an extra-dimensional continuum, and take full advantage of that extra dimension.

The UFO phenomenon is an extra-dimensional one, but the standard extraterrestrial hypothesis, which at first seemed a good one, refuses to go away. It has become something of a dogma in itself and, like all dogmas, is extended by its proponents to accommodate new and incongruous manifestations of the phenomenon. Our government has actually played an important role in this. For while it knows the phenomenon is beyond being merely extraterrestrial, it has helped perpetuate the extraterrestrial hypothesis and use it for its own purposes, while at the same time disaffirming the whole phenomenon. Sound confusing or conspiratorial? It is, but then again, given the real nature of the phenomenon, the government could almost not do anything but this.

It started in the late 1940s with a wave of UFO sightings all over the country, and our military did what it was supposed to do—investigate it. The Air Material Command was given the assignment, and in September 1947, Lieutenant General Nathan Twining, AMC Chief of Staff, wrote to his superior, the Commanding General of the Army Air Forces: "The phenomenon reported is something real and not visionary or fictitious . . . There are objects probably approximately the shape of a disc, of such appreciable size, so as to appear to be as large as man-made objects . . . [it appears] some of the objects are controlled either manually, automatically, or remotely."[3]

Several months later, the Air Force established Project Sign to investigate further, and by 1948, Sign had prepared a similar estimate of the situation, concluding that UFOs could only be otherworldly vehicles. At that point, things changed rapidly.

Project Sign was changed to Project Grudge, proponents of the otherworldly hypothesis were reassigned or encouraged to leave the service, and a pattern of debunking UFO reports and attempting to defuse interest in the phenomenon began. Grudge (appropriately named) concluded that UFOs that could not be explained in conventional terms could be in psychological ones as misperceptions, illusions, or hoaxes, even though 23 percent of its cases were still left categorized as "unknown." Project Grudge was then terminated.

For almost the next twenty years it would be more of the same. UFO sightings would continue, the public would smell an official cover-up, and the government would be forced to respond with an occasional study. But Project Blue Book, the CIA's Robertson Panel, and the infamous Condon Report all would reach the same convenient conclusion, though by the most questionable scientific methods; in 1969, the Air Force disengaged itself from the field of UFOs, stating that further study "could no longer be justified on grounds of national security or in the interest of science."[4] This final verdict had the intended effect of discouraging UFO research by independent scientists and private groups. Governments of other countries, who took their cue from the United States, began adopting a similar posture of (outward) official indifference.

Looking back however, it is certain that the government knew of the physical reality of UFOs and took a twofold approach to it. One was to assemble research groups, complete with prestigious scientists, to ward off the attention of the public and scientific community, in effect, to mount a public relations exercise. The other was to have a secret program that did real research.

Yet all this is understandable. The concern of military agencies is national security, not science. The most technologically sophisticated war in history had just ended (WW II); the UFO phenomenon held awesome implications for military hardware; and we had been caught unprepared before at Pearl Harbor, all of which necessitated a secret research program into an unknown phenomenon.

This program, in the hands of a small, top-secret group, must still exist, and it must be no closer to understanding, in conventional terms, the UFO phenomenon today than it was then. For it is not just a case of deciphering the secrets of an advanced science and technology, *the UFO phenomenon is extra-dimensional,* and as such, the principles and technology involved *must* be incomprehensible by conceptual means.

Astronomer J. Allen Hynek (1910–1986) served as scientific consultant for the Air Force on UFOs from 1947 to 1969. Though initially an avowed skeptic, he gradually became convinced of the reality of the phenomenon, and of the government's facade of a real scientific study. Hynek also began to find the standard extraterrestrial hypothesis lacking and started to speculate that UFOs were the product of a nonhuman intelligence from a kind of alternate or parallel reality, "operating outside the established laws of physics."[5]

He also saw that the phenomenon was somehow related to other kinds of paranormal phenomena, a view reflected in *The Encyclopedia of UFOs:*

> The subject is much more complex than any of us have imagined. It has paranormal aspects but certainly it has very real physical aspects too . . . If we are finally forced by the evidence itself to go into the paranormal, then we will. . . .[6]
>
> Certainly the phenomenon has psychic aspects . . . UFOs seem to materialize and dematerialize . . . people who've had UFO experiences (claim) to have developed psychic ability. There have been reported cases of healings in close encounters and there have been reported cases of precognition, where people had foreknowledge or forewarning that they were going to see something. There has been a change of outlook, a change of philosophy of person's lives . . . those are rather tricky things to talk about openly, but it's there.[7]

Hynek felt the solution to the UFO phenomenon would have a profound effect on the current worldview, saying "it will prove to be not merely the next small step in the march of science but a mighty and totally expected quantum jump"[8] and "perhaps even be the springboard to a revolution in man's view of himself and his place in the universe."[9]

Hynek was on the right track, as was Dr. Jacques Vallee, computer scientist and young associate of Hynek during the Blue Book years. Vallee, now one of the world's most experienced researchers, has written several books on the subject and believes that it represents "a yet unrecognized level of consciousness."[10] He speculates that: "UFOs operate on properties of space-time we have not yet discovered."[11] And: "In a multi-dimensional reality of which (our) space-time is a subset."[12] In his 1988 book *Dimensions,* he states: ". . . I believe that the UFO phenomenon *represents evidence for other dimensions beyond space-time;* the UFOs may not come from ordinary space, but from a multiverse which is all around us, and of which we have stubbornly refused to consider the reality in spite of the evidence available to us for centuries."[13]

In *Confrontations* (1990), he stated: "I have argued that an understanding of the UFO phenomenon would come only when we have expanded our view of the physical universe beyond the classic four-dimensional model of space-time. Like other paranormal phenomena, UFOs seem to be able to operate outside of known space-time constraints."[14]

If private researchers, basically working alone, have reached the conclusion that UFOs represent not just something extraterrestrial but another *level* of consciousness operating on another *level* of reality, then the government, with all the resources it can marshal toward the phenomenon, must surely have done so long ago. Our government, and undoubtedly others, knows of the reality of UFOs, that the phenomenon is not just extraterrestrial, and they must realize our vulnerability to such a superior, virtually godlike race operating within a realm we cannot fathom. They also know of the abduction phenomenon and the grim reality that any U.S. citizen can be taken out of his own home.

Abduction researcher Budd Hopkins comments: "Every single abductee I've worked with is sure that it may happen again. 'If they want me, they can get me,' is the general sentiment. One young man said to me that if his father were president of the United States, and he lived in the White House, guarded by the Secret Service, he would still feel that 'if they wanted to pick me up again they could.'"[15]

We have no defense against them, in the skies or in our homes. This is why no government will *ever* disclose the truth about UFOs. It is also why our government prefers to keep the focus on the extraterrestrial hypothesis. Vallee, in *Revelations* (1991), points out that intelligence operations are structured with concentric layers, like an onion. The first layer debunks and then appears to ignore the UFO phenomenon; the second, after investigative efforts have peeled away the first layer, appears as if there is a massive conspiracy to hide the truth of *extraterrestrial* visitation and sometimes leaks false documents to that effect or has inside informants announce they are ready to come forward with proof, only to recant or disappear at the last moment.

As a bonus, besides masking the real nature of the phenomenon, this program can serve another purpose: to provide a cover for other, top-secret operations, such as test flights of advanced conventional craft, or perhaps test flights of experimental models of UFOs themselves, based on guesses of what just might make them tick. As Vallee points out, it can be used as a cover for the testing of UFO "imitations," to be potentially used in tactical and counterterrorist operations.

What better way to penetrate a well-guarded enemy base than to create an atmosphere of chaos and confusion, where reactions are delayed and normal procedures suspended, since gaining just a few minutes is the difference between securing the base and being repelled? The illusion of a UFO landing or close encounter, accomplished by a combination of mechanical devices and optical and sound effects, could be used toward just that end.

Vallee reports: "In the failed Desert One operation of April 1980, organized by the Carter administration to attempt the heroic rescue of the American hostages from Tehran, some witnesses claim to have seen a disk resembling a UFO. It was said to be a platform for nonlethal weapons, intended to paralyze or otherwise disable the Iranian guards."[16]

Of course, such UFO imitations need to be tested, and responses and reaction times evaluated. What better test subjects than our own unknowing servicemen? Besides, the results would be invaluable in assessing how we would react to a similar phenomenon, whether a real enemy invasion or a real UFO.

Tests of these various types of projects can explain alleged UFO landings at or near military bases, flybys of missile silos, and rumors of crashed UFOs recovered by the military. The last are of course impossible with an *extra-dimensional* race of beings, for, unless intentionally abandoned, the craft could be easily retrieved against even the tightest security just by "extracting" it through extra-dimensional space.

The government's UFO program (debunking and disinformation) works. But ironically, it is not needed to dissuade mainstream science from addressing the phenomenon. It is already satisfied that UFOs don't exist. An alien intelligence, it reasons, even if more advanced, must surely have an advanced form of scientific know-how. This could not account for: (1) the surreal aerial maneuvers; (2) the paranormal (psychic) aspects; (3) the volume of traffic, weighed against the perceived space-time obstacle of interstellar travel; and (4) the fact that their first priority isn't establishing meaningful dialogue with us.

In short, an alien intelligence would not act the way UFOs do. The UFO phenomenon, as observed, is not logical, and any other form of intelligence *must* be logical. So the scientific approach is to search the universe for extraterrestrial radio signals, as in NASA's S.E.T.I. (Search for Extraterrestrial Intelligence) program. Another intelligence, it reasons, must use these means because we would. This attitude must be the conceptual counterpart to the Earth-centered universe, if not the plane-world-centered universe. As with other aspects of the paranormal, it is predictable. In 1961, a NASA study conducted by the Brookings Institution, a Washington, D.C., think tank, acknowledged: "If superintelligence is discovered, the results become quite unpredictable. It has been speculated that of all groups, scientists and engineers might be the most devastated."[17]

Thus mainstream science defends the prevailing worldview and its own superior standing within it. It searches the vastness of space for intelligence of its own kind but fails to acknowledge the alien intelligence that is already here.

Alien Abductions

The emergence, perhaps explosion, of the abduction aspect of the UFO phenomenon has been relatively recent, yet its implications are so mind-boggling it may seem fantastic to anyone still unacquainted with it. It started in 1961 with the case of Betty and Barney Hill of New Hampshire who, while returning home from a trip, saw a UFO and strange humanoid beings. The next thing they knew, it was two hours later; they were closer to home, but had no recollection of what had happened. This period of "missing time," plus recurrent nightmares (Betty) and headaches and ulcers (Barney), eventually led them to seek psychiatric help, whereupon under regressive hypnosis they independently recounted being taken aboard a craft, undergoing medical examinations, and being given telepathic instructions to "forget" the experience, a mental block later overcome by the hypnosis.

This was a sensational case at the time, a novelty, and researchers found it difficult to accept, despite the Hills' sterling reputation. But slowly, similar stories began to emerge. And like other aspects of the UFO phenomenon, they were coming from sane, credible people. They were at first incorporated into the standard extraterrestrial hypothesis, that the aliens needed to examine some humans to learn our physiological and biochemical makeup. But as these cases began surfacing in ever-increasing numbers, it again seemed like too much activity.

In 1981, New York artist Budd Hopkins hinted at the potential scope of the phenomenon in his book *Missing Time*. Hopkins explored abduction accounts retrieved under hypnosis and speculated that thousands more people may have had such experiences but consciously remember almost nothing about them.

Then in 1987, Hopkins, who by this time had worked with over one hundred abductees, revealed in *Intruders* the most startling aspect of abductions: they are not random, one-time events but part of a continuous process starting in childhood, with the individual systematically reabducted many times over the course of his life as part of an ongoing study. This includes "cell sampling"; marking the child by incision; sometimes "tagging" him with a tiny implant, usually through the nasal cavity (much as we might tag an animal in the wild to periodically monitor it for an experiment); and after puberty taking ova or sperm from the individual to combine human and alien genetic material in the creation of a hybrid race, the embryos of which are incubated in laboratories inside UFOs.

Fantastic as this may sound, Hopkins and other researchers have since seen a steady stream of people come "out of the closet" with similar accounts. Though skeptics say these people have been influenced by previous stories, preprogrammed, as it were, to produce like versions, the reverse is appearing ever more likely: these individuals have had real experiences, the inklings of which were so bizarre, they had no context in which to put them until they read the accounts of others.

It now appears, based on surveys, that several hundred thousand Americans (and upwards) may have had abduction experiences. Hopkins has now worked with hundreds of abductees, and other researchers with hundreds more. They are both male and female, from all walks of life, of every race and religion. All psychological tests they have been subjected to, by a growing number of mental-health professionals, have shown them to be sane and balanced. In fact, at the 1987 meeting of the American Psychological Association in New York, participants agreed that in-depth studies of alleged abductees showed them to be normal people. Furthermore, reports starting to filter in from other countries (about 20 now) seem to indicate that the abduction phenomenon, like the UFO phenomenon in general, is worldwide.

An abduction may begin while one is driving along a lonely stretch of road. The person sees a UFO just above the car, then all of a sudden it is an hour or so later, and she cannot account for that period of missing time (like the Hills). Other times, and surprisingly often, it begins in the individual's home, usually at night. Small humanoid beings appear in the bedroom, place the subject in a suspended or trancelike state that renders him incapable of resistance, and transport him to a waiting UFO. There, he is physically examined (and biological samples taken), mentally probed by mind-scanning techniques, shown terrifying visions of the human race destroying itself and our planet, and in some cases, allowed to engage the entities in communication.

Then he is returned to wherever he was abducted from and told telepathically to forget the experience. However, with either abduction scenario, the person may retain trace memories of the encounter and, sensing something extraordinary has happened to him, eventually see a psychiatrist (of late, an "abduction researcher") and under regressive hypnosis let the story unfold.

The fact that most abduction experiences are retrieved under hypnosis lends itself to controversy. Skeptics charge that subjects are encouraged or led into fantasizing accounts that fit the hypnotist's (or researcher's) preconceived belief patterns. But the evidence contradicts this.

First, though abduction accounts may vary, there is too much consistency of detail in them, despite different hypnotists and cultures. Dr. Thomas Bullard, a well-respected folklorist at the University of Indiana, published an exhaustive study of more than 300 abduction reports from 17 countries in his two-volume 1988 *UFO Abductions: The Measure of a Mystery*. He found no significant differences in accounts despite the beliefs of the subjects and the expectations of the hypnotists. Bullard says: "Hypnosis makes far less difference than critics have claimed."[18]

Second, many abduction accounts are remembered spontaneously either whole or in part without hypnosis. Hopkins reports in *Intruders* 14 abductees who fully recalled their experiences normally, and Bullard's study showed 30 percent were consciously recalled. These accounts show no differences from those that emerge under hypnosis. Bullard again: "Comparison of cases spontaneously revealed with those revealed by hypnosis shows few differences in content . . . These findings weigh against hypnosis as a causal agent in the abduction story."[19]

Third, abduction experiences are often further corroborated by physical evidence. There are power outages, broken tree branches, and imprints consistent with UFOs being on or near the ground, and abductees bear physical signs of their examination, such as permanent scars, lesions, or bloody noses. Moreover, they are physically missing from the place they are supposed to be, and family members and friends attest to their late arrival and confused state.

There can only be two explanations. Either we are seeing the advent of a mass psychosis (which can also produce physical effects) of unprecedented proportions, one for which no such psychological hypothesis has, even tentatively, been offered; or abductions are really happening.

It is here that we come face to face with beings who are truly extra-dimensional. They (the aliens) have complete possession of the higher faculty that apprehends an extra dimension, mastery of that consciousness (brief glimpses of which are the mystical experience and psychic phenomena), and freedom of movement within that extra dimension. They are as far above us as we are above animals or plane-world beings. We see this unmistakably demonstrated in the accounts of abductees who have encountered these beings and in the communications of the beings themselves.

We see this in the works of the major abduction researchers and pioneers. These are Hopkins (who also wrote *Witnessed* [1996]); David Jacobs, professor of history at Temple University, and his two books *Secret Life* (1992) and *The Threat* (1998); Massachusetts researcher Raymond E. Fowler, five of whose books, *The Andreasson Affair* (1979), *The Andreasson Affair, Phase Two* (1982), *The Watchers* (1990), *The Watchers II* (1995), and *The Andreasson Legacy* (1997), chronicle Betty Andreasson's ongoing abduction experiences in what must be the most thoroughly documented case ever, and also Fowler's 1993 book *The Allagash Abductions*. There is also John E. Mack, M.D., whose *Abduction* (1994) has been a work of major impact; he also wrote *Passport to the Cosmos* (1999). Mack, credentialed to the hilt, was a Pulitzer prize-winning author and professor of psychiatry at Harvard Medical School (he died in 2004) and was a researcher not easy for mainstream science to dismiss.

These researchers came to different conclusions about the meaning of abductions. Hopkins and Jacobs emphasize the nuts-and-bolts aspects: the appearance, attitude, and procedures of the aliens, and their genetic engineering program. They see them as calculating and sinister, coldly carrying out their own agenda strictly for their own benefit. Hopkins speculates that they may have become physically weak as a race and need to "revivify their own species from our ostensibly more primitive and more vital gene pool."[20] Jacobs fears the alien/human hybrids could be made to integrate into human society and help the aliens assume control of the planet.

Mack and Fowler acknowledge the genetic crossbreeding aspect but also recognize other, more transcendent, sides of the phenomenon. Mack sees a transformative one:

> The other important, related aspect of the abduction phe-
> nomenon has to do with the provision of information and the

alteration of consciousness of the abductees. This is not a purely cognitive process, but one that reaches deeply into the emotional and spiritual lives of the experiencers, profoundly changing their perceptions of themselves, the world, and their place in it. The information concerns the fate of the Earth and human responsibility for the destructive activities that are taking place on it.[21]

Fowler describes the aliens and their technology as "paraphysical in nature" and says some of their abilities include: communicating telepathically; passing through physical objects with ease; materializing and dematerializing into and out of our space-time frame; existing in a timeless realm; and predicting our future.[22] These are exactly what we should expect of a race endowed with extra-dimensional consciousness.

But all these differences of interpretation are understandable with a phenomenon so bizarre and multifaceted and whose true nature is just becoming known. These researchers are just emphasizing different aspects of one problem, different pieces of one puzzle, which will now be put together.

First and foremost, this is no mere extraterrestrial phenomenon; it is an extra-dimensional one. Abductees are actually taken right out of our world, through this extra dimension, into a larger world. Mack says:

[Abductees say] at least some of their experiences are not occurring within the physical space/time dimensions of the universe as we comprehend it. They speak of aliens breaking through from another dimension . . . entering our world from "beyond the veil." Abductees . . . will speak of the collapse of space/time that occurs during their experiences. They experience the aliens, indeed their abductions themselves, as happening in another reality, although one that is as powerfully actual to them—or more so than—the familiar physical world.[23]

An abductee comments:

The ETs have the ability to enter into our space and time dimension or leave it any time they want . . . I was taken out to

another dimension that has no space and time as we know it . . .
There are different dimensions, worlds existing within worlds
. . . [outside of linear time and space].[24]

Mack (says of this patient):

[She] repeatedly describes the access she gains during
her abductions to another dimension (or other dimensions) of
existence, an expanded reality in which human concepts of
space and time do not apply.[25]

Other abductees say: "I got the impression that there was another
dimension there . . . that the dimension I was in was, was coexisting
with this, this other dimension."[26] And: ". . . they are in a different plane.
They're in a heavier space than we are."[27]

Fowler comments: "We find that UFOs and their occupants are
perfectly capable of traveling between at least two different *planes of
existence.*"[28]

Of course we're precluded from perceiving this extra-dimensional
reality by our level of consciousness, as Fowler hints:

If the recalled memories of UFO abductees like Betty actually reflect genuine physical events then our comprehension of
reality is indeed limited. We could be compared with lower animals that experience life within the confines of their particular
physical and mental capabilities. Such animals are completely
oblivious to the coexisting world of man and his technology.
Even so, the forces that operate behind UFOs appear to be
functioning on an infinitely higher plane of awareness that man
is just becoming aware of through experiences like Betty's.[29]

Even Hopkins, who eschews the paraphysical side of abductions,
remarked in 1994 at a college lecture that he didn't think the phenomenon could be understood "until we've expanded our space-time
parameters."[30]

The extra dimension abductees are taken along is best conceived of (as we've seen before) as in an inside-out direction. Recall the first abductee quote, "different dimensions . . . *worlds existing within worlds.*" Also from Mack's patients: "In the transition from one reality to another, you feel like you're contracting and expanding at the same time . . . [it's the] secret of moving from one dimension to another."[31] And: "Energy, like folds into itself, and you're just somewhere else . . . everything folds, inverts into, and folds inside itself."[32]

Other abductees have recalled: "I believe we were [out] in space, and somehow I believe we were in the center of the Earth. Now how can you be in both?"[33] And: "It [the UFO] took me somewhere . . . I think it pulled me somehow . . . it's just a feeling of a—suddenly exploding. Like it was pulling me apart and then I was inside something . . . This room (in the UFO)."[34]

The fact that UFOs are extra-dimensional craft makes another strange aspect of abductions understandable—abductees may describe UFOs as being much larger inside than outside. "It's funny, this thing didn't look that big from the outside. Didn't look like there was that much room in it."[35]

Another abductee says: "I can see where the edge of the ship would be on the left, but it's very far away—maybe fifty feet away. I don't understand how it could have been that far because the other room was only like ten feet wide and this one is so really far away . . . It doesn't make sense! . . . It wouldn't have fit. It wouldn't work."[36]

Physical maneuvers that are impossible in a framework of space-time are easily accomplished with the use of an extra dimension—as with UFOs themselves. And in abductions, we see the same antics, which of course seem miraculous to those in lower space. Jacobs says: "Aliens do things that seem like magic to us. They make humans and their clothes go through solid matter like windows, walls, and ceilings. They cause themselves, humans, and other matter to be invisible when they are outside the confines of the UFO."[37]

Invisible? Only because they are at that time in extra-dimensional space. Just as UFOs seem to materialize from out of nowhere and dematerialize, the aliens do the same, initiating an abduction by just appearing in an abductee's home, or entering through walls, then removing their subject the same way. "They are starting to come through the door now . . . right through the wood, one right after another. It's amazing! Coming through! . . . Now they are all inside. . . . I was going *through* the same thing (the door), the wood, that they were."[38]

Fowler says of this feat: "It was as if each alien were moving in and out of our plane of existence and temporarily into an unseen parallel dimension in order to pass through the solid wood of the *door*. The question that immediately arises is: *Where* were their bodies when they disappeared?"[39]

The answer to the above is obvious: extra-dimensional space. Imagine how a three-dimensional being like you or I could abduct a plane being out of his home the same way. We'd all of a sudden enter "right through the wall or floor," take him in tow, and then exit, again going right through solid, two-dimensional matter, *simply by going over or under it—in the third dimension.* And when we were done with him, we'd return him the same way. The aliens do likewise. Jacobs says: "If the abduction took place from her home, the abductee usually goes directly through the window (wall or ceiling, in some cases) and 'rematerializes' in her room."[40]

Another abductee adds: "Floated (in) . . . Right through the door . . . I don't know how it could be . . . just floated to bed."[41]

This method of extraction—extra-dimensional—explains a finding in Bullard's study that he thought odd and called "doorway amnesia." Abductees were unable to remember passing through any type of door on the craft when either entering or exiting.

In abductions all communication by aliens is telepathic (as it should be), but their ability here is far more powerful than the mere glimpses seen in the mystical experience or psychic phenomena. Abductees feel their mind is completely laid bare to the aliens and they cannot keep thoughts from them. "I feel like my thoughts are available to everyone, and there's nothing to hide."[42] When abductees are addressed, it is in the form of receiving a mental impression of the intended message. "I see the words in my head. It's like—it's weird! It's like I see the words and hear them in my head."[43] "I think it was in my head that they were calling me, so they knew my name or they knew how to call me in my head."[44] "He called me Betty. It seemed like an oral sound but it . . . it . . .—ah, I think it was a transformation of thought."[45]

In the Hill case, Barney said, "He did not speak by word. I was told what to do by his thoughts making my thoughts understand," and Betty said she "knew what they were thinking."[46]

The communication between aliens appears to be telepathic as well. "They're . . . understanding each other, but they're not talking. I don't hear anything."[47] "They're talking among themselves but not with their mouths, just with their minds."[48]

Through telepathic communication, which is a direct tie-in to higher consciousness, abductees may get a sense of the higher thought process, or logic, and their descriptions of it are unmistakably transfinite—one in all, all in one, all is one. This is as we have seen before and again just as it should be. Here are some examples:

• "I understand that *everything is one*. Everything fits together . . . No matter what it is!"[49]

• "Everything has been formed to unite and I don't, I can't really understand what they say, what they mean."[50]

• "It's like you become on the one hand, part of everything, and everything becomes part of you."[51]

• "[It] allowed me to feel this aloneness yet to feel totally connected with that one individual source . . . [there's] a great web [of connection] . . . a consciousness of the whole . . . I am them, and they are me."[52]

Of course all this is made possible by the higher faculty, which apprehends an extra dimension that for us exists in time. Therefore, the aliens can see past and future aspects of our three-dimensional world laid out at once along the extra dimension. Fowler says: "They insisted that our concept of time was *localized* and that time as we understood it did not really exist. The human concept of time was illusory . . . They are not bound by such a limitation . . . *Time*, as we know it . . . does not exist for them! . . . To them, the past, present, and future are now! . . . All is Now."[53]

The aliens say: "Time with us is not your time. The place with you is localized. It is not with us. Cannot you see it?"[54] And an abductee says: "The future and the past are the same as today to them . . . Time to them is not like our time, but they know about our time."[55]

Bullard comments: ". . . such understanding of time as they have somehow differs from ours."[56]

Indeed, they live in a different, larger world of space-time. The aliens also show a keen interest in abductees' sense of time. Some have assumed this is intelligence gathering, but it is much more likely intelligence or consciousness *testing*. For if one's ascent to higher consciousness is through the expansion of the time sense (to extract an extra dimension of space), an appraisal of that time sense, as a measure of its potential for higher consciousness, would probably include simple inquiries of the abductees.

Now for the part of the UFO phenomenon that so intrigued Hynek. He couldn't have anticipated it would be associated with abductions, but it is the apparent transformation of abductees after their experiences, spiritually and otherwise, sometimes including new psychic abilities.

In the mystical experience, the person is elevated by the higher sense in all ways—physically, intellectually, morally, spiritually, and psychically; in fact, the effects can then be passed on to others in second-hand fashion. Thus we should expect that direct exposure to beings with complete possession of that faculty would produce even more dramatic results, almost akin to a mystical experience, which we indeed find in abductions. Some abductees report spontaneous healings of injuries, mostly minor but in some cases serious conditions such as pneumonia or diphtheria.

Others are intellectually enlightened. Jacobs states: ". . . a few (abductees) have displayed isolated factual knowledge about scientific topics that they have never studied, and others have shown inexplicable interest in physics or astronomy."[57] One of the Allagash abductees, an artist, related to Fowler: "Immediately after the Allagash abduction, my interests changed completely. I lost all interest in creating traditional art. I became obsessed with new technologies. My new interests suddenly included science, mathematics, engineering, architecture, geometry . . ."[58]

But by far the most profound aftereffect is a spiritual awakening. Abductees come to realize a larger universe and consciousness, one previously hidden from them. Mack says they become "open to other realities beyond space/time, realms that are variously described as beyond a 'veil' or some other barrier which has kept them in a 'box' or in a consciousness limited to the physical world."[59] They now come to acknowledge a larger self within that world, one that is intimately connected with all reality. Mack again:

> As their experiences are brought into full consciousness, abductees seem to feel increasingly a sense of oneness with all beings and all of creation . . . Each abductee experiences in some sense an expansion of his or her self, of identity in the world. Paul wondered how we had come to mistake the "shell" of our being for the "whole" of it; and Eva . . . [is moving] from fragmentation toward wholeness. The change that abductees experience is fundamentally that they may no longer feel themselves to be separate from other beings. They shed their identification with a narrow social role and gain a sense of oneness with all creation, a kind of universal connectedness.[60]

Abductees know they have experienced another realm of existence and a higher consciousness, and they are never quite the same again. They become more spiritual, yet less religious, more moral, and less materialistic. They have new values and goals, may adopt different lifestyles, and even change professions.

Many also experience the onset of psychic phenomena, such as telepathic, clairvoyant, and precognitive abilities; poltergeist-related phenomena, such as electrical disturbances, or strange noises may start. The ESP is a sign of the stirring of higher consciousness, from which all psi springs; and the poltergeist activity is caused by the same condition as in traditional poltergeist outbreaks—a new "feel" for higher consciousness, and stress, which is part of the aftermath of the abduction experience. Bullard's remarks on these aftereffects suggest just this: "The paranormal ambience of abduction aftermaths may hint that the experience ties into whole realms of human potential as alien to our everyday conceptions as humanoids are alien to our physical earth."[61]

But all these aftereffects of abductions are not unique. They're found in all human introductions to higher consciousness, whether it's UFO abductions, mystical experiences, or near-death experiences. Kenneth Ring, in his 1992 *The Omega Project*, a comparative study of such effects in abductees and near-death experiencers, reports they are virtually identical and he speculates it holds true for mystical experiencers as well. He postulates a kind of alternate reality coexisting with ours, one that can be perceived only with a new kind of psychospiritual sense, and believes this new sense represents a next step in the evolution of Man.

This is in harmony with extra-dimensional theory, and it is, in the broadest sense, what the abduction phenomenon is all about—evolution. It is also what the aliens represent—the next step in the evolution of consciousness. So now let's try to understand just how that next step was made, and how it resulted in the kind of aliens we're now confronted with.

Some scientists maintain that any intelligent life elsewhere must have evolved along different lines and so be radically different from us in appearance, that is, look anything but humanoid. Another line of thought holds that the humanoid form is the most advantageous for survival *anywhere*. A large brain mass, sense organs elevated above the ground and near the brain, upright posture which leaves two hands free to experiment with and wield tools—it may be Nature's best bet to have a species survive and eventually reach self-consciousness.

If this is the case, then intelligent life on another planet (or planets) may have evolved along a very similar course as ours, with something resembling self-conscious Man evolving from something resembling apes. Given this, can we extrapolate what type of humanoid form a still higher level of consciousness might take? Yes, through a biological phenomenon called neoteny.

In neoteny the normal physical development of a species is suspended in the fetal stage, yet the organism still matures sexually. Since it can reproduce, it can pass this trait on and a new life form will appear, one in which infantile features are retained in the adult form. This is what may have happened in the transition from ape to Man: fetal apes sexually maturing and reproducing. (It is well known that, physically, humans and apes are remarkably similar in the fetal stage.) Because a fetus' brain is more developed than the rest of its body, we might expect such neotenates to rely on thinking, problem-solving, and the further development of consciousness for survival.

Or, a species already headed in the direction of increased cerebral function may find a new, neotenous form allows for further mental development and perhaps the acquisition of a new, higher form of consciousness. This may have been the case with the evolution of ape into Man, Nature gradually approaching a threshold over which it didn't crawl, but leaped, neotenously. The fact that this was a neotenous jump rather than a gradual transition would explain why we are still searching for signs of that transition between ape to Man, from simple to self-consciousness, the "missing link."

So what is the next step in this neotenous scenario, one that goes hand-in-hand with the blossoming of a higher faculty or level of consciousness?

Obviously it would be a life-form that looks like a human fetus, which perfectly describes the aliens encountered in abductions: small humanoid beings (3 to 4 feet tall), with thin hairless body, large head and eyes, small mouth and nose, and no visible sex organs. Neoteny has been brought out before to explain the aliens' appearance, but it has always overlooked the most dramatic difference between ape and Man—the ape's lower, simple consciousness (controversy over flashes of conceptual thought aside), and Man self-consciousness. Isn't this the real difference, in comparison to which physical distinctions pale? And isn't a different level of consciousness the real distinction between the aliens and us?

In evolution, such a change or mutation in a species endures only if the change is advantageous for survival. The benefits in going from sensation to simple consciousness and from simple consciousness to self-consciousness are obvious: the successor is better equipped to prevail over natural enemies and its environment. But is there a benefit in going from self-consciousness to extra-dimensional consciousness? Are there more natural enemies or environmental perils to overcome?

History shows that civilizations rise, mature, and vanish, and even mainstream science acknowledges that we are in a crisis stage now, where either our self-destructive tendencies, magnified a millionfold by technology, will destroy us, or we will go on to further glories, like colonizing other star systems (again, always within the context of self-consciousness). But evolution is often preceded by crises and the next evolutionary step takes place in response to survival instinct.

An alien race may have been in such a crisis stage, heading as we are toward technological and ecological collapse. It faced a new natural enemy—*self-consciousness itself;* for this species now had the technological power to render inhospitable and incapable of supporting life that very environment that allowed it to blossom in the first place. But it changed, by evolving neotenously. It acquired the higher faculty, which provided the wisdom and unifying spirit needed to avoid its demise.

We are in that crisis stage right now. Our faculty's crowning achievement, technology, has in just the last few centuries emerged as a natural enemy, one that is threatening the planet's habitability. Nuclear proliferation, even with the end of the Cold War, is a constant danger, perhaps even more so now. Recent U.N. disclosures (2004) suggest that 40 nations have the ability to make a nuclear bomb, and some of these are in the most volatile regions on Earth, including the Middle East. The proliferation of chemical and biological "weapons of mass destruction" could also have devastating consequences as the global war on terrorism unfolds.

Insatiable greed and corruption (inescapable by-products of self-consciousness?) are destroying plant and animal species at a dizzying pace, in forests, coral reefs, and wetlands. Estimates range from between 10 to 100 animal species are lost every day. If this continues, one-fifth of the world's living species will vanish in the next 30 years, taking with them each one's unique biochemical and genetic material, which could be used to produce new medicines or pest-resistant crops. The planet is undergoing an extinction event the likes of which has not been seen since the dinosaurs and countless other plants and animals disappeared about 65 million years ago, and which by our own making we may reach by the middle of the next century.

There's more bad news. The ozone layer is dissipating at an ever-increasing rate. The greenhouse effect (global warming) may already be making its mark in the recent rise of climactic disasters, floods, hurricanes, droughts, the alarming resurgence of infectious diseases, and perhaps most ominously, a measurable and significant decrease in the Pacific Ocean of plankton—the bottom of the planet's food chain.

Natural resources are fast becoming depleted, and toxic wastes and other poisons and garbage are being dumped back into our planetary system so fast that natural pollutant-absorbing mechanisms are themselves polluted, increasing still more the rate of damage. Eventually, we will drown in our own waste products.

The human socioeconomic system as well is headed toward collapse. The world population is growing at a staggering rate (100 million born in 1997), raising the specter of mass-starvation if technological advances cannot keep pace. Virtually every country in the world is barely holding its head above water in the face of impending bankruptcy. There's still more: the oceans, ever more polluted, are being fished empty; acid rain; pesticide poisoning; and more.

The expansion of society as we know it, that began with the advent of self-conscious thought, has reached its limit. But the old atavistic tendencies—hunt, conquer, build, and expand at any cost—remain. Clearly the need now is for a more moral, benign, and comprehensive way of thought. But do the inherent qualities of self-consciousness— isolation, duality, nationalism, self, Self, SELF—preclude this? Is self-consciousness, unless superseded by a broader, gentler mode of thought, ultimately self-defeating? Must we have, at the deepest level, a common thread of morality and unity, without which a fragmented society turns its technological demons upon itself, in effect devouring itself?

It may be no coincidence that the U.S., the most advanced nation on Earth, leads the world in major-crime statistics (murder, rape, and robbery), prompting the Senate Judiciary Committee in 1991 to acknowledge it as "the most violent and self-destructive nation on earth."

Scientists have long speculated about a possible next step in Man's evolution, usually along the lines of a symbiotic link with a super-computer, the ultimate union of Man and his machine. But the reality is that the next step *must* be to extra-dimensional consciousness, or none at all—which brings us to the purpose of abductions, indeed the core of the UFO phenomenon. The answer involves the main themes in abductions: the creation of a human-alien race, messages of the impending destruction of our race, and the expansion of abductees' consciousness.

The aliens are producing a hybrid race. The objective is to preserve our genetic seed and in an improved evolutionary form bred to carry the higher faculty, if we, as they clearly expect, do not survive our crisis stage. Presumably, this hybrid race will then be raised and prepared to either repopulate the Earth or start anew on some other planet. Here are some comments on this:

• "They said . . . they keep the seed from man and woman so the human form will not be lost. . . . And one of them is saying, 'We have to because as time goes by, mankind will become sterile. They will not be able to produce.'"[62]

• Mack: "The purpose of this hybridization program, Joe said, was evolutionary, to perpetuate the human seed and 'crossbreed' with other species on the ships and elsewhere in the cosmos. Joe spoke sadly of the inevitable further deterioration of the earth. Many humans will die, but the species will not be eradicated."[63]

• "They're breeding us . . . there's no doubt . . . this is absolutely clear."[64]

• "There's a reason they're doing this (I feel they're) making—whatever you want to label it—another whole civilization (I don't know) whether they're going to place it somewhere else, or its going to be introduced here."[65]

Mack says the abductee, "like many abductees, has dreams of the world as we know it coming to an end and relates her breeding role to this eventuality."[66] Betty Andreasson was told, "It is better to lose some than all,"[67] and others have been told of the need to preserve "biological diversity." Fowler believes this preservation program is not limited to us but extends to all life-forms on Earth, as suggested by this message:

"Man is destroying much of nature . . . He's [the alien] saying that they have *collected the seed of Man* male and female . . . And, that they have been collecting *every species* and every *gender* of plant for hundreds of years."[68]

Just the human abduction program alone would be quite an exercise, enough to account for the extravagant amount of general UFO activity that has always baffled researchers; but if the program includes all life on Earth, then the UFO activity observed may actually be only the tip of the iceberg.

Almost all abductees are given messages about impending catastrophes that will render Man sterile if not extinct. They are in the form of visions, produced either telepathically or on holographic-like screens. Here is a typical telepathic vision: "Yeah, they kept putting images in my mind, about the destruction of the planet, and time when people will be starving, and there won't be energy because we're using up the resources."[69] Jacobs describes the viewing screen method: "(The abductee) is shown a screenlike apparatus and images begin to appear on it. The scene is often abhorrent and disturbing—death and destruction, calamity and war, atomic explosions, the end of the world, and so forth."[70] Mack describes the images as: "Scenes of the earth devastated by a nuclear holocaust, vast panoramas of lifeless polluted landscapes and waters, and apocalyptic images of giant earthquakes, firestorms, floods, and even fractures of the planet itself."[71]

Some prefer to interpret all this as a warning to change our destructive ways or these scenarios may come to pass. But taken at face value, the truth seems to be that humankind, with just the use (or misuse) of self-consciousness, is far enough down the path of self-annihilation that its demise is virtually inevitable.

The second part of the aliens' abduction program is the redirection of human consciousness necessary for us to avoid our own destruction. This of course seems contradictory and even absurd when considered in conjunction with the first part, but remember that any transfinite concept borne from the higher faculty *must* seem contradictory and absurd by our standards. In fact, if it did not appear so, we could be sure it was *not* a product of higher logic.

The objective here seems to be raising the consciousness of abductees, in effect, introducing them to the higher but latent faculty within. And though some of this could be just the natural result of exposure to the higher faculty, it seems to go well beyond this. Some abductees, Betty Andreasson, for example, have been afforded a long and in-depth interchange with their captors, typical of a concerned teacher with a prize pupil. In general, abductees deeply feel, or just seem to *know*, that there is a lesson to be learned here.

Ring's *Omega* study showed that "fully 85 percent of UFOERs (abductees) report an increase in their concern for planetary welfare following their UFO encounter, and of these, nearly 60 percent state that it is strongly increased."[72] Moreover, two thirds of UFOERs felt that: "(1) There are higher order intelligences that have a concern with the welfare of our planet; (2) the changes (they've) undergone since (their) UFO experience are part of an evolutionary unfolding of humanity; and (3) the widespread occurrence of UFO experiences is part of a larger plan to promote the evolution of consciousness on a specieswide scale."[73]

The aliens' efforts to help us in this particular fashion may seem minimal by our standards of colonial intervention, but it may be for good reason. History clearly shows that primitive cultures are devastated by superior ones who change and "educate" them. It renders them stagnant, dependent, spiritless, and incapable or undesiring of further *self*-development. It appears that though the aliens want us to survive, they will not directly intervene or provide easy answers. Isn't this how it must be? For doesn't any good teacher prod the student to think for himself, to discover how to arrive at the answer himself? Isn't this, and only this, what warrants a passing grade? The aliens appear to be showing us how to arrive at the answer by pointing out the direction in which it lies—within.

Remember the Perennial Philosophy: Man is part of a larger self and vaster reality, and our life purpose is to seek union with it by a higher faculty of mind. It appears that this is all we need do. Abductees are often told, or later come to realize, that our normal selves are part of a greater whole, that there is another aspect, or dimension, to reality and to ourselves that we've completely overlooked.

For example, Fowler writes: "[The aliens] told Betty that Man *is more than just a physical being* but has not realized this truth because of lack of interest and research . . . there is a paraphysical or spiritual side of life that he has basically ignored . . . If Betty's experiences are truly grounded in reality, then Man's body of flesh and blood now existing in what 'The Watchers' call localized time is vastly more complex than anyone could ever have imagined. Our bodies of intricate living proto-plasm would be a mere shadow of our true nature and abilities."[74]

The aliens stated: "Man is not made of just flesh and blood . . . The (higher) knowledge (and technology) is sought out through the spirit . . . It is through the spirit, but man will not seek out that portion."[75] They also said: "You think that you know yourselves, but you do not know yourselves. You do not know what you are made of. You do not know the powers that you possess."[76]

The abductees attest to this also: "It's (the vaster reality) a whole new thing. It's (our reality) like a little layer. It's one little layer, and you've got that being your whole universe . . . It's like one little layer of appearance."[77] "[They want us to] realize we're part of something greater."[78] "Listen, there is a whole other reality out there that is just as real, just as valid as what you think is the only reality. Open your minds. Look into this."[79]

But we don't. The path is clear—"through the spirit," or expanded consciousness; the way is simple—just seek it out, "look into it"; or even failing this, let Nature take its course without getting in its way. But we don't. We're our own worst enemy, obstructing the natural flow of things—the Law, one that should have been so easy to follow. Mack says: "The aliens . . . seem genuinely puzzled about the extent of our aggressiveness toward one another and especially our apparent willing-ness to destroy the planet's life."[80] "It appears (to them) . . . as if we have deliberately chosen death over life."[81]

To them, we're a spiritually arrested species, hopelessly out of touch with our greater selves, increasingly self-destructive. Here are some examples of this:

• "I was told that because of our violent nature toward each other, and a disrespect for all living things in the environment, we are evolving against the naturalness of the Universal Flow."[82]

- "Human beings think they're it, that that's it. But there's so much else here . . . There's so much life, yet human beings want death. They're choosing destruction, and they keep choosing it over life, over connection, over creation."[83]

- ". . . they told me terrible things would happen to the Earth . . . and they said that it's bad because people can't stop being greedy."[84]

- "(The aliens): Man is very arrogant and greedy and he thinks that all worlds revolve around him . . . Man seeks to destroy himself. Greed, greed, greed, greed. And because of greed, it draws all foul things. Everything has been provided for man. Simple things. He could be advanced so far, but greed gets in the way."[85]

We need a new way of thought, a new way of looking at things, a way where the higher faculty can naturally blossom. We need a new worldview. Mack states: "UFO abductions have to do, I think, with the evolution of consciousness and the collapse of a worldview that has placed man at a kind of epicenter of intelligence . . ."[86] "It has become clear to me also that our restricted worldview or paradigm lies behind most if not all of the major destructive patterns that threaten the human future . . ."[87] On the other hand, Fowler says the consciousness expansion the aliens are trying to bring about on Earth, if effected in time, will "revolutionize every aspect of our lives—science, religion, philosophy, sociology—nothing will be spared . . . mankind is on the verge of a revolution in thought of a magnitude far greater than the Copernican revolution. In fact, there can be little comparison."[88]

One part of the abduction phenomenon *is* about the gradual cultivation of the higher faculty in the human race. This can help explain two other aspects of the phenomenon that have baffled researchers. First, why are these particular abductees selected? It's obvious that the abductees have something the aliens want. *It is that person's capacity for the higher faculty.*

Researchers have noted that abductees seem to be mystically and/or psychically inclined even before their abduction, a sign of their proximity to higher consciousness. Ring's *Omega* study showed that children UFO experiencers seem to be "apparently already sensitive to nonordinary realities."[89] The aliens can somehow detect this capacity, perhaps even communicate with it on some subconscious level. "They let me know that . . . I'm special . . . though just a kid . . . they said that I can understand them and that's what makes me special."[90] They are simply better specimens, whose capacities for higher consciousness are then stimulated still more. "It's about evolving to a higher consciousness . . . They need my consciousness to expand. They need more of my brain to be awake . . ."[91]

Second, why do abductions run across family generations? Bucke and Gopi Krishna both felt that only those born with a special quality—a hereditary gift—could attain the higher faculty; and J. B. Rhine speculated that ESP (a lower branch of the faculty) was inheritable as well. Abductees have it, and the aliens are accelerating the evolutionary process in these, the most suitable bloodlines, to bring about in succeeding generations a new genotype, one better endowed with the natural ingredient for the higher faculty. "(The beings were) acting to breed for the highest qualities of mankind . . ."[92] "(They're trying) genetically (to take) the higher human qualities and somehow, I want to say, reincorporate them into our race."[93]

In true transfinite fashion, the expansion of consciousness would be more profitable with subjects closer to where the aliens need them to be to begin with, and improved over generations (all this for *our* benefit); and they would also be better specimens for interbreeding with *their* race, with the most desirable quality in offspring being the higher faculty.

In what seems to be the final chapter in an abductee's experiences, and especially so for women, one is shown a hybrid baby and told, or one knows, that it is hers. The woman is then asked or made to hold the infant in what seems to be a bonding procedure. Presumably, the babies need to be physically touched to nourish the human side (once seems sufficient). Who better to provide this than an actual parent? The babies, who are described as listless and frail, seem to absorb the experience and afterwards appear better, stronger. But beyond their physical form, the babies have another distinct difference—*consciousness*. The hybrids display unmistakable signs of the higher faculty: they appear telepathic and their eyes have the same hypnotic "knowing" quality.

For example, ". . . he looked so wise . . . more wise than anybody in the world . . . there was (in the eyes) something more there . . . I just fell into them . . . It's like the whole world was in this little baby's eyes. It was like, God, he knew, he *knew* what I felt. He just knew . . ."[94] "I get the sense that she is receiving everything that I'm saying in my head . . . I was transfixed on her eyes . . . I'm drawn into her . . . There's a sense of joining."[95]

Abductions are about the future, our future. Mack says: "The abduction phenomenon, it seems clear, is about what is *yet to* come."[96] But without accelerated progress toward the higher faculty, we may not have a future. While it is difficult to suppose a time frame for our day of reckoning, many have begun to sense an escalation in abductions, as if time is growing short. Fowler notes: "Today . . . their genetics program appears to have accelerated to vast proportions. The Watchers are diligently collecting the seed from earth's lifeforms. Their purpose is to preserve them for existence elsewhere because of their impending extinction on this planet."[97]

And Hopkins says: "I also sense an escalation of their abduction activities, a widening of scale, and a lessening of the attempt to operate covertly. I do not know where all this is leading, but I am not encouraged . . . I fear the (some kind of upcoming) crisis may be deeper and more profoundly wrenching than human history has ever known."[98]

But the last words should belong to the abductees, and the aliens. In fact, these three passages sum up the entire abduction phenomenon:

- "They have the ability to see into the future . . . They can see what's about to happen to us, and they're just watching us . . . These are physical beings that have mastered an awareness of time or space or whatever. They can see what's going on. They can see what the possibilities are . . ."[99]

- "Somehow I feel as if time is running out, as if something big is about to happen. Don't ask me to explain it any better, for I can't. All I know is that this is important—it's a feeling I have, that's all!"[100]

- The aliens: "Observe the children [hybrid babies] . . . These are our children, and they're your children. They're the children of the future . . . Observe the children of the future."[101]

<u>8</u>

Life after Death

For in that sleep of death what dreams may come, when we have shuffled off this mortal coil, . . .

—*Hamlet,* William Shakespeare

What happens when we die? The visible body disintegrates, this we know. But what of the innermost part of us, the mind, consciousness? Science says that since the mind is only a product of neurological and biological processes, consciousness is extinguished the moment those processes cease. But those who have been there tell a different story. They say that far from outward appearances, death is a transition, from our three-dimensional world to a vaster, timeless world of light. It may happen like this:

The victim of a serious accident is rushed to a hospital emergency room, and before his condition can be stabilized, his life forces flicker out. But at the moment of apparent death, he finds himself outside his body. From this new vantage point, he sees the attending medical personnel, their desperate attempts to revive a lifeless body, and recognizes the body as his own. He is at first startled by this strange state of affairs, but as he begins to come to terms with it, something stranger happens. The world of space around him collapses into a kind of tunnel through which he is drawn into another reality, a world of brilliant golden light.

Here, a being of light appears before him and fills him with feelings of love. The being communicates with him telepathically and asks him to evaluate his life; he is surprised that he sees a panorama of it laid out before him, and not just his *entire* past, but aspects of his future as well. At the same time, he notices he is taking all this in with a strange, new sense, which makes him feel somehow united or one with all of creation.

He is told it is not yet "his time," and he must return to his life on Earth. He is reluctant to do so, as he has never experienced such feelings of peace and love, and he also senses that, in some way, this is his real *home.* But the next thing he knows, he is back in his physical body and recovers.

The experience continues to affect his life profoundly. Something has been awakened in him, something greater, something spiritual. And he will never again fear death, for he *knows* it is not the end. Yet when he tries to describe the episode to others, he cannot; there are no words to portray it—the experience is ineffable.

This is a model near-death experience (NDE), a composite of the main features found in thousands of such experiences reported worldwide (and these out of the many millions that may have actually occurred). Their number has increased dramatically in the last few decades as modern resuscitative techniques now almost routinely bring back accident and heart attack victims from the brink of death. In such numbers, they send a strong message. There is life after death, in the form of a shift to another, transcendental kind of consciousness and an entrance into another, higher realm of existence.

But this creates a problem. It is impossible under the current worldview, which acknowledges no such kind of consciousness or other realm of existence. Therefore, the near-death experience as described can't happen and skeptics say it doesn't. They attribute all near-death experiences to dreams, fantasies, wish-fulfillment of religious expectations, hallucinations, release of endorphins, sensory detachment, autoscopy (a condition where one sees another self), hypoxia (oxygen deprivation), limbic lobe seizures, the effects of anesthetics, and so on.

But taken individually and collectively, these "normal" explanations don't measure up.

Even though no two near-death experiences are exactly alike, there is an uncanny similarity to them, whereas if they were dreams or fantasies, it would be just the opposite: there would be a bewildering assortment of visions. The general content of the experience is also the same for the devoutly religious (of all religions and cultures), agnostics, and even atheists, which negates any religious wish-fulfillment theory.

As for the other explanations—hallucinations, anesthetics, seizures, and the like—the psychological states these conditions give rise to are all categorized as distorted, unpleasant, and widely varied, nothing like the one state of clarity, peace, and joy *consistently* described by NDErs. Furthermore, those who have experienced any of these states, and an NDE at another time, say they were altogether different, and that they could clearly distinguish between the two.

In addition, NDErs have amazed their doctors by recounting *exactly* what was going on during their resuscitations, a period when they were unconscious and oftentimes clinically dead! They have accurately described medical procedures, clothing worn by those present, and even what was going on in other rooms of the hospital. Still there's the aspect of the phenomenon that many find the most compelling—the sheer "realness" of the experience to the NDErs. Honest and sincere people from all walks of life describe it as "realer than here,"[1] or "as real as you and I are,"[2] while others say:

- "It's reality. I know for myself that I didn't experience no fantasy. There was no so-called dream or nothing. These things really happened to me. It happened. I know. I went through it."[3]

- "I've had a lot of dreams and it wasn't like any dream that I had. It was real. It was so real."[4]

- "I *know* it was real . . . I could swear on a Bible that I was there . . . There's no way you can prove it, but I was there!"[5]

No appeal to scientific validation or what is possible under the current worldview is needed for these people. They have been there, they have seen, they *know* what death is, and no longer fear it. "I saw the place you go when you die. I am not afraid of dying . . . [it] is hard to explain because it is very different from life in the world."[6] "After you've once had the experience that I had, you know in your heart that there's no such thing as death. You just graduate from one thing to another . . ."[7] "The reason why I'm not afraid to die . . . is that I know where I'm going when I leave here . . . I've been there before."[8]

Does a dream make a person lose all fear of death? A hallucination cause him to swear on a Bible that he was somewhere else? Can a lack of oxygen allow someone to see what is going on in other rooms of a hospital? Do anesthetics completely change people's outlooks on life and reality? Raymond A. Moody, Jr., the pioneer and unofficial dean of NDE research, says he has talked to almost every NDE researcher in the world, and most of them believe that NDEs are a true glimpse of life after life. They just can't scientifically prove it.[9]

Moody speculates that the real problem may be a "limitation of the currently accepted modes of scientific and logical thought."[10] Kenneth Ring, probably the most prominent NDE researcher, echoes this sentiment and calls for a paradigm shift, or an "openness to concepts that remain generally unacceptable to the scientific community." He says: "It is my opinion that without such concepts the near-death experience cannot be understood."[11]

Moody and Ring are right. The NDE, like all paranormal phenomena, doesn't work under the current scientific worldview or paradigm. But in an expanded framework of space, time, and consciousness, it not only works, it *must be,* for the most basic axiom of extra-dimensional theory is that we are all extra-dimensional beings, and the greater part of us, our higher selves and consciousness, exists in higher space. Or as Ouspensky says: "We are ourselves beings of four dimensions, and *really* live in a four-dimensional world but are conscious of ourselves *only* in a three-dimensional world." The near-death experience is the beginning of the transition to that higher self and consciousness, a transition we will all someday make.

In fact, *all* pathways to higher consciousness lead to this conclusion. Jesus said, "In truth, in very truth I tell you all, you shall see heaven wide open."[12] What could he have meant by this? As one who accessed that higher, extra-dimensional consciousness, he saw that a part of us will exist after death in a higher reality. Mohammed said: "And those who disbelieve will not cease to be in doubt thereof until the Hour comes upon them unawares, or they come into the doom of a disastrous day."[13] What could he have meant by this? That even if someone did not acquire the higher sense, to see this larger world *sooner,* they'd see it *later,* when they died.

Those with complete possession of higher, extra-dimensional consciousness? "You yourself, will see the universe as I have seen it,"[14] the aliens told one abductee, while Betty Andreasson was told that her real home was a world of light, where the "One" was, and that *everyone* would someday experience it (more on this later). Many abductees, their consciousness stimulated, in effect raised, by the aliens, have sensed this, as Mack observes: "A number of abductees with whom I have worked experience at certain points an opening up to the source of being in the cosmos, which they often call Home (a realm beyond, or not in, space/time as we know it), and from which they feel they have been brutally cut off in the course of becoming embodied as a human being."[15]

These are different paths that will cross many times in this chapter but lead to the same place: our place of origin and our destination. We are indeed more than flesh and blood; we are extra-dimensional beings whose real home is in higher space, who enter this three-dimensional world as a point (birth), and exit as one (death).

The Out-of-Body Experience

The out-of-body experience (OBE) is not only the first step in the near-death experience, it is a distinct and well-documented psychic phenomenon in itself. There are millions of OBE reports from all over the world, just as with other kinds of psychic phenomena, and many of these experiences (probably more than half) occur independently of near-death situations. Furthermore, these spontaneous OBEs are virtually identical to those that initiate the near-death sequence of events. A person may be lying in bed, or in some other restful state, when suddenly he (or she) finds his conscious self outside of and above his body. "I was lying on my back, with the light out, when suddenly I found myself in mid-air, looking down at myself."[16]

At first, the individual is surprised at this separation of consciousness and body, but finds that it quickly feels quite natural. He also finds that he is still aware of his surrounding environment and can see anything taking place there (in the case of NDErs, usually a lot). He fully realizes that what is happening is impossible in the world as he knows it, yet he knows that nevertheless it *is* happening; it is a *real* experience.

Spontaneous occurrences such as these and the OBE phase of the NDE are essentially the same up to this point. Indeed some near-death experiences consist of only this. But many NDErs progress to a next phase, they are drawn into another, higher reality, or as Ring says, "[They] go on to experience events outside of the time-space coordinates of ordinary sensory reality."[17]

How can the out-of-body experience be understood? The key to understanding OBEs is the recognition that they are, like all examples of psi, lesser experiences of higher, extra-dimensional consciousness. Spontaneous OBEs are a dim "feel" of that consciousness but a unique one. Here, that dim feel allows normal self-consciousness, normally contained, as it were, in a point of space, to be temporarily freed where it can then wander in (but not beyond) three-dimensional space. That is, the effect is not so much the transcendence of self-consciousness or the apprehension of higher space, but the transcendence of self-consciousness's relation to its normal space. The person's consciousness may be expanded and, in fact, it usually is, but not to the level of the mystical experience or more complete near-death experience, both direct apprehensions of an extra dimension.

Spontaneous OBErs are in an in-between state in virtually every way. Mentally they are somewhat above self-consciousness; they may report great mental clarity ("my mind was clearer and more active than ever before"[18]) and occasionally even a vague sense of higher knowledge ("everything you could think you could get an answer"[19]), but they are nevertheless still below the threshold of extra-dimensional consciousness. In similar fashion, other aspects of the OBE fall along the spectrum between just above normal consciousness/space to just short of higher consciousness/space. OBErs may describe a mysterious illuminating light during the experience, but typically soft and diffuse, nothing like the brilliant, radiant light in mystical and (deeper) near-death experiences. One OBEr calls it a "curious grey radiance,"[20] while another relates: "At some stage during the night, I was aware of myself being high up in the air, looking down at the room which was illuminated by a hazy light, and at my bed and something in it."[21]

Also, some OBErs say that the physical world about them appeared normal, while others, evidently *right at* the (inside-out) threshold of extra-dimensional space, have described objects as "transparent," that is, they were able to "see" *through them*. As one NDEr puts it, it was "as if I could, if I wanted to, see the inside as well as out."[22]

The sign of extra-dimensional consciousness that is most often reported is a change in the time sense. OBErs may say that time seemed to pass more slowly than usual ("I was watching . . . and time seemed to pass very slowly"[23]) or even seemed to stand still ("I had no idea of time"[24]). But even so, one does not find, or at least not nearly to the same extent, the panoramic views of the past and precognitive visions of the future (laid out along higher space) as in the mystical experience and more complete NDEs. Also lacking is the sheer power of an extra-dimensional experience, which transforms the person for the rest of his life, and the unmistakable higher transfinite sense (one in all, all in One), which allows for the apprehension of that extra dimension in the first place.

The near-death OBE is basically the same. The person is outside of his body; his thinking is acute; time slows down or seems to stop; there is a mysterious light source ("Everything seemed to be lighter and brighter"[25]); and he may have other faint signs of extra-dimensional consciousness, such as being telepathically aware of what others around him are thinking ("You understand them without them having to say words . . . like reading their minds"[26]). At first perplexed by the experience, he knows that it is *real*. At the same time, there is a sense of peace and well-being, and a feeling that all this is perfectly natural, that somehow, everything is happening as it is meant to: "It seemed perfectly right. Everything about it seemed right."[27] "It was part of what you were supposed to do . . . very natural."[28]

The OBE is the beginning of movement toward that person's

higher self and consciousness in extra-dimensional space. It's reasonable, or natural, that this transition would begin with a loosening of *all* one's bonds to normal space and consciousness. But as said, many near-death experiences go no further than the OBE, and some only a little further—the transition is apparently terminated. Why? Simply because the person did not actually die or stay "dead" long enough. As Moody notes: "In general, persons who were 'dead' seem to report more florid, complete experiences than those who only came close to death, and those who were 'dead' for a longer period go deeper than those who were 'dead' for a shorter time."[29]

Those who go deeper progress to the next profound stage of the NDE where one's consciousness undergoes a dramatic transformation and the action shifts from our normal three-dimensional world into another reality. Ring calls this next stage the "core experience," while Michael Sabom, an Atlanta cardiologist and highly respected NDE researcher, calls it the "transcendental NDE," because "it contains descriptions of objects and events that transcend or surpass our earthly limits." For example, this includes the "passage of consciousness into a foreign region or dimension quite apart from the earthly surroundings of the physical body."[30] This passage, we'll see, can be into only one kind of region or dimension—an extra dimension, as portrayed by extra-dimensional theory.

The Tunnel

The direction to higher space is inside-out. Try to imagine traveling this route or being turned inside-out. What would it feel like? "Contracting and expanding at the same time." "Everything folding inside itself—and then you're somewhere else." This is how abductees have described it. Mystics call it an involution or passing through oneself. Imagine this happening slowly, as time itself is slowing down and as part of a transition from our world to an extra-dimensional one. What might this be like?

The space around you would probably appear to slowly close in, contract, and collapse, which, coupled with the sensation of your own movement, could create the impression that you were beginning to move "through" something. What if, at the same time this was happening, your normal senses and consciousness were fading out to be replaced by a new sense and consciousness as an accompanying part of the transition? Everything may temporarily seem to go black and this movement would then be through a strange, dark void—a tunnel—as these statements suggest:

- "There was total blackness around me. I want to say that it felt like I was moving very fast in time and space. I was traveling through a tunnel . . . all you see is blackness around you. If you move very fast you can feel the sides moving in on you whether there are sides there or not because of the darkness."[31]

- "I remember . . . a tremendous rushing sound . . . but almost pulling me, and I was being pulled into a narrow point from a wide area."[32]

- "That's when I went into a tunnel. I just felt like I was in a rolling tunnel, black tunnel. Just darkness."[33]

The NDEr is making the transition to higher space and consciousness. Not through an actual tunnel, for there is none, but through the *semblance* of one, with the effect created by a gradual change in these two factors of reality: (1) his subjective interpretation of inside-out movement, which transforms collapsing space-time parameters into a sort of personalized "black hole"; and (2) a shift in consciousness from the slightly elevated state of the OBE to the higher consciousness that will soon realize an extra-dimensional reality.

The World of Light and Higher Space—Home

"At the end of that tunnel was a glowing light . . . That's what it looked like at the end of that tunnel."[34] "And then before you is this . . . the most magnificent, just gorgeous, beautiful, bright, white or blue-white light. It is so bright, it is *brighter* than a light that would immediately blind you, but this *absolutely* does not hurt your eyes at all."[35]

This is where it all happens. The most powerful and profound elements of the NDE come together here, and more and less at once! For in emerging into this other reality, in the *very process* of apprehending it, the person has shifted to a new state of consciousness, one with a new sense of time, one where everything that has happened, is happening, or will happen does so simultaneously. He is immersed in a world of brilliant light, the radiance and glory of which surpass anything he could ever imagine; the light embraces him, nourishes him, surrounds him with feelings of peace, love, and joy. He senses that everything in the universe is vibrant, alive, all connected, and part of one order, one plan; he begins to realize—All is One.

At just this point, he becomes aware of a presence before him, a magnificent being of light, who somehow knows him completely, every facet of him and everything about his life, down to the most intimate detail. Feelings of deep and unconditional love pour into him from this being, and he is completely overwhelmed by its affection for him. The being mentally communicates, and thoughts beyond all normal human comprehension flood into his mind.

All at once he understands the meaning and purpose of the universe, has knowledge of all things in it, sees the past and future of his life, the past and future of the human race, of all Creation. It all pulses in, around, and through him as if he were the universe and it him. "Of course," he thinks. "It's so incredibly simple. Everything makes sense; everything is connected; everything *is* everything else. Of course!"

At the same time, he is aware of another curious sensation, the feeling that he has always known this but somehow has forgotten it. The being seems familiar too; it's almost as if he should know it. He is irresistibly drawn to this being, taken by it, and despite the awe it inspires in him, he is perfectly at ease.

Who is this being? It is his own higher self!

The NDEr does not recognize it. Though right in front of him, and even though it seems familiar, he does not make the connection. Strange, yes, but under extra-dimensional theory it is predictable. For the NDEr is just beginning the transition to his higher self and consciousness. As such, he has the first glimpse of the faculty, not the whole thing, and not enough possession of it to recognize himself. If this sounds odd, consider the fact that it works much the same way in the transition from simple to self-consciousness; that is, it takes not just temporary possession of the faculty but a certain degree of acquaintance with it to realize that what is in front of one is actually oneself.

Take an animal with simple consciousness, say the dog Samson, and place him in front of a mirror. He does not recognize the image; this would take conceptual thought. The same holds true for an infant who has not yet acquired self-consciousness. Place him in front of a mirror and he does not recognize the image, does not realize that it is himself. This recognition will come later, at about the age of three, when he begins to acquire self-consciousness. But even then, *during the transition,* his first few flashes of higher consciousness will not immediately lead to the right conclusion.

The child, who has just begun (only moments ago) to sense his own self, will see an image in the mirror, and perhaps even realize it is a "being," but he will not make the connection between that being and himself. At least not right away. More experience with the faculty is needed, more time to acquaint himself with its higher form of conception, its higher, expanded sense of consciousness and self. Shouldn't it work the same way with a still higher, more expanded consciousness and self?

The NDEr, though directly in front of his higher self, in direct contact with it, and sampling its higher consciousness, does not realize who that being is. He does not make the connection. If the near-death experience is a link or bridge between self-consciousness and higher, extra-dimensional consciousness, then the NDEr is not far enough along, or will not be there long enough, for the concept of a higher self to dawn upon him.

Besides, the being of light is so beautiful, so magnificent, that the person cannot conceive of it as related to his earthly self. NDErs invariably think of it as something completely distinct and supernatural such as a divine presence, a spirit guide, or God Himself. This is significant, and in fact predictable. It is not just the case with NDErs! Virtually everyone who has experienced flashes of the *same* higher, extra-dimensional consciousness have interpreted the "source" of it the same way.

The mystical experience is the dawning of a higher evolutionary faculty that apprehends an extra dimension, but this faculty is at the same time accessing one's own higher self and consciousness in extra-dimensional space. And just as with NDErs, mystics sense an identity—a completely separate and divine one—associated with this consciousness.

Mohammed saw the heavens open up and a radiant being appear before him. At first terrified by this higher presence for fear it would possess him, he came to accept it as the Archangel Gabriel, a messenger sent by God. He could never have imagined that the beatific visions and thoughts this archangel imparted to him were coming from a higher aspect of himself.

Jesus saw the heavens rent asunder and a "Spirit" descend to speak to him. Greatly alarmed at first, he retreated into solitude to reflect on the experience and the possibility that it was some kind of impending madness. In the end the realness of the experience was inescapable; he emerged from the desert convinced it was his destiny to teach what was revealed to him. He would later call this Spirit "the Father," a higher presence that glorified him and provided him with his teachings, clearly distinguishing it from God. "Not that anyone has seen the Father except him who is from God, he has seen the Father."[36] In other words, only those who could apprehend the vaster (extra-dimensional) Kingdom of God would be able to see this presence.

In similar fashion, mystics through the ages have attributed their experiences of enlightenment to visits from a higher and informing "Other." Paul called it the "Christ," Socrates his "daemon," and Dante "Beatrice." Like NDErs, they were never aware that this Other was their own higher self, and that the consciousness that proceeded from it was their own higher consciousness. They, too, thought of it as a separate being and generally interpreted it according to cultural and religious expectations. NDErs do exactly the same. In fact, the *only* real difference in interpretation of the near-death experience is the *interpretation* of the being of light. Some may call it God or Jesus, others Allah or Vishnu. Is it not reasonable that there is only one kind of being behind these various interpretations? That it is the same presence encountered in *both* the mystical and near-death experience?

Ring, a brilliant theorist, has made some tantalizing speculations in this regard. He conjectured that the being of light in NDEs may be one's more "complete or higher self."[37] He recognized that the near-death experience is just one of several pathways to a remarkably similar type of higher consciousness, and he surmised that these experiences are related in such a way that there cannot just be an explanation for the NDE alone: there must be one comprehensive explanation that includes all of them. "Any interpretation that purports to explain NDEs must also be capable of accounting for the *general family* of transcendental experiences—and their aftereffects—of which the classic NDE is but one member.[38]

This is the point of extra-dimensional theory. The near-death phenomenon, like the UFO phenomenon, psychic phenomena, and the mystical experience, cannot be understood separately. In each type there are connections, associations, and implications for the others. They must be understood *together* as the assorted but intimately related workings of an extra-dimensional reality of space, time, and consciousness. As Bucke first realized that *all* mystical experiences were of the *same* higher consciousness, we must now realize that *all* near-death experiences are too, and moreover, that all of both types—and abduction experiences as well—are experiences of that *same,* higher consciousness.

Here are four accounts of contact with higher consciousness, two arrived at by the NDE pathway, one the mystical, one the abduction. Can you tell which is which?

• "I became aware that it was part of all living things and that at the same time all living things were part of it."[39]

• "I have a greater awareness of all living things and that we are ALL a part of one another and ultimately a part of a greater consciousness . . ."[40]

• "One big thing I learned . . . was that we are all part of one big living universe. I look at a forest or a flower or a bird now, and say, 'That is me, part of me.' We are all connected with all things."[41]

• ". . . everything's connected, canyons, deserts, and forests. One cannot exist without the other . . . and I was connected with all these other things and I can't separate out as I've been trying to do."[42]

Are not these interchangeable? Is there any doubt that these experiences are of the same *kind* of consciousness? Can it be any other kind than the next level of consciousness under extra-dimensional theory? The transfinite perception of the whole contained in each and every part (all in one, one in all), and that they are all connected by a medium that connects everything in our three-dimensional world? This transfinite apprehension is the root of extra-dimensional consciousness and *must* be present in all experiences of that consciousness, just as the sense of Self, the root of self-consciousness must be present in all experiences of self-consciousness.

Thus in the previous quotes a mystic describes the higher sense as "a feeling of all in each and of each in all"; an NDEr as "simultaneously comprehending the whole and every part"; and an abductee as "it's like you become on the one hand, part of everything, and everything becomes part of you." Each of these could just as easily be the other. They embody the same sense, the same consciousness, the same transfinite root.

And the same reality, too: "I was free in a time dimension of space,"[43] said one NDEr, an explanation given him by a higher presence he called his "mentor." He is indeed in a time dimension of space, or more precisely, in a dimension of space that was previously included in his idea of time. It is an *extra* dimension, the same one the mystic mentally extracts from time, and the same dimension or other, yet equally real reality that abductees are taken into. NDErs know they are somewhere else, somewhere beyond the normal world of space-time:

- "... where I was and what I was experiencing was not of this world ... It was another place, another time, and perhaps it was even another universe."[44]

- "I came into a place that was at a different level, a different height. This is hard to explain."[45]

- "It's sort of like if you went through another passageway ... you walked right through a wall into another galaxy or something."[46]

Gallup's 1982 study showed the most commonly reported sensation was that of "being in an entirely different world." Further, by virtue of now apprehending this extra dimension (extracted from time), the NDEr perceives the past, present, and future laid out before him; he is in what appears to be a "vast timeless realm." Compare the NDEr's perception of time in this realm to the mystical (or abduction) accounts we've already seen. "There was no time."[47] "It was timeless."[48] "It seemed like time had no meaning."[49] "Time there isn't like time here."[50] "I realized that time as we see it on the clock isn't how time really is."[51] "Everything that [normally] happens in time had been brought together into a concrete whole."[52]

How about this NDE transfinite description of time: "You could say it lasted one second or that it lasted ten thousand years and it wouldn't make any difference how you put it."[53] Compare to Peter's New Testament description: "One day with the Lord is as a thousand years, and a thousand years as one day."

Are not mystical and all these NDE accounts of time interchangeable as well? Is it not reasonable that these are descriptions of *one* timeless realm seen from different vantage points? They show the same transfinite consciousness, the same expanded sense of time, the same apprehension of another reality. All the main features of any one type of experience are the same main features of the others, and they show the last unmistakable hallmark of higher space: the Light. NDErs describe a realm of brilliant, radiant light, so powerful that it should hurt their eyes but doesn't. "Like a golden sun . . . magnificent," [54] or as a glorious sun now seen through a "veil which had suddenly been opened."[55]

Compare these with what we've seen in the mystical experience. The Upanishads say, "Thou art the fire, Thou art the sun." The Bhagavad-Gita: "brilliant like the sun, like fire, blazing, boundless." Can it be anything but the *same* world of Light entered by different pathways? A world illuminated by faster-than-light particles like the proposed tachyon? It is the world of higher space that the abductee, inside an alien ship, does not normally get to see. But Betty Andreasson was given an extraordinary initiation into it. The aliens induced an out-of-body experience in her, then ushered her through a "door" into a "world of light" where she experienced an overwhelming and ineffable sense of joy and "Oneness." They told her that this was her real "home," where the "One was,"[56] and that *everyone* would experience this for themselves someday.

Fowler comments on the larger meaning of this in *The Watchers:*

> Betty's visit to what "The Watchers" referred to as "home" implies that this indescribable "world of light" was the place of her origin. That she could not enter it in her "physical" body obviously tells us that "home" exists on another plane of existence. Betty was told that "home" was going to be experienced by everybody . . . "The Watchers" seem to be telling us that Man's true essence can coexist in more than one plane, not only in this life but the next. Their message also implies that Man, in some form, may have preexisted in the "world of light" prior to being born into the plane of existence which we call "Life." The place called "home" is both the origin and destination of Man's true essence: "Man is not made of just flesh and blood!"[57]

Here we come to a profound implication for life after death under extra-dimensional theory: it is really a matter of life *before* and after death. For we are more than just our three-dimensional physical bodies; we are in the most real sense higher and ageless beings, whose nature we, in our current state, are either scarcely aware of or oblivious to. That is, we exist in this three-dimensional world with only one aspect of our being, just one of our sides. Only this small part of us lives and changes in time, while the larger part exists in a timeless state in higher space. Like a three-dimensional body passing through a plane world, we enter this world as a point, grow or expand (mature), recede or shrink (age), and exit again as a point (death). Our point of origin and point of destination are the same, and our real home is in an extra-dimensional world of light.

NDErs often have a strange feeling that this Light world is their real home, that they have in some way been reacquainted with their true nature during the experience. Ring relates that one NDEr said, "When he experienced the higher knowledge, it was not that he acquired it but that he *remembered* it."[58] Another said that when the being of light imparted the knowledge to him, he felt "it was something that I had always known and somehow I'd forgotten it until he'd reminded me of it."[59] One described the being of light as inspiring tremendous awe, but at the same time seeming familiar. "I felt I knew this being extremely well."[60] Still others: "It's like I was always there and I will always be there, and my existence on earth was just a brief instant."[61] "Peace. Homecoming. It's strange, because I never verbalized that before. It was really like a homecoming . . ."[62]

This is not a place where we have never been. The higher part of us has been there all along! Bucke, as well as others, apparently sensed this when he said that eternal life is not something one *will* have, but something one "has already." This might seem to cinch the case—everlasting life for all. But does it?

Eternal Life?

When you're in love everything's wonderful. Intoxicated by that potent elixir, one sees the positive everywhere; birds sing, faces smile back at you, and it's hard to imagine that anything, anywhere, could ever be wrong again. All is right with the world, and this is how it will be forever.

Yet there is a state of intoxication far beyond this, one beyond all normal human conception. One where mind, heart, and soul are swept up into a seeming eternity of breathless and unutterable rapture. Mystics call it ecstasy, a state so blissful that a person, having once experienced it, will devote the rest of his life to training and techniques to return to it. NDErs who have encountered it say that at that moment they would gladly and without hesitation give up all they have known and loved in Earth life for it. Surely this is how wonderful the higher life will be forever, they think. Surely everyone else will experience it just as I have.

But is the NDEr (and the mystic), in proclaiming eternal, joyous life for all, like the lover in allowing the euphoria of the experience to color his perceptions, to confuse any and all calculations of what lies ahead? Is he seeing the world through rose-colored glasses?

Under extra-dimensional theory, everyone and everything in our world has extension in an extra dimension, and so *must* have existence in higher space beyond and after this world. *Existence:* This is not what we normally have in mind when we think of life after death. We think of a continuation of ourselves, retaining a sense of personal identity, remembering all that has gone before. Will we have this? The NDEr is not there long enough to find out. He is, after all, just beginning the transition to his higher self and consciousness. Or put yet another way, he is beginning what must be an eventual *merging* with that higher self and consciousness, to be reclaimed—absorbed?—by it. What will be left of his old self and consciousness when this transition is complete?

We humans like to think we're the crowning glory of consciousness in the universe, and if there is life after death it is reserved for *only* us as *"higher"* consciousness (lower forms of life do not qualify). What if this is correct, that only higher consciousness will have life after death, *but we're off by one level?* That is, only that part of us that has in some way touched upon or gained *some* familiarity with that higher state of being will survive the transitional merging intact and so retain an independent awareness of Self.

There is reason to think this may be the case. Most mystical traditions maintain that we have a divine aspect in a higher reality; and our purpose in life is to rediscover that divine nature and work towards unification with it. They also stress that herein lies the key to immortality, for this higher awareness is all we can take with us at death. Thus, all human beings will not automatically *have* life after death; each individual must by his own efforts in this lifetime *earn* it. The Bhagavad-Gita states:

> At the hour of death, when a man leaves his body, he must depart with his consciousness absorbed in me. Then he will be united with me . . . Whatever a man remembers at the last, when he is leaving the body, will be realized by him in the hereafter; because that will be what his mind has most certainly dwelt on, during this life.
>
> Therefore you must remember me at all times, and do your duty. If your mind and heart are set upon me constantly, you will come to me. Never doubt this.[63]

Lama Govinda says:

> Man is mortal as long as he tries to hang on to his present state of mind and body, as long as he does not endeavor to rise above his present condition, i.e., the state of his present ignorance, his contentment with the irrelevant and partial phenomena of his existence. Immortality is not a gift of nature or of a god: it has to be acquired.[64]

Yet just as in acquiring the mystical experience, there is no reason why mystical training should be required here. Plotinus pointed out that the higher sense can be cultivated in any way that elevates the mind or spirit, whether prayer, science, philosophy, or just plain love, the choice simply depending on one's particular turn of mind. The important thing is that we must do *something*.

NDErs sense this. They come away from the experience with a feeling that we *do* have a purpose here on Earth, that the normal pursuit of the sensual and material must give way to "something else," a more spiritual way of life for a more significant eventual reward. Ring describes a man whose life was transformed from seeking material wealth to following a new, deeper purpose and direction, one of spiritual understanding, with an overpowering conviction that there would be a reward at the end of his life similar to "a pot of gold at the end of the rainbow."[65] Another came to understand: "We have a more important mission in our lives than just the material end of it ... It showed me the spiritual side is important ... That's all I can say."[66]

Indeed, NDErs are left with an understanding that the only thing we can take with us when we die is the higher part of us; moreover, they understand that it can be cultivated in the simplest of ways, by learning and loving, pursuits obviously within the reach of all. Sounds easy, but there's another side to it. Also found in mystical teachings is the admonition that for those who have not sought out and developed their higher sense, the transition into this world of fiery light will be anything but blissful.

Mohammed said: "And as for those who do evil, their retreat is the fire ... Unto them it is said: 'Taste the torment of the Fire which ye used to deny.'" Jesus spoke of how the righteous will have eternal life in the Kingdom but those who have rejected the higher way will be separated from God's essence and suffer forever in the "everlasting fire."[67] Paul preached, "If you live according to the flesh you will die, but according to the spirit, you will live,"[68] and that in the end "the fire will assay the quality of everyone's work."[69] It is the same world of light, but one that some will find heavenly, others downright hellish. What do we make of this?

Forget about the wrath of God; in an extra-dimensional universe, it may simply be the survival of the fittest. For without the refinement of the higher sense necessary to adapt to life in a new world, one where this sense is the operative, native faculty, the transition could well be a calamitous one. In fact, the transition to higher consciousness is not without peril in our world.

Gopi Krishna says that the onset of the mystical experience through kundalini can be unimaginably frightening and disorientating, to the point of actually causing madness in some. (This, he relates, almost happened to him; also, remember Jesus' and Mohammed's initial trepidations.) Krishna also maintains that as psychic ability and genius are lower, though positive, by-products of the energy of kundalini, so many mental illnesses are negative ones to those who cannot handle or balance this tremendous force.

In addition, Aldous Huxley in *Heaven and Hell* points out the haunting parallel between the gloriously radiant world of the mystic and the "infernally glaring" one of the schizophrenic, citing how in France that world of madness has been called "le Pays d'Eclairement"[70]—the country of lit-upness. Most mystical disciplines indeed stress that the arduous training mystical trainees undertake is for the purpose of fortifying the mind against the (possible) sudden and sometimes terrifying awakening of kundalini.

How does this bode for us at death? It depends. There are several possibilities in what is admittedly the most speculative area of extra-dimensional theory. To begin with, although virtually all NDEs are overwhelmingly positive, those who report them (not everyone at death does) seem to have a distinct advantage going into death. For Ring's *Omega* study showed that those who do have had since childhood "an extended range of human perception beyond normally recognized limits."[71] In other words, they have some development of or at least heightened capacity for higher consciousness. And if this is the determining factor, then the transition should be smooth and pleasant, and strongly suggest a continuation of life and identity. "It's just going to be another life somewhere else. Maybe in a different form, but I'll still have my soul."[72]

Still, there is a point in the experience called the "life review" that no NDEr goes past. And after this, in *real* death, must come a final stage of the transition, when the person's self-consciousness is assimilated into the higher Self and consciousness. But if the capacity for higher consciousness is the determining factor, the NDEr's "self" should survive. Let's assume it does, more or less (this I'll return to shortly), and that it works like this: By virtue of incorporating that higher aspect into his self-consciousness during earthly life, his self-consciousness is in turn incorporated *into it* so a sense of (the old) self will remain after the transition is complete.

On the other hand, what of those who are just as close to death and do not report an NDE? One possibility is that these people (or some of them) simply were not close enough to death or "dead enough," at least for them, for the transition to begin. Another is the view, held by many researchers, that everyone at the threshold of death has an NDE, some just don't remember it. The question then is why not?

One reason may be that anesthetics, far from being the cause of a NDE, may actually inhibit its recall, essentially erasing it from the person's memory. This almost surely accounts for some. Moody, for example, relates the case of a woman who "died" twice, once without any drugs and with a deep NDE, and once accompanied by anesthetics with no NDE; he states that in general those who have had the least amount of anesthetic seem to have the most powerful NDE experiences.

So far, so good. But another explanation could be that, though everyone has an experience, it is recalled only by those with a heightened capacity for higher consciousness. This leads us into other, less comforting possibilities.

What if those without that capacity (or enough of it) indeed had an "experience," but one they would rather not remember? Gallup (and others) have come across some who came just as close to death as the NDErs and reported only vague recollections of "fear, discomfort, and confusion."[73] If these individuals had the same difficulty in balancing the energy of kundalini that Gopi Krishna described, it's understandable how the experience could be a negative and deeply disturbing one; the person may subconsciously suppress as much of it as possible. Projecting this into a *real* death situation, if the person is unable to adapt during the course of the transition, any negative feelings could intensify, or along with what remains of the old self, fade into a state of insentient existence.

If everyone at death has an NDE (minus the return), then the sensations one receives during the experience may depend *entirely* on what capacity for higher consciousness that person had beforehand. If he had none, then in a situation where his customary sensory and mental functions were completely inoperative, he may experience what other NDErs do, but be oblivious to it from the start. Such a person could hardly be expected to retain a sense of self through the transition.

Yet even so, this would not really be death. For remember that in an extra-dimensional reality, everything is "alive." Everyone *must* have eternal existence *and* eternal life but not necessarily awareness of it. It just may be that, for those without the requisite development of the higher sense, one may have existence and life in an extra-dimensional reality but lack the awareness of it (of the old, three-dimensional self) in the same way that a dog with only simple (two-dimensional) consciousness has existence and life in our three-dimensional world but likewise lacks an awareness of self.

So far, we've looked at these situations strictly in a pass/fail context. But with the NDEr, there may be more to it. Why do these people consistently stress the importance of developing the higher side if *just* survival is the end in itself? They feel strongly they *will* survive. Could it be that the degree of spiritual development we take with us into our higher life is consequential in determining the degree of awareness, individuality, and perhaps even autonomy that the old self will have in relation to the higher Self? Or that its development and capacity for still further development is more the end in itself, as part of a process of spiritual growth that continues in the afterlife?

NDErs seem to sense it is; one advises: "No matter how old you are, don't stop learning. For this is a process that goes on for eternity."[74] And why not? We've seen the inexorable evolution of life and consciousness in our world—its benefits, beauty, and ceaseless striving to transcend itself. Isn't it reasonable that life and consciousness continue to evolve in a higher world?

This is the most speculative area of extra-dimensional theory, yet one thing remains certain, and another reasonably so. Everyone at death *will* make that transition to their higher self and consciousness in extra-dimensional space, and what happens then *may* depend to a large degree on what we do now. We have a higher side that we must recognize and develop. The rest will follow. This is what mystics tell us. This is what NDErs tell us. It is the Perennial Philosophy. The aliens who live in this larger world tell us we're part of something greater, something higher, that we should "seek it out and develop it." Our very survival as a race depends on it, in accordance with a universal law. Shouldn't this law, whether it's purposeful evolution or a higher form of natural selection, apply on an individual basis as well?

The Return from the NDE

When the NDEr says he sees a tunnel, at the end of which was a glowing light, he has just arrived. All that has happened has been in the blink of an eye, or an eternity. Such is the nature of time in the higher realm. As he views his entire life laid out at once along an extra dimension, the being of light communicates one last thought to him: it is not yet his time. The NDEr returns to normal reality, sometimes traveling back through the tunnel, sometimes just finding himself back in his physical body.

Yet as with all apprehensions of higher, extra-dimensional consciousness, the NDEr loses his grasp of it when he descends back to his normal conscious state. Here, the transitional link between him and his higher Self and consciousness is severed; or as one NDEr lamented, he felt his "mind splitting into two parts, with the part that understood everything left behind."[75] The NDEr then finds, as all those who've experienced that same higher consciousness have found, that the higher conception cannot be adequately represented in conceptual terms. "There are not words . . . It can't (be conveyed). And it cannot be fully understood,"[76] or "I could never explain it in a million years."[77] The experience is ineffable.

Nevertheless, the nature and realness of what the NDEr has experienced will remain etched into him; and it will change him completely. Like anyone who has apprehended the transfinite order of "one in all, all in One," he will forevermore have a special understanding that all living things are on some level connected and a part of one another. How can he not now have a deeper appreciation for all life, more compassion and empathy for it? I earlier postulated that this moral sense is a lower abstraction of the transfinite sense. The connection should be apparent here, as the essence of the person's moral sense is raised to another level by just a momentary tie-in with that higher faculty.

The NDEr's heightened awareness leads to other realizations. He sees that true spirituality is not to be found in any church or creed but only within, and he realizes the importance of developing it. His priorities change; the old, materialistic goals in life are gone, replaced by the pursuit of knowledge and spirituality, and with a sense that there *is* a reason for it. "[I developed an] . . . awareness that something more was going on in life than just the physical part of it . . . There's more than just consuming life."[78] "I think that my greatest desire is to develop cosmic consciousness, greater awareness . . . And I feel that I'm being drawn closer to something meaningful . . . I feel that I'm *going* somewhere. I feel that I'm *reaching* something . . ."[79]

The NDEr's transformation centers on a moral and spiritual awakening, but there are other aspects to it, many of which are paranormal. His consciousness now elevated near the threshold of the higher faculty, he begins to exhibit additional signs of it, as psychic phenomena. We've seen how these work as fragments of extra-dimensional consciousness filtering down into one's normal state. We've also seen how when one's consciousness is raised closer to higher consciousness, his capacity, or penchant for them, is markedly increased. It is the same with NDErs.

After their experience, they consistently report classic psi intuitions, i.e., telepathy, clairvoyance, precognition; also electrical disturbances, and other minor poltergeist activity. Some have been spontaneously healed of their infirmities, while others feel they have increased intelligence, sometimes extending into areas they had no prior interest in or aptitude for. Dr. Melvin Morse documents all these changes (psychic, moral, spiritual, and more) in his 1992 *Transformed by the Light*, a comprehensive work on the aftereffects of NDEs; Ring's *The Omega Project* shows basically the same results in NDErs and abductees.

All these aftereffects demonstrate once again, and yet in still another way, that it is one and the same consciousness encountered in NDEs, abductions, and mystical experiences. Must not these same *effects*, virtually identical from one phenomenon to another, spring from a common *cause?* In fact, taken together with psi, these phenomena complement one another, and their inherent associations strengthen the case for an extra-dimensional reality of space, time, and consciousness. How can there not be striking similarities and endless parallels among them?

Still, those who have experienced these phenomena will share one last thing in common. Their accounts will be dismissed by mainstream science. These things cannot happen in reality as we know it—therefore, they don't happen, even though these reports come from millions upon millions of normal, competent observers whose testimonies would be unquestionably accepted in a court of law, if it were on any other matter. How strange it should be so. In the next chapter, we'll see that the observations of normal, competent observers are an *inseparable* component of reality.

PART III

A New Worldview

9

Extra-Dimensional Theory
and the New Physics

At the turn of the twentieth century, the worldview was of three dimensions of space plus time, and time, as described by Newton's classical mechanics, flowed throughout all space simultaneously. However, there was a growing interest in the notion of a fourth dimension, sometimes envisioned as another dimension of space, sometimes as time itself. Some even thought that travel along the axis of time might be possible, just as is travel along the three spatial dimensions.

Remember H. G. Wells's *The Time Machine*? An inventor builds a device that can transport him forward or backward through time. This machine was nothing if not user-friendly: simply move the control lever in the desired direction and travel into the past or future while remaining in the same space. But as we've seen, the Earth is moving through space *and* revolving about its axis, so any such sojourn would result in the traveler appearing not only in a different time but in a different space as well.

The idea of the fourth dimension was not only pondered by writers and philosophers, it was taken seriously by scientists; in fact, during the early twentieth century there were more than a thousand academic papers on extra-dimensional geometry. Adding intrigue to this was the possibility that this invisible domain could account for spirits and other psychic phenomena, which were quite the rage. Only Russian P. D. Ouspensky saw that the fourth dimension was not just one of space nor time, but a *component* of time that had to be extracted mentally with a higher faculty. At this time, there were two developments that soon put an end to any respectability the image of the fourth dimension might have.

Spiritualism, the belief that departed souls can be accessed through mediums and séances, was especially popular at the time. These spirits, emanating of course from the fourth dimension and routinely produced at sessions, were said to be composed of ectoplasm or energy of some sort. But eventually, under watchful eyes, it became apparent that many of the most prominent practitioners were using sleight-of-hand and other assorted gimmickry on an all too credulous public.

Some of these tricksters and showmen had a field day before they were exposed. Other, less obvious mediums and psychics, including the most credible, were unable to produce under the controlled conditions now imposed on them by scientists and a chagrined public. The golden age of Spiritualism had come to an end, and not surprisingly, the fourth dimension had lost some of its luster along the way.

Right on the heels of this began what is now called the golden age of physics, highlighted by Einstein's special theory of relativity (1905) and general theory of relativity (1915). Under special relativity, time is indeed the fourth dimension but taken as is, as a self-evident, no-further-explanation-needed phenomenon, flexible yet permanently bonded to the three spatial dimensions. The positivistic current of thought now predominant was responsible for stunning advances occurring regularly in physics, and little consideration was left for the idea of the fourth dimension as an arcane realm of Spiritualism and the like. Paranormal phenomena then went underground, outside the attention and interest of mainstream science.

Looking back on this era now, with an eye turned to extra-dimensional theory, we see that the idea of the fourth dimension need not have been abandoned so readily. Time is the fourth dimension, but it is a *composite* dimension, consisting of all extra dimensions (of space) either not apprehended or imperfectly apprehended by us. However, given the confluence of events in the early 1900s, the demise of the fourth dimension is understandable.

Now extra dimensions are again in vogue, in the paranormal and in science. We've come full circle back to a concept that was rejected almost a century ago. Is there something strange in this? Not at all. In the history of worldviews, it's the way it usually happens. They pop up and get shot down, but the good ones keep coming back. The idea that the Earth was round instead of flat was alternately proposed and dismissed for thousands of years before Columbus. Copernicus, who is credited with bringing an end to the worldview of an Earth-centered universe, was aware he was reviving a sun-centered theory that had been rejected long ago.

Why do these ideas keep coming back? Because the long-standing problems they once held hope for solving still remain. So the old theory is resurrected and new versions of it are tried until one works. Extra-dimensional theory is a new version of the turn-of-the-century fourth dimension model, but with the factors of expanded time and consciousness incorporated into it. It works. We've already seen how it can explain paranormal phenomena. In this chapter we'll see how it can explain long-standing problems in quantum theory and lead to a new worldview.

The New Physics

The first thing to say about the new physics is it's not really new. It's just a new way of looking at the physical world that started in the early 1900s with Einstein's relativity theory. This did away with one of two sacred concepts—the idea of absolute time or space—and for the first time, the factor of mind entered the equation. Now, not only must time and space be considered together as space-time, they must be considered together with consciousness, and as coordinates of that consciousness.

The other sacred notion to be shattered was the nature of matter itself. Up until this point, it had always been assumed that matter could be divided into smaller and smaller units of the same kind of "stuff," until the ultimate building blocks of nature were revealed; at first it was atoms, then later their constituents—electrons, protons, and neutrons. But in the next few decades, hundreds more subatomic particles were discovered under a new, highly specialized field of study called quantum mechanics. Under quantum mechanics theory, the great number of particles now identified can only be understood as forces or transactions rather than "things." It is the relationships between these particles as they interact that are the "particles." The essence of matter at this level is mostly empty space, highlighted by exchanges of information, or particles.

As quantum theory developed, things got stranger. These particles, or "quanta," did not seem bound by our space or time. They pop into our reality from out of nowhere (quantum creation), disappear without a trace (quantum annihilation), go from one point to another without being in between (quantum tunneling), instantaneously change from one state of being to another, depending on how you look at them (quantum jumping), and are connected to each other in a way that transcends our time (the quantum connection). Sound familiar? Quantum theory was fast becoming a scientific Wonderland, replete with more quanta and bizarre paradoxes, prompting Neils Bohr, one of the field's pioneers, to muse that anyone who is *not* shocked by quantum theory doesn't understand it.

What was also becoming apparent was the role that our consciousness played in all this. By the 1920s, it was known that light sometimes exhibited the properties of a wave and sometimes of a particle. But the scientific community was stunned when this proved to be the case with the electron as well. Thus, at the subatomic level, matter and energy must be seen as both wave and particle, but never both at once, only one or the other per observation. What seems to determine which property is displayed is the act of observation itself. The choice of the experimenter as to how the observation takes place in effect produces the result.

This factor of consciousness runs right to the core of quantum theory, for herein lies the uncertainty principle first put forth by physicist Werner Heisenberg. This states that the quantities of a particle—its position and momentum (mass x velocity)—cannot both be measured at the same time. The more precisely one is determined, the less is certain about the other. This is not due to any limitation in our instruments of measurement; it's due to the influence the actual act of observation has on the state of the particle. Therefore, a quantum act is a relationship between an observer and a possible event. There is no way to eliminate *our* consciousness from the equation; it is a determining factor in *our* reality.

Because of the problems associated with wave-particle duality and the uncertainty principle, matter at the quantum level is best described statistically, as probabilities or tendencies to be in different forms at different times in different places; these probabilities are inextricably linked to us, the observers. The world of the very small suggests that reality must be seen as one inseparable phenomenon, a universal web of matter, energy, and consciousness.

Does this sound a little more familiar? Kind of transfinite? Suggestive of the all-encompassing oneness described by mystics and NDErs? Isn't this what we should expect? For if reality is extra-dimensional, shouldn't we pick up hints of this at the limits of our science through quantum theory? Shouldn't these hints have the earmarks of mystical accounts of the direct apprehension of that extra dimension?

Fritjof Capra devoted a book, *The Tao of Physics,* to the parallels between the new physics and Eastern mysticism. He finds these parallels striking, as if they were just two different ways of describing the same underlying reality.

> These changes, brought about by modern physics, have been widely discussed by physicists and philosophers over the past decades, but very seldom has it been realized that they all seem to lead in the same direction, toward a view of the world which is very similar to the views held in Eastern mysticism. . . .[1]
>
> At the atomic level, then, the solid material objects of classical physics dissolve into patterns of probabilities, and these patterns do not represent probabilities of things, but rather probabilities of interconnections. Quantum theory forces us to see the universe not as a collection of physical objects, but rather as a complicated web of relations between the various

parts of a unified whole. This, however, is the way in which Eastern mystics have experienced the world.[2]

This interconnecting oneness is just one of many extra-dimensional signs, *all* of which we've seen before. Capra also notes how quantum theory reveals reality to be ever-changing, dynamic, virtually alive: "The closer we look, the more alive it appears."[3] He also says: "Modern physics, then, pictures matter not at all as passive and inert, but being in a continuous dancing and vibrating motion whose rhythmic patterns are determined by the molecular, atomic, and nuclear structures. This is also the way in which Eastern mystics see the material world. . . . that nature is not in a static, but a dynamic equilibrium."[4]

We've seen that things that are separate, or even opposites, in our world are one in higher space, connected through the medium of an extra dimension, and that the expression of this concept is ineffable to those in lower space. Capra again:

> The exploration of the subatomic world has revealed a reality which repeatedly transcends language and reasoning, and the unification of concepts which had hitherto seemed opposite and irreconcilable turns out to be one of the most startling features of this new reality. . . . where particles are both destructible and indestructible; where matter is both continuous and discontinuous, and force and matter are but different aspects of the same phenomenon.[5]

We saw this in chapter 3. As a being's consciousness (on any level) approaches a threshold in understanding its world, beyond which a higher faculty is needed, its mental tools begin to register confusing input—contradictions and absurdities—as it dimly senses the new order. Recall Ouspensky's example of the dog who begins to sense that this house and that house, or "this" and "that," are both unified as plurals with a higher, extra-dimensional consciousness. Chuang Tzu, a Taoist popularizer, described a still higher consciousness: "The 'this' is also 'that.' The 'that' is also 'this.' . . . That the 'that' and the 'this' cease to be opposites is the very essence of the Tao."[6]

These are the kind of paradoxes we've come to now in quantum theory, at the farthest reaches of our scientific and perceptual abilities. We are flirting with the apprehension of an extra dimension, picking up bits and pieces of its higher order, an order that we cannot *grasp* but can *infer*. Particles just appearing and disappearing from our space or reappearing elsewhere (as in teleportation); particles violating our sense of time; an underlying, all-pervading oneness; and intimations of a dynamic ineffable reality in which opposites are unified. We've seen all this throughout the book, in the line- and plane-world analogies, in different levels of time and consciousness, and especially in the paranormal. *They are all the signatures of an extra dimension.*

Extra Dimensions in the New Physics

At the turn of the twentieth century, extra dimensions were depicted as just like our three and as unrelated to time or consciousness. But relativity firmly established time as the fourth dimension, and other extra-dimensional theories quickly became dated. Still, the idea was kept alive by a small number of higher space aficionados who began to refashion their theories into versions more in keeping with the new scientific paradigm.

The best of this early lot was put forth by in 1919 by Polish physicist Theodor Kaluza. His five-dimensional version of general relativity was a bold attempt at unifying the two basic forces that were then known—electromagnetism and gravity (the strong and weak nuclear forces had yet to be discovered). Kaluza's theory made a favorable impression on Einstein, who eventually helped get it published in the scientific journal *Sitzungsberichte der Berliner Akademie.*

But by the time Kaluza's theory came out, it was already obvious there were three major problems with it. One, it didn't seem compatible with the emerging quantum theory; two, it failed to explain how planetary orbits could still work with a fifth "normal" dimension; and three, that old bugaboo—why can't we see it?

In 1926, Swedish physicist Oskar Klein seemed to have all three problems worked out. He demonstrated that a five-dimensional theory was indeed compatible with quantum theory. The other two problems he solved at once. Klein proposed that we couldn't detect this fifth, extra dimension, and it wouldn't affect planetary orbits because it was rolled up or "curled up" to practically nothing at 10^{-32} centimeters in length, just large enough for the necessary field activity to take place.

To envision a rolled-up dimension, picture a sheet of paper as a two-dimensional plane world, then imagine rolling the paper up from the side. There are still two dimensions, the length of the paper, and the contracting surface around the now cylindrical shape. But as the paper is rolled up tighter, the dimension around the surface continues to shrink. When this surface becomes so curled up it almost disappears from view, what is essentially left is a one-dimensional line, which is actually a world of two dimensions, one large (the line), and one tiny or rolled up.

By the 1930s, it was known that there were two more forces of nature besides electromagnetism and gravity—the strong and weak nuclear forces—and these could not be incorporated into the Kaluza-Klein theory, as it was called. Thus work was abandoned on the idea, and for decades it lay all but forgotten.

Then, in the late 1960s, some physicists began developing extra-dimensional "string" theories in which they attempted to unite all four fundamental forces by proposing that elementary particles are really tiny bits of "string" existing in up to 22 dimensions of space, with all but our normal three curled up out of sight. The way the strings vibrate, they suggested, gives rise to differences which show up in our space as ordinary particles. But mathematical inconsistencies and just the strangeness of the idea caused these extra-dimensional theories, too, to fall out of favor, with all but a few persistent adherents.

Both the Kaluza-Klein theory and "strings" have since undergone a tremendous renaissance. In the 1970s, physicists working on unifying gravity with the other three forces found some startling connections between their "supergravity" theories and the Kaluza-Klein model. One is that if the simplest of the eight different supergravity theories is proposed in 11 dimensions (four "big" [space-time] ones and seven rolled up ones), it corresponds to the most complicated theory in just four dimensions. This suggests that physical laws become simpler and more comprehensive from a higher dimensional view, something we have seen before. Also, supergravity theories are only workable in up to 11 dimensions, and 11 is just what is needed in the Kaluza-Klein theory to accommodate all four basic forces.

In the late 1980s, string theory made a big comeback. Spruced up with some new math (supersymmetry), the new versions are called "superstrings," and are usually proposed in either 10 or 26 dimensions, although one model goes as high as 506 dimensions. As before, the most elementary "objects" are vibrating multi-dimensional strings; and just as violin strings produce different frequencies (tones), harmonics, and secondary resonance, so do these strings. We perceive these differences in our space as a vast assortment of elementary particles. As before, the extra dimensions are curled up tightly.

Extra-dimensional theories in science have had their ups and downs over the years, but it now appears they're here to stay. They're our best approximations yet of reality, and yet, approximations nonetheless. We've expanded our framework of space but ignored the factors of time and consciousness. Can it just be coincidence that in these theories, tachyon particles (speculative particles faster than light and our time) and mathematical infinities (our closest transfinite concept) keep popping up? Physicists do their best to cancel these "bugs" out by introducing other infinities into the equations. The problem is they keep popping up. Is this telling us something?

Supergravity and superstring theories *begin* to point in the right direction. Both assume a larger, extra-dimensional reality where natural laws are simpler and more comprehensive. Their tiny but just large enough dimensions do allow for *some* of the bizarre antics of subatomic particles, by providing a medium for them to "tunnel" in and out of our space and just appear elsewhere, etc. But they offer nothing for the other esoteric aspects of quantum theory—the ineffability, the unification of opposites, the transcendence of our time, the life, the oneness, not to mention the entire range of paranormal phenomena. And these are theories that aspire to be *the* Theory of Everything, or T.O.E. There's clearly something missing.

Bucke gives it here, and at the same time puts the quest for the T.O.E. in perspective. "Especially does he obtain (with cosmic consciousness) a conception of THE WHOLE, or at least of an IMMENSE

WHOLE, as dwarfs all conception, imagination or speculation, springing from and belonging to ordinary self-consciousness, such a conception as makes the old attempts to mentally grasp the universe and its meaning petty and even ridiculous"[7] (emphasis in original).

Expanded consciousness—we seek the Theory of Everything, and yet strangely are content with the little we know of consciousness and time. We need an expanded framework of space, time, and consciousness. This is why we can't "see" an extra dimension; it takes a higher faculty of mind; and this is why an extra dimension doesn't affect planetary orbits—it cannot be incorporated into our mathematical context. It has its own higher space-time context, one that our world must be incorporated into. These conventional extra-dimensional theories and their mathematical constructs of curled-up extra dimensions are still just extensions of our self-consciousness.

We can go no further without an expanded framework. Gopi Krishna noted: "But no attempt made by the intellect, assisted by all the inventions of science, can penetrate the veil, because the veil itself is the creation of the intellect. It is only by self-transcendence that light begins to penetrate into the darkness, dissolving the problem, as shadows melt at the approach of dawn."[8]

Let's now look at the most profound paradoxes in quantum theory for which these extra-dimensional theories offer no solution. We'll look at them under the light of an expanded framework of space, time, and consciousness, and see if the problems dissolve with a transcendent point of view.

The one that best illustrates the bizarre nature of quantum theory is the classic double-slit experiment. Electrons are propelled toward a screen with two holes in it, and behind this screen is another screen that acts as a detector. Remember that electrons sometimes manifest as waves, sometimes as particles. When the electrons reach the first screen, they can pass through either of the two slits; as they reach the second or detector screen, there is evidence not of particle traces but of a wavelike interference pattern, meaning that the electrons were wavelike and canceled each other out upon impacting the second screen. This is surprising, since electrons are generally treated as particles; but it gets stranger.

If one of the slits in the first screen is covered, the electron(s) traveling through the other slit now reveals itself as a particle. In other words, the act of observation has apparently changed the electron's nature from wave to particle. Now for the pièce de résistance. If the covered slit is then uncovered, even as the electron is between the two screens, a wave pattern instantaneously appears on the second screen, as if the electron *knew* at that instant that the second slit was now open. Even if the experimenter utilizes a device to observe which slit the electron has passed through, the wavelike effect still changes to that of a particle.

The standard explanation of this is called the Copenhagen interpretation. It says a wave and particle are different yet complementary aspects of the same phenomenon, and both descriptions must be employed. It also describes particles in terms of probabilities (location and momentum) known as "wave functions." Now, because of the uncertainty principle, it is impossible to know the exact location *and* momentum of a particle at the same time, so the wave function is a system of probabilities as to a particle's status. And when a measurement is taken, the wave function is said to "collapse" into a specific value.

The Copenhagen interpretation says that out of those many possibilities, the observer *causes* one—the "measurement"—to become objective reality. In the double-slit experiment, the "wavelike" electron has two possibilities of travel through either slit until a measurement alters the wave function and fixes a specific value for the electron which is now a particle.

The Copenhagen interpretation still is the prevalent one in the scientific community, but even so, many physicists are wary of it. They feel it is deeply unsatisfactory, partly because it offers no explanation as to exactly *when* in the course of an observation the wave function collapses into objective reality. Far more troubling is the fact that without an observation, no particle can be said to physically exist at all, and it is hard to imagine how an act of observation can affect reality to that extent. Paul Halpern in *Time Journeys* (1990) remarks:

> It seems as if quantum mechanics provides an answer to a hackneyed philosophical question: If a tree falls in a forest where there are no listeners, can it be said to make a sound?

> The Copenhagen interpretation of quantum mechanics implies that the answer is no. Only when there is a measurement (observation), can the falling tree be said to make a sound at a definite time.[9]

No observer, no sound? You're probably thinking this isn't reasonable, and you're not alone. Many physicists, even ones who support the Copenhagen interpretation, think so too. They'd prefer to believe that there is an underlying objective reality independent of observation or measurement. So to get out of this quandary, they postulate that the Copenhagen interpretation is "operative" only below a certain threshold, at the microscopic level. This seems a safe escape. But then again, there's that famous "Schrödinger's cat" paradox, where those consequences supposedly confined to the quantum world turn into real ones in ours.

Austrian physicist Erwin Schrödinger, one of the founders of quantum theory, proposed a thought experiment in 1935 that, under the Copenhagen interpretation, allows a cat to be dead *and* alive at the same time—until an observation settles the matter. The experiment begins with a cat sealed in a box along with a vial of poison gas. There is also a device such as a Geiger counter, and attached to it a lever set to break the vial of gas. Now, a radioactive particle is sent inside, and it exists in two possible states, decayed and undecayed, until it is observed. Possibility number one: The particle decays, which sets off the Geiger counter, which triggers the lever, which releases the gas, which kills the cat. Possibility number two: The particle remains undecayed, and the cat lives.

Since the particle's status is undetermined until it is observed, and the particle's status is a matter of life or death for the cat, the cat's status is likewise undetermined, until someone opens the box and looks. (Until then it is in some complex "wave-function-like" state of dead plus alive, dead minus alive, dead plus the square root of alive, etc.) And there's no reason why we couldn't take this one step further, that until someone actually observes the person who opened the box, then he exists in the same kind of undetermined state as well, somebody who finds a live cat, or somebody who finds a dead one.

It should be apparent by now that the Copenhagen interpretation lends itself to some enigmatic profundities. Yet it's actually tame compared to its only real competition to date, the "many-worlds interpretation." This theory, put forth in 1957 by Hugh Everett, a Princeton graduate student, maintains that all of the different possibilities in the wave function represent different possible universes; any time a quantum observation or measurement is made, another world is forged, carrying the observer with it, until another observation is made, and the process repeats itself, with that world then splitting off into different branches. The observer is unaware of all this, as the reality he finds himself in is to him the only one.

What this amounts to is that there are countless billions of worlds constantly branching into billions of others and still others, with countless copies of each of us inhabiting them, but aware of only the one we're in.

The theory is compatible with observation, and in the case of the double-slit experiment, it says that in the act of observing which slit the electron passes through, the observer "splits" into two worlds, one for each slit. Instead of collapsing, the wave function splits into duplicates, accompanied by each possibility's respective observer. In the case of Schrödinger's cat, there are two worlds, one with a live cat, and one with a dead one, and by making an observation, we branch off into one or the other.

As far-out as this theory may sound, it does have some proponents in the scientific community, and it is impossible to prove or disprove. However, most physicists still favor the Copenhagen interpretation, despite its inherent two-at-a-time type problems, finding the many worlds theory simply too much, not to mention it's impossible to ever observe.

Both of these interpretations of quantum theory are shocking if taken at face value and constitute completely new and different worldviews. Paul Davies, in *Other Worlds*, says:

> Science, it is usually believed, helps us to build a picture of objective reality—the world "out there." With the advent of quantum theory, that very reality appears to have

crumbled, to be replaced by something so revolutionary and bizarre that its consequences have not yet been properly faced . . . one can either accept the multiple reality of the parallel worlds, or deny that real world exists at all, independent of our perception of it.

Scientific revolutions tend to be associated with a major restructuring of human perspectives (new worldview) . . . It is therefore remarkable that the greatest scientific revolution of all time has gone largely unnoticed by the general public, not because its implications are uninteresting, but because they are so shattering as to be almost beyond belief—even to the scientific revolutionaries themselves.[10]

But the thing is, neither the Copenhagen or many-worlds interpretations are "scientific" theories. They are *philosophical* interpretations of the outcome of scientific experiments. The structure itself of quantum theory is undisputed; the results have been verified repeatedly. But what do these results mean? What is the underlying reality that gives rise to these paradoxes? As with any worldview, some philosophy must be added.

Davies, as quoted, said the Copenhagen and many-worlds interpretations were "almost beyond belief—even to the scientific revolutionaries themselves," and the "revolution . . . has gone largely unnoticed by the general public." These two situations are related. One senses a reluctance on the part of scientists to promote these theories because they are so bizarre, virtually "beyond belief," *even to themselves*. It may be most accurate to say that, in general, physicists are ill at ease with *both of them*, and only align themselves with one or the other for lack of another alternative.

But there is one. We may consider these paradoxes in an expanded framework of space, time, and consciousness—extra-dimensional theory.

This starts with the assumption that our normal world of three dimensions of space plus time is but a cross-section of a vaster, extra-dimensional ground. Thus, in contrast to the Copenhagen and many-worlds interpretations, there is one objective reality independent of our perception of it. Our perception of it is just limited to a cross-section at a time. In quantum mechanics, we are at the absolute limit of our powers of perception, not the limit of reality, the limit of *our* means of intelligibly perceiving it, with logic and its extension, science. Therefore, even though the cross-section we experience in everyday life is clear and distinct, when we get right up to our perceptual limits, the picture becomes hazy and ambiguous. Our view of reality then becomes a mode of possibilities for different cross-sections.

This is exactly what happens in the case of the wave function. It represents a set of different variations that we are *capable* of apprehending. Then when a measurement or observation is made, that part becomes registered in our cross-section or imprinted on our three-dimensional map of reality.

A simple analogy to the collapse of the wave function can be made by bringing back our old friend Samson, a being who mentally inhabits a world of two dimensions of space plus time. Imagine him at play once more, this time with a multicolored, three-dimensional cube. As Samson jostles his new toy about, the spatial dimensions of the cube change for him *in time*. Now when he pauses, and the cube comes to rest, he will register just one of the cube's surfaces, out of several possibilities.

Samson, as the observer, is not creating reality with his observation; he is just inadvertently choosing which variation is seen at a given time. He doesn't split into different Samsons either. For we know that in higher, three-dimensional space, all possible views of the cube are just different vantage points of the same object; that is, they are all parts of one extra-dimensional phenomenon. Similarly, in quantum mechanics, we dimly sense an extra-dimensional reality as motion in time, and with a measurement we reduce it to a tangible impression in our space.

Thus our wave function is an incomplete description of reality in that it is only a collection of possible views accessible to us. It does not collapse with a measurement but disappears, as our apprehension is limited by our psychic state to one cross-section at a time. This makes understandable the most baffling part of the double-slit experiment: how an electron traveling between screens can instantaneously "know" that the covered slit in the first screen has now been uncovered. The wavelike interference pattern immediately appears again because it was there all along, and having shifted our focus, we again detect it.

For example, consider this analogy. We know that each of our eyes registers a two-dimensional image which is then combined in the brain to form a three-dimensional one. Now in theory, if we were to cover one eye, we would revert back to a two-dimensional picture. (This works only to some extent as it is impossible to exclude natural conceptual adjustments.) At any rate, if we look at a three-dimensional object, then cover one eye, we see a two-dimensional surface; uncover the eye, and the three-dimensional image returns. We have not changed the nature of the object by observing it differently, just our *representation* of it. Similarly, in quantum physics, we reduce a set of potential points of view, a wave function, to one, with a measurement.

In the case of Schrödinger's cat, however, the status of the cat is determined before the observation by the Geiger counter. It serves as a tool capable of extracting a possibility of the particle's state (decayed or undecayed) and permanently recording an impression of it in our three-dimensional world. Some adherents of the Copenhagen interpretation likewise maintain that the matter is settled here, but the difference lies in the fact that under the Copenhagen interpretation reality is produced there. Under extra-dimensional theory one side of it has been selected randomly by the Geiger counter to be registered on our "map." Correspondingly, the proverbial act of the tree falling in the forest will be recorded in our world as soon as the extra-dimensional activity that sets the appropriate forces in motion are registered as "cleanly" within our cross-section with or without an observer.

Thus to resolve these paradoxes in quantum theory, we begin by acknowledging that they are built on false premises. These are: (1) that the wave function is a complete portrait of objective reality, albeit prospective ones; and (2) that our observational capacities can perfectly apprehend all of reality. Still, the Copenhagen interpretation, the many-worlds interpretation, and extra-dimensional theory are all compatible with observation. But let's look at one more quantum paradox, one that transcends time itself, or, at least, "our" time.

It was discovered in 1935 that once two quantum particles interact, they seemingly retain an influence with each other, no matter how far apart they may later travel. And the effect is instantaneous, even if the distance between them is such that the influence must be faster than light. Einstein called this "spooky action at a distance," and was so vexed at this apparent superluminal link, as well as other quantum oddities such as the uncertainty principle, that he never accepted quantum theory as a coherent system. In fact, in a classic debate with Neils Bohr on "probabilities," Einstein was prompted to utter the famous line—"God does not play dice [with the universe]." We now see that Einstein was right; it just appears dicelike when we apply "three-dimensional logic" to an extra-dimensional reality.

Einstein proposed a thought experiment, suggesting there was a hidden variable (or variables) that could effect a more conventional explanation for these superluminal connections and quantum theory. But in 1965, Irish physicist John Bell developed a mathematical way to test for such variables. The result was that faster-than-light influence must be maintained—the so-called quantum connection is real.

The connection can be envisioned by starting with two electrons in an interactive state. These have a characteristic spin about their axis, either up or down; when one is up, the other one must be down. When these particles separate, no matter how far apart or how fast they are traveling, even right up to the speed of light, if the orientation of one is altered, say from up to down, then the other particle will *instantaneously* register the opposite orientation, maintaining the original symmetry.

The Copenhagen interpretation implies that when a measurement of one particle shows that its orientation is changed, then that information somehow travels to the other particle at faster than light speed so it can also change. This explanation in itself might seem to be a problem seeing as how the transmission of that information would supersede special relativity and cause and effect. Physicists have managed to get around this by adding the aforementioned causal ordering postulate (COP) to relativity, which "allows" superluminal connections as long as they do not constitute an intelligible signal; and they are not intelligible here because the information of the particles' status must be compared at below light speed.

A larger problem is that the Copenhagen interpretation of the quantum connection suggests that an act of observation *creates* reality not only in the immediate area, but *also creates it simultaneously* at an unlimited distance as well. This is scarcely conceivable. Fortunately, there's a much simpler explanation, already offered by Dr. Bohm: an extra-dimensional one. Bohm has us understand the symmetry of the quantum connection as an extension of this setting.

Picture a fish tank stocked with swimming fish, two television cameras aimed at the tank at right angles (one in front, one on the side), and two television screens at different locations receiving images from the cameras. What is seen is a relationship between the two images. In other words, two complementary, two-dimensional images represent one higher-dimensional actuality. If a fish shows a certain movement on one screen, a *corresponding* movement will instantaneously be seen on the other screen, from a different vantage point. The content of one screen does not *cause* the content of the other to change, nor does any information pass between them; they are merely two-dimensional images simultaneously reflecting different views of a three-dimensional reality. Similarly, Bohm postulates, the quantum connection demonstrates a non-causal abstraction of a still higher-dimensional reality. Bohm states:

> One finds, through a study of the implications of the quantum theory, that the analysis of a total system into a set of independently existent but interacting particles breaks down in a radically new way. One discovers, instead, both from considerations of the meaning of the mathematical equations and from the results of the actual experiments, *that the various particles have to be taken literally as projections of a higher-dimensional reality which cannot be accounted for in terms of any force of interaction between them.*[11] (Emphasis added.)

Bohm's theory says that what we perceive as separate particles within our "subtotality" are really parts of one multi-dimensional whole. Extra-dimensional theory says that which is separate in our space is connected and part of one phenomenon in higher space. In this respect, they are the same; in regard to the quantum connection, they offer the same simple solution that works. These related particles only seem separate because we can't apprehend the extra-dimensional whole. As the Bhagavad-Gita says: "Undivided, He seems to divide into objects and creatures."[12] In higher space, all these parts are joined together by a faster-than-light medium that connects; it is that which connects everything in our normal three-dimensional world—an extra dimension.

With this in mind, let's make a comparison between the three contenders for a new worldview: the many-worlds interpretation, the Copenhagen interpretation, and extra-dimensional theory. The many-worlds interpretation is a lot to accept. Billions upon billions of universes being created every second seems so uneconomical. The world we do perceive is so frugal, with matter and energy continually recycled, that it is hard to conceive of such outright ostentation, not to mention the fact that it seems to sidestep the first law of thermodynamics, that energy cannot be created from nothing.

Even some proponents of the many-worlds theory have had second thoughts about it. Bryce DeWitt admits, "It is not easy to reconcile with common sense. Here is schizophrenia with a vengeance."[13] John Wheeler, who helped Everett formulate his theory, has given up on the idea. "I once subscribed to it. In retrospect, however, it looks like the wrong track . . . its infinitely many unobservable worlds make a heavy load of metaphysical baggage."[14] Quantum physicist J. S. Bell probably sums it up best in *Quantum Mechanics for Cosmologists*, "If such a theory were taken seriously it would hardly be possible to take anything seriously."[15]

The Copenhagen interpretation tries to keep strictly to observation and the simplest way to explain experimental results. This is the scientific way, and it's generally commendable. But ironically, by virtue of trying to exclude any philosophical implications here, it ends up being the most philosophical of the three theories, for it postulates that there is no objective reality without measurements and observations, even if the reality is separated from the observation by vast expanses of space and time.

Extra-dimensional theory reinstates what science has always endeavored to study and what most physicists have always felt most comfortable with: *one* objective reality, independent of any particular perception. It is said that a good scientific theory helps explain phenomena in other areas of study, and extra-dimensional theory does this by providing an expanded framework within which the paranormal can be included and understood.

There is a trade-off in this, though. We must abdicate Man's assumed position as the summit of mental evolution in the universe. Heretofore, it has been thought that all of reality could be rendered subservient to logic and science. This is just the scenario that quantum mechanics clings to so tenaciously, hence the problematic Copenhagen and many-worlds interpretations. But has the evolution of consciousness come so far just to end with our self-consciousness? Just as it was hard but necessary to accept that our physical world is not the focal point of the entire universe, it is now so for the conceptual nature of Man.

In *The Structure of Scientific Revolutions,* Thomas S. Kühn points out that normal science *presupposes* a certain conceptual framework of reality, one that is accepted without question by a scientific community; given such a framework, scientific research tends to gear toward filling in the missing pieces of the puzzle rather than the exploration of the unknown. This is where we stand today in the age of specialization where every scientific discipline is broken down into ever more specialized fields of study, to tie down those loose ends. Are we at the point where we can no longer see the forest for the trees? For as we carve up that which is to be studied into smaller and smaller parts, the specialist comes to know more about less, while new worldviews are always broader, more comprehensive.

This is all too often the case in paranormal research as well. Researchers specialize in a particular phenomenon (or aspect of that phenomenon) and try to explain it in terms of current scientific knowledge, within the accepted framework. (A fine approach if there were just one or two types of phenomena, but the sheer number of them calls for a new framework.) For example, as mentioned in chapter 6, psi subjects in the lab have been able to affect subatomic particles in devices such as random number generators (RNGs); some parapsychologists have proposed a way of how this might be done, in accordance with "acceptable" quantum theory, i.e., the Copenhagen interpretation.

The tests involve the random rate of decay of radioactive particles which are truly quantum events in that prior to each psi measurement the particle exists in the probabilistic "wave function" state. Since the wave function can be thought of as a range of information of the particle, some parapsychologists feel that the subject's consciousness may be able to somehow interact with this information to either intuit the next outcome (precognition), or actually cause it (PK).

But such a hypothesis neglects *all* other forms of PK and precognition, all other psi phenomena, and all other paranormal phenomena as well. Yet an extra-dimensional framework of space, time, and consciousness, which can explain those other phenomena, can also explain these "micro-results." I'll demonstrate with one more plane-world analogy.

Figure 16 shows the plane world existing on the surface of water, say a pond, and near the shore; here fine particles of dust, sand, and dirt are constantly being blown out over the pond, causing tiny "points" to instantaneously appear and then disappear from the plane world. Plane beings consider this to be the activity of "elementary particles" moving about their world.

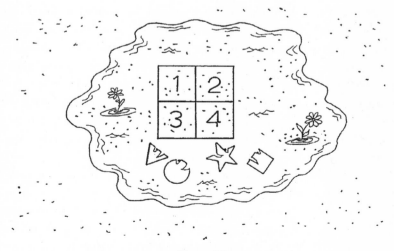

Figure 16

Researchers on this world elect to study this phenomenon by setting up a laboratory of sorts, consisting of a grid or square (as in the illustration). They wish to see if there is a pattern to the way the particles act in the lab; they will discover that the distribution seems to be a random process, that is, in the long run an equal number of particles appear in each of the four quadrants of the square. For example, with 1,000 particles, roughly 250 will be within each quadrant. They cannot predict exactly when the next particle will appear *or in what quadrant* as each quadrant has a one-in-four chance. So prior to each particle's "registration," it would exist in a probabilistic state—a wave function— which then collapses into a specific measurement or quadrant.

Now the researchers will conduct a two-part experiment, to test a special plane being's alleged ability to: (1) *predict* which quadrant the next particle will appear in, by a score better than chance—more than 25 percent—which would be precognition; and (2) *cause* a greater number of particles than chance predicts (25 percent) to fall in a selected quadrant, which would be PK.

In the experiment, the Star is once more the subject and the Square, Triangle, and Circle the observers. In part one, the Star is able to utilize his higher, three-dimensional consciousness, with which he can mentally rise above his normal two-dimensional space and "see" particles traveling toward the grid through the third dimension (a dimension that before existed to him only in time, and in an inside-out direction). He is able to see that some of the particles are definitely headed for certain quadrants. Accordingly, he makes his prediction. Because he has only partial use of the higher sense, he will succeed only a small percentage of the time, but this percentage is enough to boost his score above chance. Let's say that after 1,000 guesses, he was correct 31 percent of the time, instead of the expected 25 percent. This would be a significant score and suggest precognition.

In part two (PK), the Star again utilizes a part of higher consciousness, this time to maneuver his extension in higher space (a part of himself he is scarcely aware of, if at all) and "deflect" some of the particles into the desired quadrant, say number four. He must cause more than the expected 25 percent to fall in it and again he succeeds—this time scoring 32 percent. This is also a significant result, and suggests PK.

The researchers of the plane world might try to explain these scores within the accepted framework of their science, by hypothesizing that the Star's consciousness interacted with the wave function of the particles, and thus knew how it would collapse (precognition), or somehow caused it to collapse in a certain way (PK). Of course we know that's not how it happened. This micro-psi was originated in extra-dimensional space by the awareness and utilization of higher consciousness—as is all psi activity, in any world of space and time.

It's also apparent that their wave function is incomplete; it consists only of components capable of registration on the plane world. Yet there are other possibilities. For example, particles could continue to drift in the third dimension right over the plane world, or settle on trees, plants, etc., and in such cases remain in extra-dimensional space. Indeed, *most* of the wave function (set of possibilities) exists in extra-dimensional space—*as it does for us.*

New worldviews are also simple. The Earth is round. The Earth orbits the sun. Even with the seeming complexities of the last few, they are still basically simple, just new, broader ways of looking at reality. Einstein for example, in his best years, favored simple yet compelling reasoning and thought experiments over complicated mathematics. In fact, he demonstrated the relativity of the present using mathematics no more advanced than arithmetic.

We're at the threshold of a new worldview. But which one? The Copenhagen and many-worlds theories, though worlds apart, are simple. Which would you choose? There's no need to defer to the experts, for your choice is as good as theirs; it's a simple philosophical preference. Yet maybe you feel there is something more to reality, something our science has not yet grasped, or *cannot grasp.* If you're one of the many millions who have had a paranormal experience, you know this.

Another level of reality? Another realm of existence? A spiritual world, different and separate from the sense-world? No. There is only one Reality, embracing all worlds, interpenetrating all realms of existence, and connecting all levels of reality.

Extra-dimensional theory is simple. Which do you choose?

Endnotes

Chapter 2: Worlds of Space

1. "The Fourth Dimension" in *A New Model of the Universe*, p. 86.
2. *Life After Life*, p. 26.
3. *Adventures in Immortality*, p. 200.
4. Ibid., p. 31.
5. *Life at Death*, p. 255.
6. *Fabric of the Universe*, p. 43.
7. *Dimensions*, p. 241.
8. *Revelations*, p. 259.
9. *Forbidden Science*, p. 421.
10. *Abduction*, p. 404.
11. Ibid., p. 32.
12. Ibid., p. 393.
13. *The Watchers*, p. 198.
14. Ibid., p. 183.
15. *Abduction*, p. 250.
16. Ibid., p. 224.
17. "In the Labor Prophet," as cited in R. M. Bucke's *Cosmic Consciousness*, p. 249.
18. *Tertium Organum*, p. 48.
19. *Creative Meditation and Multi-Dimensional Consciousness*, p. 116.
20. A near-death experience, from Kenneth Ring, *Life at Death*, p. 245.
21. A mystical experience, Hiroshi Motoyama, "Theories of the Chakras," as cited in Kenneth Ring, *Heading Toward Omega*, p. 233.

22. From Michael B. Sabom, *Recollections of Death,* p. 15.

23. Lin Yutang (editor), *The Wisdom of Laotse,* p. 101.

24. *Homer's Odyssey.*

25. *The Republic of Plato,* pp. 209–12.

Chapter 3: Levels of Consciousness

1. Rene Descartes (1596–1650).

2. R. M. Bucke, *Cosmic Consciousness,* pp. 9–10.

3. Ibid., p. 73.

4. Ibid., p. 11.

5. Ibid., pp. 13–4.

6. Ibid., p. 94.

7. Ibid., pp. 245–6.

8. As cited in Irving Oyle, *Time, Space, and the Mind,* p. 50.

9. *Cosmic Consciousness,* p. 26.

10. From E. A. Burtt, *The Teachings of the Compassionate Buddha,* p. 194.

11. *The Synthesis of Yoga,* p. 989.

12. As cited in *Tertium Organum,* p. 280.

13. As cited in Stephen Mitchell, *The Enlightened Mind,* p. 48.

14. Svetasvatara Upanishad, the Upanishads, p. 127.

15. Bhagavad-Gita, p. 122.

16. *The Enlightened Mind,* p. 51.

17. As cited in I. K. Taimni, *The Science of Yoga,* p. 211.

18. *Creative Meditation and Multi-Dimensional Consciousness,* p. 271.

19. Ibid., p. 287.

20. *Tertium Organum,* pp. 37, 71.

21. *Cosmic Consciousness,* p. 73.

22. Ibid., p. 17.

23. Surah III:1, *The Meaning of the Glorious Koran.*

24 The First Epistle of John, 1:1–3.

Chapter 4: What Time Appears to Be, and What It Really Is

1. As cited in *Time Machines,* p. 65.

2. Ibid., p. 214.

3. As cited in *The Art of Time,* p. 134.

4. Kaivalya Upanishad, the Upanishads, p. 115.

5. From his "Summa Theologiae," cited in *Time Machines,* p. 112.

6. In "From Adam's Peak to Elephanta," as cited in *Cosmic Consciousness,* p. 242.

7. Ibid., p. 192.

8. As cited in *Tertium Organum,* p. 279.

9. *Tao Te Ching,* p. 51.

10. From Michael Talbot's *The Holographic Universe,* p. 249.

11. *Vital Signs,* a quarterly digest of news for the membership of the International Association for Near Death Studies (December 1981):12.

12. As cited in *Time's Arrows,* p. 123.

13. As cited in Nick Herbert, *Faster than Light,* p. 191.

14. From a personal letter written in 1955, cited in Larry Dossey, M.D., *Space, Time, and Medicine,* Shambhala Press, Boulder, Colo., London, 1982, p. 157.

15. From a conversation with Rudolph Carnap at the Institute for Advanced Study at Princeton, cited in *Time Machines,* p. 141.

16. *The Synthesis of Yoga,* p. 854.

17. *Life After Life,* p. 69.

18. Ibid., pp. 133–4.

19. Bhagavad-Gita, p. 92.

20. Svetasvatara Upanishad, the Upanishads, p. 123.

21. From Kenneth Ring, *The Omega Project,* p. 96.

22. *Life at Death,* p. 239.

23. Ibid., p. 56.

24. *Wholeness and the Implicate Order,* p. 169.

25. Ibid., p. 42.

26. In Ganga Sahai, *Metaphysical Approach to Reality,* pp. 50–1.

27. *The Science of Yoga,* p. 314.

28. In *Time Machines,* p. 103.

29. From Mally Cox-Chapman, *The Case for Heaven,* p. 172.

30. *Creative Meditation and Multi-Dimensional Consciousness,* p. 286.

31. Ibid., pp. 259–60.

32. Ibid., p. 199.

33. *On Indian Mahayana Buddhism,* pp. 148–9.

34. *Heading Toward Omega,* p. 82.

35. Ibid., p. 39.

Chapter 5: The Mystical Experience: Dawn of a New Species

1. Mark 1:10.

2. John 18:36–7.

3. Luke 17:21.

4. Surah XXV:25.

5. Surah II:268.

6. Surah XX:110.

7. Surah III:185.

8. Svetasvatara Upanishad, the Upanishads, p. 127.

9. *The Enlightened Mind*, Stephen Mitchell's excellent compilation of mystical/religious essays, pp. 48–9.

10. Ibid., p. 56.

11. *Creative Meditation and Multi-Dimensional Consciousness*, p. 270.

12. In J. Kennett, *Selling Water by the River*, p. 140.

13. *The Synthesis of Yoga*, p. 857.

14. Ibid., p. 853.

15. 2 Corinthians 4:17–8.

16. Revelation 1:18.

17. Peter 3:8–9.

18. From "Compendium Theologiae," as cited in *Time Machines*, p. 103.

19. *The Enlightened Mind*, p. 24.

20. As cited in *Mysticism*, p. 116.

21. Bhagavad-Gita, p. 111.

22. *Tao Te Ching*, p. 32.

23. *The Enlightened Mind*, p. 48.

24. Ibid., p. 80.

25. Ibid., p. 68.

26. *The Synthesis of Yoga*, p. 107.

27. Ephesians 4:6.

28. Romans 12:4–6.

29. *Tao Te Ching*, p. 1.

30. Surah XXIX:64.

31. Colossians 3:34.

32. John 14:6.

33. Matthew 23:13.

34. *The Teachings of the Compassionate Buddha*, p. 38.

35. *Cosmic Consciousness*, p. 3.

36. *The Enlightened Mind*, xiii.

37. As cited in Roger Walsh, *The Spirit of Shamanism*, p. 141.

38. Luke 17:20.

39. Matthew 25:13.

40. Surah VII:187.

41. *Tao Te Ching*, p. 73.

42. *The Kingdom of God Is within You*, p. 61.

43. *Cosmic Consciousness*, p. 5.

44. *The Enlightened Mind*, p. 114.

45. *The Biological Basis of Religion and Genius*, p. 12.

46. Matthew 12:2.

47. Luke 9:29–30.

48. *The Biological Basis of Religion and Genius,* p. 13.

49. Peter 3:12.

50. John 1:5.

51. Bhagavad-Gita, p. 92.

52. Brihadaranyaka Upanishad, the Upanishads, p. 84.

53. Prasna Upanishad, the Upanishads, pp. 35–6.

54. *Tao Te Ching,* p. 10.

55. Surah XXIV:35.

56. Surah XXXII:20.

57. *The Secret of Yoga,* p. 89.

58. 2 Corinthians 12:4.

59. 2 Corinthians 5:17.

60. 1 Corinthians 1:20.

61. Ephesians 3:18–9.

62. Katha Upanishad, the Upanishads, p. 17.

63. *The Teachings of the Compassionate Buddha,* p. 56.

64. *The Secret of Yoga,* p. 34.

65. Colossians 3:2–3.

66. Romans 12:2.

67. 1 Corinthians 2:14.

68. Matthew 19:23–5.

69. Surah CII:1.

70. "Dhammapada," in Vol. X of *Sacred Books of the East,* translated and edited by F. Max Mueller, The Clarendon Press, Oxford, in forty-eight volumes, 1879–1885, as cited in *Cosmic Consciousness,* pp. 95–6.

71. Ibid., p. 261.

72. Matthew 13:44.

73. As cited in *Mysticism,* p. 235.

74. As cited in *The Enlightened Mind,* p. 169.

75. From *Auguries of Innocence.*

76. *Cosmic Consciousness,* p. 381.

77. *The Biological Basis of Religion and Genius,* p. 112.

78. *Abduction,* pp. 3–4.

79. As quoted in C. D. B. Bryan, *Close Encounters of the Fourth Kind,* p. 420.

Chapter 6: Psychic Phenomena

1. As cited in S. Ostrander and L. Schroeder, *Psychic Discoveries behind the Iron Curtain,* p. 165.

2. *Cosmic Consciousness,* p. 367.

3. *The Science of Yoga,* p. 181.

4. Ibid., p. 195.

5. 1 Corinthians 12:8–11.

6. Surah XX:98.

7. John 2:25.

8. From Louisa Rhine, *ESP in Life and Lab,* pp. 215–6.

9. Ibid., pp. 54–5.

10. *The Collected Works of St. John of the Cross,* p. 217.

11. Bhagavad-Gita, p. 79.

12. *ESP in Life and Lab,* p. 70.

13. Ibid., p. 10.

14. S. Aurobindo, *The Synthesis of Yoga,* p. 864.

15. A mystical experience from the Old Testament, Wisdom 7:18.

16. As cited in Martin Ebon, *Prophecy in Our Time,* pp. 211–2.

17. *ESP in Life and Lab,* p. 3.

18. 1 Thessalonians 5:2–3.

19. *Tao Te Ching,* p. 14.

20. Ibid., pp. 156–7.

21. *ESP in Life and Lab,* pp. 266, 259.

22. Ibid., p. 377.

23. As cited in *Prophecy in Our Time,* pp. 165–6.

24. From "Synchronicity," in *The Interpretation of Nature and the Psyche.*

25. Ibid., p. 27.

26. Ibid., p. 5.

27. Ibid., p. 38.

28. Ibid., p. 300.

29. Kena Upanishad, 3, *The Thirteen Principal Upanishads.*

30. *Tao Te Ching,* p. 14.

31. Matthew 13:13–4.

32. *Extra-Sensory Perception,* p. 220.

33. Ibid., p. 223.

34. Ibid., pp. 18–9.

35. *The Science of Yoga,* p. 355.

36. *The Enlightened Mind,* p. 93.

37. Ibid., p. 73.

38. *The Poltergeist,* p. 74.

39. Hans Bender's poltergeist investigations were given in his presidential address to the Parapsychological Association, "New Development in Poltergeist Research," contained in *Proceedings of the Parapsychological Association,* 5, 1968, pp. 29–38. As cited in *The Poltergeist Experience,* p. 126.

40. Ibid., pp. 129–30.

41. From the *Journal of the Society for Psychological Research,* XII:260–266.

42. As cited in *Mysticism,* p. 61.

43. Matthew 11:5.

Chapter 7: UFOs and Abductions

1. *The UFO Experience,* p. 139.

2. *American Weekly,* October 24, 1954.

3. A well known document in UFO circles and now a matter of public record.

4. Acting secretary of the Air Force, Robert C. Seaman, Jr., at a press conference on December 17, 1969.

5. *The UFO Experience,* p. 232.

6. From an interview for *Fate* magazine, June 1976, p. 180.

7. From an interview for *Today's Student,* April 3, 1978.

8. *The UFO Experience,* p. 234.

9. *The Hynek UFO Report,* p. 27.

10. *Confrontations,* p. 99.

11. *Revelations,* p. 259.

12. *Forbidden Science,* p. 421.

13. Ibid., p. 253.

14. Ibid., p. 100.

15. *Intruders,* p. 149.

16. *Revelations,* p. 251.

17. House Report No. 242, "Proposed Studies on the Implications of Peaceful Space Activities for Human Affairs," 1961, p. 225.

18. In "Hypnosis and UFO Abductions: A Troubled Relationship," *Journal of UFO Studies,* n.s. 1, 1989, pp. 3–40.

19. In "Abductions in Life and Lore," *International UFO Reporter,* Vol. 12, No. 4, 1987, p. 14.

20. In *Selected Articles: A Collection of Articles on the UFO Abduction Phenomenon,* p. 8.

21. *Abduction,* p. 39.

22. *The Watchers,* pp. 183, 198.

23. *Abduction,* p. 404.

24. Ibid., pp. 250, 257.

25. Ibid., p. 261.

26. *The Allagash Abductions,* p. 236.

27. *The Andreasson Affair,* p. 144.

28. *The Watchers,* p. 147.

29. Ibid., p. 58.

30. In April, 1994, at Bristol Community College, Fall River, Mass.

31. *Abduction*, p. 250.

32. Ibid., p. 224.

33. *The Andreasson Affair*, p. 86.

34. *The Allagash Abductions*, pp. 206–7.

35. *Missing Time*, p. 68.

36. *Abduction*, p. 158.

37. *Secret Life*, p. 220.

38. *The Andreasson Affair*, pp. 23, 33.

39. *The Watchers*, p. 148.

40. *Secret Life*, p. 208.

41. *The Allagash Abductions*, p. 172.

42. *Abduction*, p. 184.

43. *The Allagash Abductions*, p. 169.

44. *Missing Time*, p. 196.

45. *The Andreasson Affair*, p. 26.

46. From John G. Fuller, *The Interrupted Journey*, New York: Dial Press, 1966. As cited in *The Andreasson Affair*, p. 177.

47. *Missing Time*, p. 59.

48. *The Watchers*, p. 121.

49. *The Andreasson Affair*, p. 143.

50. *The Andreasson Affair, Phase Two*, p. 195.

51. *Abduction*, p. 250.

52. Ibid., pp. 316–7.

53. *The Watchers*, pp. 185, 209, 345.

54. *The Andreasson Affair*, p. 159.

55. Ibid., p. 143.

56. *On Stolen Time*, p. 12.

57. *Secret Life*, p. 197.

58. *The Allagash Abductions*, p. 336.

59. *Abduction*, p. 49.

60. Ibid., pp. 408–9.

61. *On Stolen Time*, p. 25.

62. *The Watchers*, pp. 25, 49.

63. *Abduction*, p. 186.

64. *Secret Life*, p. 158.

65. *Abduction*, p. 135.

66. Ibid., p. 135.

67. *The Andreasson Affair*, p. 121.

68. *The Watchers*, p. 203.

69. *Secret Life*, p. 148.

70. Ibid., p. 136.
71. *Abduction*, p. 40.
72. Kenneth Ring, *The Omega Project*, p. 181.
73. Ibid., pp. 282–4.
74. *The Watchers*, pp. 201, 347.
75. *The Andreasson Affair*, p. 121.
76. Ibid., p. 158.
77. *Abduction*, p. 226.
78. Ibid., p. 329.
79. *The Omega Project*, p. 188.
80. *Abduction*, p. 403.
81. Ibid., p. 238.
82. *The Omega Project*, p. 182.
83. *Abduction*, p. 225.
84. *Secret Life*, p. 147.
85. *The Andreasson Affair*, pp. 140–1.
86. *Abduction*, p. 422.
87. Ibid., p. 3–4.
88. *The Watchers*, p. 200.
89. *The Omega Project*, p. 129.
90. *Secret Life*, p. 135.
91. *Abduction*, p. 308.
92. Ibid., p. 329.
93. Ibid., p. 311.
94. *Intruders*, pp. 263–5.
95. *Secret Life*, pp. 184–5.
96. *Abduction*, p. 422.
97. *The Watchers*, pp. 212–3.
98. *Selected Articles: A Collection of Articles on the UFO Abduction Phenomenon*, p. 8.
99. *Abduction*, pp. 306–10.
100. *The Omega Project*, p. 188.
101. *Secret Life*, pp. 312–3.

Chapter 8: Life after Death

1. *Recollections of Death*, p. 16.
2. *Life at Death*, p. 83.
3. *Recollections of Death*, p. 165.
4. Ibid., p. 165.
5. Ibid., p. 180.
6. *The Light Beyond*, pp. 50–1.

7. *Life After Life*, p. 97.

8. Ibid., p. 96.

9. *The Light Beyond*, p. 151.

10. *Life After Life*, p. 182.

11. *Life at Death*, p. 219.

12. John 1:51.

13. Surah XXII:55.

14. The Herb Schirmer case. Cited by Coral and Jim Lorenzen in *Abducted*.

15. *Abduction*, p. 397. Inset: "Home—an inexpressibly beautiful realm beyond, or not in, space/time as we know it." p. 48.

16. Green, *Out-of-the-Body Experiences*, p. 108.

17. *Life at Death*, p. 221.

18. *Out-of-the-Body Experiences*, p. 81.

19. Ibid., p. 119.

20. Ibid., p. 78.

21. Ibid., p. 77.

22. Ibid., p. 79.

23. Ibid., p. 93.

24. Ibid., p. 92.

25. *Life at Death*, p. 48.

26. *The Light Beyond*, pp. 92–3.

27. *Life at Death*, p. 49.

28. Ibid.

29. *Life After Life*, p. 24.

30. *Recollections of Death*, p. 41.

31. Ibid.

32. *Life at Death*, p. 94.

33. *Recollections of Death*, p. 40.

34. Ibid.

35. *Heading Toward Omega*, p. 57.

36. John 6:46.

37. *Life at Death*, p. 240.

38. *Heading Toward Omega*, pp. 228–9.

39. A near-death experience. Ibid., p. 66.

40. A mystical experience. Ibid., p. 220.

41. A near-death experience. *The Light Beyond*, p. 34.

42. An abduction experience. *Abduction*, p. 173.

43. *Mysteries of the Inner Self*, p. 83.

44. *Heading Toward Omega*, p. 64.

45. *The Case for Heaven*, p. 165.

46. *Closer to the Light,* p. 110.
47. *The Case for Heaven,* p. 100.
48. *Heading Toward Omega,* p. 62.
49. *Life at Death,* p. 97.
50. *Reflections on Life After Life,* p. 94.
51. *Transformed by the Light,* p. 75.
52. From Carl Jung's account of his near-death experience. Cited in *Life at Death,* p. 245.
53. *The Light Beyond,* p. 14.
54. *Heading Toward Omega,* p. 60.
55. Ibid., pp. 65–6.
56. *The Watchers,* p. 333.
57. Ibid., p. 345.
58. *Heading Toward Omega,* p. 199.
59. Ibid., p. 63.
60. Ibid., pp. 64–5.
61. Ibid., p. 54.
62. Ibid., p. 60.
63. Bhagavad-Gita, p. 75.
64. *Creative Meditation and Multi-Dimensional Consciousness,* p. 189.
65. *Heading Toward Omega,* p. 99.
66. *Life at Death,* p. 165.
67. Matthew 25:41.
68. Romans 8:12–3.
69. 1 Corinthians 3:13–4.
70. *Heaven and Hell,* p. 134.
71. *The Omega Project,* p. 146.
72. *Life at Death,* p. 184.
73. *Adventures in Immortality,* p. 83.
74. *Life After Life,* p. 93.
75. *Transformed by the Light,* p. 12.
76. *Life at Death,* p. 85.
77. Ibid., p. 85.
78. Ibid., p. 143.
79. Ibid., p. 151.

Chapter 9: Extra-Dimensional Theory and the New Physics
1. *The Tao of Physics,* p. 17.
2. Ibid., p. 138.
3. Ibid., pp. 193–4.
4. Ibid., p. 194.

5. Ibid., p. 149.

6. Ibid., p. 114.

7. *Cosmic Consciousness,* p. 74.

8. *The Biological Basis of Religion and Genius,* p. 100.

9. *Time Journeys,* p. 129.

10. *Other Worlds,* pp. 11–2.

11. *Wholeness and the Implicate Order,* p. 186.

12. Bhagavad-Gita, p. 103.

13. "Quantum Mechanics and Reality," in *The Many-Worlds Interpretation of Quantum Mechanics.* Edited by B. S. DeWitt and N. Graham, Princeton, N.J.: Princeton University Press, 1973. *Time Machines,* p. 273.

14. "Frontiers of Time," in *Problems in the Foundation of Physics.* Edited by G. T. diFrancia. *Proceedings of the International School of Physics.* Course 72. New York: North-Holland, 1979. *Time Machines,* p. 274.

15. "Quantum Mechanics for Cosmologists," "On the Einstein-Podelsky-Rosen Paradox," and "Bertlmann's Socks and the Nature of Reality." In *Speakable and Unspeakable in Quantum Mechanics.* New York: Cambridge University Press, 1987. *Time Machines,* p. 201.

Bibliography

Abbott, Edwin A., *Flatland*, New York: HarperPerennial, 1983.

Arvey, Michael, *UFOs: Opposing Viewpoints*, San Diego, Calif.: Greenhaven Press, 1989.

Auerbach, Loyd, *ESP, Hauntings and Poltergeists*, New York: Warner Books, 1986.

Aurobindo, Sri, *The Synthesis of Yoga*, Pondicherry, India: Aurobindo Ashram Trust, 1971.

Barrow, John D., *Theories of Everything*, Oxford, England: Clarendon Press, 1991.

Bender, David L., and Leone, Bruno (series editors), *Paranormal Phenomena*, San Diego, Calif.: Greenhaven Press, 1991.

Blake, William, *Auguries of Innocence: A Poem*, Providence, R.I.: Ziggurat Press, 1997.

Bloom, Harold (editor), *Homer's Odyssey*, New York: Chelsea House Publishers, 1996.

Bohm, David, *Wholeness and the Implicate Order,* New York: Ark Paperbacks, 1983.

———, *Unfolding Meaning,* New York: Ark Paperbacks, 1985.

Bragdon, Claude, *A Primer of Higher Space,* New York: Alfred A. Knopf, 1913.

Briazack, Norman J., and Mennick, Simon, *The UFO Guidebook,* Secausus, N.J.: The Citadel Press, 1978.

Broughton, Richard, S., *Parapsychology: The Controversial Science,* New York: Ballantine Books, 1991.

Brunstein, Karl A., *Beyond the Four Dimensions,* New York: Walker and Company, 1979.

Bryan, C. D. B., *Close Encounters of the Fourth Kind,* New York: Alfred A. Knopf, 1995.

Bucke, Richard Maurice, *Cosmic Consciousness,* New York: E. P. Dutton and Company, 1923.

Bullard, Thomas, E., *On Stolen Time,* Mount Rainier, Md.: Fund for UFO Research, 1987.

———, *UFO Abductions: The Measure of a Mystery,* Mount Rainier, Md.: Fund for UFO Research, 1987.

Burtt, E. A. (editor), *The Teachings of the Compassionate Buddha,* New York: Penguin Books, 1955.

Capra, Fritjof, *The Tao of Physics,* Boston, Mass.: Shambhala Publications, 1975.

Clark, Jerome, *UFOs in the 1980s* (*The UFO Encyclopedia,* Volume 1), Detroit, Mich.: Apogee Books, 1990.

————, *UFO Encounters and Beyond,* Lincolnwood, Ill.: Publications International Ltd., 1993.

Cox-Chapman, Mally, *The Case for Heaven,* New York: G. P. Putnam's Sons, 1995.

Crookall, Robert, *Out-of-the-Body Experiences,* Secausus, N.J.: The Citadel Press, 1970.

Davies, Paul, *Other Worlds,* New York: Simon & Schuster, 1980.

De Riencourt, Amaury, *The Eye of Shiva,* New York: William Morrow and Company, 1981.

Ebon, Martin, *Prophecy in Our Time,* New York: New American Library, 1968.

Einstein, Albert, *The World as I See It,* New York: Covivi Friede Publishers, 1934.

————, *Out of My Later Years,* New York: Philosophical Library, 1950.

Feuerstein, Georg, and Miller, Jeanine, *Yoga and Beyond,* New York: Schocken Books, 1972.

Fowler, Raymond E., *The Andreasson Affair,* Englewood Cliffs, N.J.: Prentice-Hall, 1979.

————, *The Andreasson Affair, Phase Two,* Englewood Cliffs, N.J.: Prentice-Hall, 1982.

————, *The Watchers,* New York: Bantam Books, rack edition, 1991.

————, *The Allagash Abductions,* Tigard, Ore.: Wild Flower Press, 1993.

Gallup, George, Jr., with William Proctor, *Adventures in Immortality,* New York: McGraw Hill, 1982.

Govinda, Lama Anagarika, *Foundations of Tibetan Mysticism,* New York: Samuel Weiser, 1969.

———, *Creative Meditation and Multi-Dimensional Consciousness,* Wheaton, Ill.: Theosophical Publishing House, 1984.

Green, Celia, *Out-of-the-Body Experiences,* Oxford, England: Institute of Psychophysical Research, 1968.

Halpern, Paul, *Time Journeys,* New York: McGraw Hill, 1990.

Herbert, Nick, *Faster than Light,* New York: New American Library, 1988.

Hinton, Charles Howard, *The Fourth Dimension,* London: George Allen & Unwin Ltd., 1976.

Holroyd, Stuart, *Mysteries of the Inner Self,* London: Bloomsbury Books, 1992.

The Holy Bible, Confraternity Version, New York: Benziger Brothers, 1950.

Hopkins, Budd, *Missing Time,* New York: Ballantine Books, 1981.

———, *Intruders,* New York: Ballantine Books, 1987.

———, *Selected Articles: A collection of articles on the UFO abduction phenomenon.* New York: The Intruders Foundation, 1991.

Hume, R. E., *The Thirteen Principal Upanishads,* New York: Oxford University Press, 1934.

Huxley, Aldous, *The Doors of Perception,* New York: Harper & Row, 1954.

———, *Heaven and Hell,* New York: Harper & Row, 1954.

Hynek, J. Allen, *The UFO Experience,* Chicago, Ill.: Henry Regnery Company, 1972.

———, *The Hynek UFO Report,* New York: Dell Publishing, 1977.

————, with Jacques Vallee, *The Edge of Reality,* Chicago, Ill.: Henry Regnery Company, 1975.

Jacobs, David M., *Secret Life,* New York: Simon & Schuster, 1992.

Jung, C. G., and Pauli, W., *The Interpretation of Nature and the Psyche,* New York: Pantheon Books, 1955.

Kaku, Michio, *Hyperspace,* New York: Oxford University Press, 1994.

Kavanaugh, Kieran, and Rodriguez, Otilio (translation), *The Collected Works of St. John of the Cross,* Garden City, N.Y.: Doubleday & Company, 1964.

Kennett, J., *Selling Water by the River,* New York: Vintage Books, 1972.

Krishna, Gopi, *The Biological Basis of Religion and Genius,* New York: Harper & Row, 1971.

————, *The Secret of Yoga,* New York: Harper & Row, 1972.

Kühn, Thomas S., *The Structure of Scientific Revolutions,* Chicago: The University of Chicago Press, 1962.

Kung, Hans (translation by Edward Quinn), *Eternal Life?* Garden City, N.Y.: Doubleday & Company, 1984.

Lorenzen, Coral and Jim, *Encounters with UFO Occupants,* New York: Berkeley Medallion Books, 1976.

————, *Abducted!,* New York: Berkeley Medallion Books, 1977.

Mack, John E., *Abduction,* New York: Charles Scribner's Sons, 1994.

Mitchell, Stephen (editor), *Tao Te Ching,* New York: Harper Collins, 1988.

———— (editor), *The Enlightened Mind,* New York: Harper Collins, 1991.

Moody, Raymond A., Jr., *Life After Life,* New York: Bantam Books, 1976.

————, *Reflections on Life After Life,* Harrisburg, Pa: Stackpole Books, 1977.

————, *The Light Beyond,* New York: Bantam Books, 1988.

Morris, Richard, *Time's Arrows,* New York: Simon & Schuster, 1984.

————, *The Nature of Reality,* New York: McGraw Hill, 1987.

Morse, Melvin, M.D., with Paul Perry, *Closer to the Light,* New York: Villard Books, 1990.

————, *Transformed by the Light,* New York: Villard Books, 1992.

Motoyama, Hiroshi, with Rande Brown, *Science and the Evolution of Consciousness,* Brookline, Mass.: Autumn Press, 1978.

Murchie, Guy, *Music of the Spheres,* Boston, Mass.: Houghton Mifflin Company, 1961.

————, *The Seven Mysteries of Life,* Boston, Mass.: Houghton Mifflin Company, 1978.

Nahin, Paul J., *Time Machines,* New York: American Institute of Physics, 1993.

Osis, Karlis, and Haraldsson, Erlendur, *At the Hour of Death,* New York: Avon Books, 1977.

Ostrander, Sheila, and Schroeder, Lynn, *Psychic Discoveries behind the Iron Curtain,* Englewood Cliffs, N.J.: Prentice Hall, 1971.

Ouspensky, P. D., translation by Nicholas Bessaraboff and Claude Bragdon, *Tertium Organum,* New York: Alfred A. Knopf, 1922.

————, *A New Model of the Universe,* 1931. Reprint. New York: Vintage Books, 1971.

Oyle, Irving, *Time, Space, and the Mind*, Berkeley, Calif., Celestial Arts, 1976.

Pickthall, Mohammed Marmaduke (translation), *The Meaning of the Glorious Koran*, New York: Penguin.

Plato, translation by Benjamin Jowett, *The Republic of Plato*, New York: Willey Book Co.; The Colonial Press, 1901.

Postle, Denis, *Fabric of the Universe*, New York: Crown Publishers, 1976.

Prabhavananda, Swami, and Isherwood, Cristopher (translation), Bhagavad-Gita, New York: New American Library, 1954.

Prabhavananda, Swami, and Manchester, Frederick (translation), Upanishads, New York: New American Library, 1957.

Ralphs, John D., *Exploring the Fourth Dimension*, St. Paul, Minn.: Llewellyn Publications, 1992.

Rawlings, Maurice, M.D., *Beyond Death's Door*, New York: Thomas Nelson Inc. Publishers, 1978.

Rhine, J. B., *Extra-Sensory Perception*, Brookline Village, Mass.: Brandon Press, 1973.

Rhine, Louisa E., *Precognition and Intervention*, New York: Sloane, 1955.

———, *ESP in Life and Lab*, New York: The Macmillan Company, 1967.

———, *Mind over Matter*, New York: The Macmillan Company, 1970.

Ring, Kenneth, *Life at Death*, New York: Coward, McCann & Geoghegan, 1980.

———, *Heading Toward Omega*, New York: Quill, William Morrow and Company, 1984.

———, *The Omega Project*, New York: William Morrow and Company, 1992.

Rogo, D. Scott, *The Poltergeist Experience*, New York: Penguin Books, 1979.

————, *Mind over Matter*, Northhamptonshire, England: The Aquarian Press, 1986.

Roll, William, *The Poltergeist*, New York: New American Library, 1973.

Sabom, Michael B., *Recollections of Death*, New York: Harper & Row, 1982.

Sahai, Ganga, *Metaphysical Approach to Reality*, New Delhi: Sagar Publications, 1969.

Servan-Schrieber, Jean-Louis, translation by Franklin Philip, *The Art of Time*, Reading, Mass.: Addison-Wesley, 1988.

Spencer, John, and Evans, Hilary, *Phenomenon*, New York: Avon Books, 1988.

Story, Ronald D., *The Encyclopedia of UFOs*, New York: Dolphin Books, Doubleday & Co., 1980.

————, with J. Richard Greenwell, *UFOs and the Limits of Science*, New York: William Morrow and Company, 1981.

Suzuki, D. T. (E. Conze, editor), *On Indian Mahayana Buddhism*, New York: Harper & Row, 1968.

Taimni, I. K., *The Science of Yoga*, Wheaton, Ill.: The Theosophical Publishing House, 1974.

Talbot, Michael, *The Holographic Universe*, New York: HarperCollins, 1992.

Tolstoy, Leo (translation by Leo Weiner), *The Kingdom of God Is within You*, New York: Farrar, Strauss, and Cudahy, 1961.

Underhill, Evelyn, *The Essentials of Mysticism*, New York: E. P. Dutton & Co., 1960.

————, *Mysticism,* New York: New American Library, 1974.

Vallee, Jacques, *Dimensions,* New York: Ballantine Books, 1988.

————, *Confrontations,* New York: Ballantine Books, 1990.

————, *Revelations,* New York: Ballantine Books, 1991.

————, *Forbidden Science,* Berkeley, Calif.: North Atlantic Books, 1992.

Walsh, Roger N., *The Spirit of Shamanism,* Los Angeles, Calif.: Jeremy P. Tarcher, 1990.

Watson, Lyall, *Lifetide,* New York: Simon & Schuster, 1979.

Weil, Andrew, *The Natural Mind,* Boston, Mass.: Houghton Mifflin Company, 1972.

White, John (editor), *Kundalini, Evolution and Enlightenment,* New York: Paragon House, 1990.

Wilson, Ian, *The After Death Experience,* New York: William Morrow and Company, 1987.

Yutang, Lin (editor), *The Wisdom of Laotse,* New York: Random House, 1948.

Zaleski, Carol, *Otherworld Journeys,* New York: Oxford University Press, 1987.

Index

About the Author

John R. Violette is an independent scholar in the field of dimensions of space and space-time, who had a few profound paranormal experiences at an early age, and ever since searched for an understanding of how such things could really "work" and be understood in a rational context. He lives in Massachusetts.

Hampton Roads Publishing Company

. . . for the evolving human spirit

HAMPTON ROADS PUBLISHING COMPANY publishes books on a variety of subjects, including metaphysics, spirituality, health, visionary fiction, and other related topics.

We also create on-line courses and sponsor an *Applied Learning Series* of author workshops. For a current list of what is available, go to www.hrpub.com, or request the ALS workshop catalog at our toll-free number.

For a copy of our latest trade catalog, call toll-free, 800-766-8009, or send your name and address to:

HAMPTON ROADS PUBLISHING COMPANY, INC.
1125 STONEY RIDGE ROAD • CHARLOTTESVILLE, VA 22902
e-mail: hrpc@hrpub.com • www.hrpub.com